Assessment in
Student Affairs

Second Edition

Assessment in Student Affairs

Second Edition

John H. Schuh
J. Patrick Biddix
Laura A. Dean
Jillian Kinzie

JB JOSSEY-BASS™
A Wiley Brand

Published by Jossey-Bass
A Wiley Brand
One Montgomery Street, Suite 1000, San Francisco, CA 94104-4594—www.josseybass.com

Jossey-Bass books and products are available through most bookstores. To contact Jossey-Bass directly call our Customer Care Department within the U.S. at 800-956-7739, outside the U.S. at 317-572-3986, or fax 317-572-4002.

Wiley publishes in a variety of print and electronic formats and by print-on-demand. Some material included with standard print versions of this book may not be included in e-books or in print-on-demand. If this book refers to media such as a CD or DVD that is not included in the version you purchased, you may download this material at http://booksupport.wiley.com. For more information about Wiley products, visit www.wiley.com.

Library of Congress Cataloging-in-Publication Data is available

ISBN 9781119049609 (Hardcover)
ISBN 9781119051084 (ePDF)
ISBN 9781119051169 (ePub)

Cover design by Wiley
Cover image: ©Studio-Pro/iStockphoto

Printed in the United States of America
SECOND EDITION

HB Printing   10 9 8 7 6 5 4 3 2 1

CONTENTS

PREFACE

Another book on assessment in student affairs? Hasn't this topic been covered in its entirety? These are legitimate questions that any prospective reader could raise about another book being published on assessment in student affairs. In fact, we, as authors, have written numerous pieces on assessment in student affairs that in many respects trace the development of the art and science of assessment in student affairs over the past 25 years. While it is very difficult to identify a contemporary book on student affairs practice that does not address topics related to assessment, such has not always been the case, as we will affirm in this volume.

Assessment in student affairs has evolved over the past several decades to the point where we believe that assessment is in the process of being institutionalized as a part of student affairs practice. But assessment still is not as common as we think it should be, and we hope that over the next couple of years assessment will become a part of routine student affairs practice, similar to staff selection, for example, in residence life. Moreover, as we point out in Chapter 1, assessment, evaluation, and research have not been differentiated clearly in the student affairs literature until fairly recently (see Suskie, 2009), and while these activities have clearly different purposes, they were used synonymously for years, incorrectly in our opinion. So, this book will try to add to the clarity of the definition of assessment and provide a myriad of examples of assessment projects.

Not only has assessment been differentiated from evaluation and research in the past several decades, the purposes of assessment have become sharper. We can thank Ewell (2009) for his elegantly written piece that discusses the tensions related to the accountability and improvement dimensions of assessment. Virtually all assessment projects fit into one of these two categories, and in some cases assessment projects can fit into both of them. Contemporary thinking about the purposes of assessment is more streamlined and fits projects neatly into one purpose or the other, or both.

The technical side of conducting assessments has evolved over the past number of years, and while we believe that predicting where technological improvements will take us in the future is difficult, we are confident that new technologies will be developed in the future. Our experience takes us back to, in effect, distributing questionnaires by hand, collecting them, copying responses onto coding sheets, transferring the data to Hollerith cards, having them analyzed by mainframe computers, and making sense of the results, in effect, by hand. This approach, while effective in its day, was incredibly time consuming and is the assessment equivalent of making long distance telephone calls by dialing "0" and asking the operator to place the call. In this book we offer what we think are contemporary approaches to the practice of assessment by using current technology that is widely available.

In this volume we also look at other aspects of assessment that are evolving continuously, such as protecting the rights of participants, developing a culture of assessment in student affairs, differentiating between individual and group assessment projects, identifying strategies for getting assessment projects started, and reporting results. This book is much more than an update of the first edition. Rather, in identifying the concepts for this book, we started from scratch and identified those topics that in our opinion will be of great practical value for our readers. In short, we have overhauled the topic of assessment and developed what we trust our readers will find is a fresh look at very important topics covered under the umbrella of assessment in student affairs.

Finally, we thought it would make sense for a book to be written with the graduate student and young professional in mind. Curricula in student affairs preparation programs, in our view, ought to have a course on assessment as the CAS standards indicate. Our view is that this volume could be used as the primary textbook for such a course. With that in mind the reader will find case studies, scenarios, and discussion questions throughout the book.

General Purpose of the Book

As the previous paragraph suggests, this book has been designed as a text for a course on assessment in student affairs. We also think that this book can be used for staff development purposes for student affairs educators and others who are interested in assessing the potency of services, programs, and learning experiences as related to student growth and development. All of the authors have offered courses, workshops, and seminars and done consulting related to assessment in student affairs. Our view is that the existing literature is valuable in providing important information about assessment for graduate students preparing for careers as student affairs educators, but we also believe that a book especially tailored for a graduate course or staff development has great utility. With that in mind we have developed this book with the purpose to provide a primer on topics that provide a foundation for students preparing for careers as student affairs educators or those staff who seek more information to inform their practice as they work with college students.

Intended Audiences

Our primary audience for this book consists of those who are preparing for careers as student affairs educators or those who work with college students and seek more information about the extent to which students learn and grow from the experiences they offer. We trust that graduate students will have a course on assessment in student affairs in their curriculum. Accordingly, this book can be used as the primary text for such a course. If an assessment course is not part of the prescribed curriculum, this book can be used for an independent study of assessment in student affairs. Because of the cases and discussion questions, our opinion is that the book will lend itself well to a formal course or an independent study.

We also realize that a number of people come to careers in ways other than through student affairs graduate programs. Included in this career path, for example, are academic advisors, career counselors, recreation coordinators, and so on. Though their career path may be outside that of those with graduate degrees in student affairs education, they are not absolved from assessment activities. Consequently, they could choose to use this book to provide a foundation for their work in assessment as student affairs educators through staff development activities offered by their institution or through independent reading on their own.

Still others enter student affairs education by switching from faculty roles or perhaps from outside higher education. They, too, have an obligation to participate and perhaps lead an ongoing program of assessment in student affairs. Included in this set of professionals are those who lead learning centers, coordinate retention programs, or serve in executive roles with student affairs being included in their portfolios. This book can provide them with background information as they work with staff in developing assessment projects.

Beyond staff in student affairs, others may have an interest in issues related to accountability and improvement in higher education. Those who serve on regional accrediting committees or governing boards, or who advise legislators or other policy groups, might find this volume useful. Our view is that oversight of higher education will continue to tighten in the future, and this volume can provide those providing such oversight with a foundation for the questions they should be asking.

How to Use the Book

While this book does not have to be used in a linear sense, meaning that one's reading should start with Chapter 1, then following with Chapter 2, 3, and so on, ultimately finishing with the last chapter, we think that might be the best approach. Our assumption is that most readers will not know a great deal about assessment, and even may not have thought about it much before beginning to read this book. The chapters are designed to build on each other with information from the early chapters providing a foundation for those that follow. So, our recommendation is that readers start with the first chapter and then follow through the rest of the book sequentially.

This book, however, is not designed to be read in isolation. That is, we have provided two features that are designed to provide a basis for group discussions and perhaps group projects. One of the features is the introduction of a case study or scenarios that can be used to apply and illustrate the elements of the chapter. The other is a set of questions found at the end of each chapter designed to stimulate discussion about its contents. The questions are designed to prompt in-class discussion, for small group work outside of class, or for reflection and contemplation by those who are reading the book outside a group exercise. Most important, the cases and the discussion questions are designed to make active learning very much a part of the experiences of those who read the book.

If the book is used for staff development in a student affairs unit, the same principles apply. That is, the cases can be used to illustrate the content of the chapter and the questions at the end of the chapter are designed to stimulate discussion and further thinking about the topic of the chapter.

We provide foundational information about assessment in Chapter 1 by differentiating between assessment, evaluation, and research. We also look at the reasons why student affairs educators should be concerned about assessment, using Ewell's (2009) primary proposes of assessment (accountability and improvement) as our taxonomy. Then we move into a review of the development of assessment through a review of selected source materials, beginning with the *Student Personnel Point of View* that was published in 1937 (National Association of Student Personnel Administrators, 1989). Finally, we identify the role of assessment in contemporary student affairs education.

Chapter 2 takes an expansive view of planning for assessment. It begins with identifying principles of good practice in assessment, followed by suggestions about how to develop an assessment plan. We look at questions to be used to guide the assessment process and then identify questions for discussion about developing an assessment. The chapter emphasizes the importance of how to develop a problem statement and identify the purpose of an assessment project.

We think it is imperative that assessment projects be conducted with the highest ethical standards. That is, the rights of participants in assessment projects should be of paramount importance at all times. Accordingly, we have positioned our discussion of ethics early in this volume. Our view is that all studies must be conducted with the highest ethical standards and, as a consequence, we think our readers should have a firm understanding of their ethical obligations before embarking on any assessment project. Chapter 3 introduces basic principles of ethical research, establishes the need for ethical practice in assessment, describes how to apply ethical standards to assessment projects, and provides recommendations for ensuring that the highest ethical standards are met in assessment work. It also describes the importance of the relationship that those who conduct assessments need to establish with their campus's institutional review board.

The change in emphasis on measuring student learning outcomes rather than organizational inputs is an important element of Chapter 4. We believe that this emphasis reflects an important change in the values of higher education. For example, accrediting agencies are interested in how institutions measure student learning and how they add value to the student experience (see for example, Standard Five of the Commission on Institutions of Higher Education of the New England Association of Schools and Colleges). Individual learning outcomes and measuring student growth are the focus of the chapter. Learning and development outcomes frameworks are provided and discussed and strategies for developing learning outcomes are provided. The chapter concludes with a discussion of how to measure learning outcomes.

Whereas Chapter 4 is designed to provide basic information about measuring individual student learning, Chapter 5 takes a look at students in the aggregate by discussing program assessment and review. The case study for the chapter is a carryover from Chapter 5, but reflects a different emphasis. A substantial part of the chapter is devoted to discussing program review, including developing a framework for program review and describing the elements of program review.

Moving into the technical aspects of assessment, Chapter 6 addresses issues related to data collection and management. Implicit in data collection are determining an appropriate sample size, deciding on a data collection strategy, and managing the data. We point out that existing data can be used in assessment projects and will accelerate the assessment process.

Chapter 7 explores various aspects of qualitative assessment. We assert that the methodological approach needs to be tied to the goals of the assessment project. A discussion of primary forms of qualitative data collection is presented, including interviewing, observing, and reviewing. Then, the chapter explores data analysis and provides questions for further discussion about qualitative techniques.

Using quantitative techniques in conducting student affairs assessment is the focus of Chapter 8. Four keywords are introduced to assist in selecting a qualitative technique: describe, differ, relate, and predict. Quantitative data analysis also is discussed in the chapter with a special emphasis on selecting an appropriate statistical technique to use in a quantitative project.

In Chapter 9 we provide a discussion of instrument development and selection. This is a key component of the assessment process, since the use of an instrument that is inappropriate for the assessment will result in a study that will not accomplish the objectives of the project. Similarly, the development of a flawed instrument will result in a study in which the consumers of the project cannot have confidence. The chapter places special emphasis on developing instruments of high quality and also provides strategies for administering instruments.

Assessing student environments is the topic of Chapter 10. We assert that the campus environment has a significant influence on student experiences and as a consequence we believe that environmental assessment projects should be of particular interest to student affairs educators and others on campus. The chapter introduces foundational theories about campus environments, discusses the purposes of assessing campus environments, and then describes various approaches to assessing campus environments. It provides an important differentiation between assessing campus culture and campus climate.

Chapter 11 looks at various ways of measuring how institutions can compare themselves with peers using external data, standards, and frameworks. It includes a discussion of assessing quality through institutional comparisons. It provides a variety of ways of assessing quality through various forms of benchmarking such as external peer benchmarking, best practices benchmarking, capability benchmarking, and productivity benchmarking.

In Chapter 12 we explore a chronic problem found all too often in student affairs divisions, and that is starting and sustaining assessment projects. Many challenges exist, sometimes real and sometimes perceived, to undertaking assessment projects. At times assessments are required, such as when an institution is facing its periodic regional accreditation. But otherwise, how can student affairs divisions weave assessment into their annual work routine? This chapter provides strategies for getting assessment projects started, identifies the role of the assessment coordinator in a student affairs division, and pinpoints barriers to undertaking assessment in student affairs, and provides recommendations for sustaining assessment projects over time.

Chapter 13 asserts that once an assessment has been completed, the results will need to be shared with stakeholders and the findings may indicate that changes need to be made. Since our concern is that too often assessment findings are reported in ways that are uninteresting to stakeholders, we provide suggestions for crafting results that are informative and attractive, and also how to use results to take action in effect applying the results to student affairs practice.

Making assessment part of an organization's routine is central to developing a culture of assessment as is recommended in Chapter 14. We define what a culture of evidence is in this chapter, identify points of resistance to developing assessment projects, and conclude with strategies designed to develop an assessment culture.

Chapter 15 features our speculation about the future of assessment. Included are our hunches about the continued sharpening of the definition of assessment, our view about the future of assessment methods, and some thoughts about reporting results and our ongoing concerns about protecting those who agree to participate in assessment projects.

The reader will find a number of internal references throughout this volume. That is, there will be suggestions in one chapter to refer to other chapters to develop a more complete understanding of a particular topic. We hope this approach will assist the reader in understanding how assessment topics inform each other. For example, some of the same strategies that can be used by staff to assist them in sustaining assessment projects over time are aspects of developing a culture of assessment. Or, the development or selection of an appropriate survey instrument is a necessary feature of undertaking a quantitative assessment.

We have provided an Appendix for instructors and graduate students that provides advice on undertaking assessment projects as part of a graduate course on assessment in student affairs. The appendix provides a 12-week framework for completing an assessment project. We believe that actual practice will help readers of this book sharpen their assessment skills and understand some of the challenges and rewards that are associated with assessment in student affairs.

We trust that this volume will provide a fresh, contemporary look at assessment in student affairs, a central element of student affairs practice. We anticipate that the readers of this volume will be able to undertake assessment projects as part of their student affairs practice. We look forward to hearing from them as they contribute to the learning and development of the college students with whom they work.

References

Ewell, P. T. (2009). *Assessment, accountability, and improvement: Revisiting the tension*. Champaign, IL: National Institute for Learning Outcomes Assessment.

National Association of Student Personnel Administrators. (1989). *Points of view*. Washington, DC: Author.

New England Association of Schools and Colleges. (2016). *Students. Standard Five*. https://cihe.neasc.org/standards-policies/standards-accreditation/standards-effective-july-1-2016#standard_five

Suskie, L. A. (2009). *Assessing student learning: A common sense guide* (2nd ed.). San Francisco, CA: Jossey-Bass.

ABOUT THE AUTHORS

John H. Schuh is director of the Emerging Leaders Academy at Iowa State University where he also is Distinguished Professor Emeritus. At Iowa State University he served as a department chair for six and a half years and he was director of the School of Education for 18 months. In a career that has spanned over 45 years, he held administrative and faculty assignments at Wichita State University, Indiana University (Bloomington), and Arizona State University. He received his Master of Counseling and PhD degrees from Arizona State.

Schuh is the author, coauthor, or editor of over 235 publications, including 30 books and monographs, 80 book chapters, and over 110 articles. Among his books are three volumes on assessment, including *Assessment Methods for Student Affairs*, *Assessment Practice in Student Affairs: An Applications Manual* (with M. Lee Upcraft), and *Assessment in Student Affairs* (also with M. Lee Upcraft). Other recent books include *Student Services* (fifth edition edited with Susan Jones and Shaun Harper), *One Size Does Not Fit All: Traditional and Innovative Models of Student Affairs Practice* (with Kathleen Manning and Jillian Kinzie), and *Student Success in College* (with George D. Kuh, Jillian Kinzie, and Elizabeth Whitt). He was associate editor of the *New Directions for Student Services* Sourcebook Series after serving as editor for 13 years. He was associate editor of the *Journal of College Student Development* for 14 years and was book review editor of *The Review of Higher Education* from 2008 to 2010. Schuh has made over 300 presentations and speeches

xviii ABOUT THE AUTHORS

to campus-based, regional, national, and international meetings. He has served as a consultant to more than 80 institutions of higher education and other educational organizations. Schuh is a member of the Evaluator Corps of the Higher Learning Commission of the North Central Association of Colleges and Schools, where he also serves as a team chair for accreditation visits.

John Schuh has received the Research Achievement Award from the Association for the Study of Higher Education, the Contribution to Knowledge Award from the American College Personnel Association, the Contribution to Research or Literature Award, and the Robert H. Shaffer Award for Academic Excellence as a Graduate Faculty Member from the National Association of Student Personnel Administrators. The American College Personnel Association elected him as a Senior Scholar Diplomate. Schuh was chosen as one of 75 Diamond Honorees by ACPA in 1999 and as a Pillar of the Profession by NASPA in 2001. He is a member of the Iowa Academy of Education and has received a number of institutional awards including the Distinguished Alumni Achievement Award from the University of Wisconsin-Oshkosh, his undergraduate alma mater. Schuh received a Fulbright award to study higher education in Germany in 1994, was named to the Fulbright Specialists Program in 2008, and had a Fulbright specialists' assignment in South Africa in 2012.

J. Patrick Biddix is an associate professor of Higher Education in the Department of Educational Leadership and Policy Studies at the University of Tennessee. His areas of expertise include college student involvement outcomes, technology in higher education, and research design. He teaches graduate courses in research methodologies, assessment and evaluation, and special topics in higher education and student affairs. In 2015, he received a Fulbright Award to study college student technology use at Concordia University in Montreal, Canada.

Biddix received his PhD in education with a concentration in higher education from the University of Missouri in St. Louis.

He holds a graduate certificate in Institutional Research from the University of Missouri in St. Louis as well as an MA in Higher Education Administration from the University of Mississippi and a BA in Classical Civilization from the University of Tennessee. His published research includes numerous articles in top-tier student affairs and communication technology venues. He currently serves on four journal editorial boards and one national commission.

Biddix is an appointed member to the University of Tennessee Institutional Review Board (IRB), the College of Education, Health, and Human Services Tenure and Promotion Committee, and serves the department of Educational Leadership and Policy Studies in a number of capacities, including serving as academic program coordinator, accreditation liaison, program review coordinator, and graduate student advisor. Prior to coming to the University of Tennessee, he worked for six years as Associate Professor and Higher Education Program Coordinator at Valdosta State University and for four years as a student affairs professional at Washington University in St. Louis. He has received three faculty excellence awards (2010, 2011, 2015).

Laura A. Dean is professor of College Student Affairs Administration at the University of Georgia; she also serves as program coordinator of the master's program. She has been an educator throughout her career, in settings ranging from high school to major research-extensive universities. She has worked as a teacher, admissions officer, counselor, director of student activities and orientation, Dean of Students, vice president for Student Affairs, and graduate faculty member. Prior to her current position, she served as the director of Counseling/Associate Dean of Student Development at Manchester College (IN), as Dean of Student Development (SSAO) at Pfeiffer University (NC), and as vice president for Student Development/Dean of Students at Peace College (NC). She also served in 2010 as the Interim Dean of Students at the University of Georgia.

Dean earned her bachelor's degree in English at Westminster College (PA). After teaching high school and working in college admissions, she then earned her master's degree in counseling and her PhD in Counselor Education/Student Development in Higher Education, both from the University of North Carolina at Greensboro.

Her publications and presentations focus largely in the areas of assessment and the use of professional standards of practice. She has served on the editorial boards of the *College Student Affairs Journal* and the *Journal of College Counseling*. Dean has been extensively involved professionally in organizations including the American Counseling Association, American College Counseling Association (ACCA), ACPA-College Student Educators International, NASPA-Student Affairs Administrators in Higher Education, and the Council for the Advancement of Standards in Higher Education (CAS). She served as president of ACCA and represented that organization on the CAS Board of Directors for nearly two decades. She was CAS president, having previously served on the executive council as Member at Large and as the CAS publications editor. She has been recognized for her contributions with awards including the ACCA Professional Leadership Award, ACPA Senior Professional Annuit Coeptis award, ACPA Diamond Honoree, NASPA Robert H. Shaffer Award for Academic Excellence as a Graduate Faculty Member, NASPA Region III Outstanding Contribution to Student Affairs through Teaching, the Georgia College Personnel Association Paul K. Jahr Award of Excellence, and the Distinguished Alumni Outstanding Achievement Award from the School of Education at University of North Carolina at Greensboro.

Jillian Kinzie is the associate director for the Center for Postsecondary Research and the National Survey of Student Engagement (NSSE) Institute at Indiana University Bloomington School of Education. She conducts research and leads project activities on effective use of student engagement data to improve educational quality, and studies evidence-based improvement in higher education. She managed the Documenting Effective Education Practices (DEEP) project and Building Engagement and Attainment of Minority Students (BEAMS), and also serves as senior scholar on the National Institute for Learning Outcomes Assessment (NILOA) project, an initiative to study assessment in higher education and assist institutions and others in discovering and adopting promising practices in the assessment of college student learning outcomes.

Kinzie earned her PhD from Indiana University in higher education with a minor in women's studies. Prior to this, she served on the faculty of Indiana University and coordinated the master's program in higher education and student affairs. She also worked as a researcher and administrator in academic and student affairs at Miami University and Case Western Reserve University. Her scholarly interests include the assessment of student engagement, how colleges use data to improve, student and academic affairs partnerships and the impact of programs and practices to support student success, as well as first-year student development, teaching and learning in college, access and equity, and women in underrepresented fields.

She has coauthored numerous publications including *Using Evidence of Student Learning to Improve Higher Education* (Jossey-Bass, 2015); *Student Success in College: Creating Conditions that Matter* (Jossey-Bass, 2005/2010); *Continuity and Change in College Choice: National Policy, Institutional Practices, and Student Decision Making*, and the second edition of *One Size Does Not Fit All: Traditional and Innovative Models of Student Affairs Practice* (Routledge, 2008/2014). She serves as coeditor of *New Directions in Higher Education*, on the editorial board of the *Journal of College Student Development and the Journal of Learning Community Research*, and on the boards of the Council for the Accreditation of Educator Preparation (CAEP), the National Society for Collegiate Scholars, and the Gardner Institute for Excellence in Undergraduate Education. In 2001, she was awarded a Student Choice Award for Outstanding Faculty at Indiana University and in 2005 and 2011 she received the Robert J. Menges Honored Presentation by the Professional Organizational Development (POD) Network, the Shaffer Distinguished Alumni Award in 2012, and in 2015, was awarded the honor of Senior Scholar by the American College Personnel Association (ACPA).

Assessment in Student Affairs

Second Edition

1

UNDERSTANDING THE CONTEMPORARY ASSESSMENT ENVIRONMENT

While assessment has not always been a central activity in student affairs practice in higher education, it is becoming an institutional imperative in contemporary times, as Kinzie (2009) points out, "Every college or university must decide how to most effectively assess student learning outcomes for institutional improvement and accountability (p. 4)." Livingston and Zerulik (2013) add the following observation about the centrality of assessment to student affairs practice as follows, "Assessment is an essential element in any successful student affairs division" (p. 15).

This chapter begins with a case study related to the potential role of assessment as part of implementing a new program. Then, we provide definitions of *assessment, evaluation,* and *research,* terms that are important to understand in the development of projects designed to determine the effectiveness of programs, activities, and experiences developed by student affairs educators. We follow that with a brief discussion of the historical development of assessment in student affairs practice and the centrality of assessment in contemporary institutional accreditation, student affairs practice and the education of student affairs educators. We conclude with questions to consider in the development of an assessment plan to address the dynamics identified in the case study.

Learning Communities at Mid-Central University

Sean is an area coordinator at Mid-Central University (MCU) in the residence hall system. As such, Sean has responsibility for four buildings, each housing about 240 students, four graduate assistants (one for each building), and 16 resident assistants. MCU is a regional institution, with most of its students majoring in education, business, or liberal arts. Predominantly, the students are the first in their families to attend college and many have significant amounts of federal financial aid.

Sean is in her second year of service at MCU and noted that as opposed to other institutions with which she was familiar, MCU did not have any learning communities (LC). Sean had served as a graduate assistant in the residence halls at State University while pursuing her master's degree and was used to having many learning communities in residence halls. She was surprised that MCU did not have any learning communities when she interviewed for her position but decided to accept the position with the hope that learning communities could be established though no promises were made that LC units would be established at MCU. She spent her first year investigating why MCU did not have any of these special residential units and it turned out that a variety of reasons contributed to the lack of learning communities, among them the philosophy of the residence department, lack of funding, and potentially, lack of student interest.

From Sean's point of view, the idea behind a learning community was to use the concept to improve retention. In the pilot project she was developing, two learning communities would be implemented in the trial program. Twenty students majoring in business would be assigned to one of the learning communities and another 20 education majors would be assigned to the other learning community. The students in each learning community would be assigned to three courses in the curriculum and a community advisor (CA) would be hired to provide support and enrichment, such as organizing study groups, arranging for tutoring as necessary, and organizing a field trip for the student participants once per month in the fall semester.

Sean briefed her staff at the end of the first academic year about wanting to implement two trial learning communities the next academic year. The concept was foreign to many of the staff and several asked this question: How did Sean know that the students needed this experience? Sean indicated that such would be a part of a pilot project of learning communities that was being planned.

She managed to convince the assistant director of student housing for residential programs that implementing two learning communities on a trial basis was worth undertaking but she was cautioned by Sami, the assistant director, that she would run into a series of hard questions as she had conversations with other member of the central office staff. And, Sami was clear about one central concern that was paramount in his mind: Whenever programs were implemented, senior staff would want to know how the program could be improved from one year to the next.

Sean also met with the fiscal officer of the residence life department who wanted to know what the cost of the program would be. Sean thought that adequate compensation for the community advisors would be a free room plus a monthly stipend of $100 for each CA plus an operations budget for each LC of $2,000 for modest programming efforts. The fiscal officer left Sean with this question: How would Sean demonstrate that the resources were used wisely?

The final discussion Sean had was with the director of the residence life department, Casey. While Casey was generally supportive of the program, there were some doubts about the effort required to implement learning communities. Would the establishment of the learning communities be worth Sean's time? Are the outcomes Sean has identified consistent with the purposes of residence halls at the university? What about staff time in organizing room assignments for the participants? Wouldn't working with the Registrar's office and the two academic programs, business and elementary education, take a lot of time? How would the benefits of the program be communicated to senior administrators? Wouldn't recruitment of

(Continued)

participants take a tremendous effort? And, most important, how would Sean determine if the program made a difference?

Sean is faced with a daunting number of questions related to assessment, because without data she really can't answer the questions posed by the various administrators who will have an influence as to whether or not the learning communities will be implemented on a trial basis and what the future of these new units might be. We cannot be certain if Sean was ready for all of the questions raised by these administrators, even though learning communities are common on many campuses (see Benjamin, 2015).

Defining Assessment, Evaluation, and Research

Before we move further into this chapter, it is important that we are clear by what we mean by assessment. We'll also compare and contrast the term *assessment* with *evaluation* and *research*, since the terms often are used interchangeably—however, to our way of thinking, each represents a very different purpose.

Assessment

We think the definition of the term *assessment* that we introduced in the first edition of this book is still relevant in contemporary student affairs practice. We defined assessment this way:

"Assessment is any effort to gather, analyze, and interpret evidence which describes institutional, departmental, divisional, or agency effectiveness" (Upcraft & Schuh, 1996, p. 18).

To this definition we would add program or initiative effectiveness. In the case of our example, an assessment of the learning community initiative at MCU would be conducted to determine the extent to which the program achieved its goals. It is also important to note that for the purposes of this book, we are interested in students in the aggregate. We will be addressing individual student learning to the extent described in chapter 4. We would, in the context of this volume, be interested in the aggregate scores of students who might have taken the College Senior Survey (http://www.heri.ucla.edu /cssoverview.php) or the National Survey of Student Engagement (http://nsse.iub.edu/) if the instrument measured an aspect of the student experience pertinent to the study being conducted.

Effectiveness, for the purpose of this definition, can take on many dimensions. Most important, we think of effectiveness as a measure of the extent to which an intervention, program, activity, or learning experience accomplishes its goals, frequently linked to how student learning is advanced. Goals will vary from program to program but typically they are linked to the goals of a unit, the division in which it is located, or the goals of the institution. So, for example, at a commuter institution with no residence halls, the development of community as an institutional goal might have a different definition than the development of community at a baccalaureate college where nearly all students live on campus.

Evaluation

We also defined the term *evaluation* in the first edition of this book but we think *evaluation* needs a bit of updating and for that we rely on the work of Suskie (2009). We defined evaluation, in effect, as the use of assessment data to determine organizational effectiveness. Suskie provides a more nuanced definition of evaluation by asserting, " ... that assessment results alone only guide us; they do not dictate decisions to us" (p. 12). She adds that a second concept of evaluation is that " ... it determines the match between intended outcomes ... and actual outcomes" (p. 12). In our LC example, we might learn that participation in the learning community programs does not result in increased retention but we might find out that students who participate earn a higher grade point average at a statistically significant level. If the LCs were established with a goal of improving retention and that did not occur, the higher GPAs may or may be sufficient evidence to determine that the LCs should continue.

Suskie (2009) adds that evaluation also "... investigates and judges the quality or worth of a program, project, or other entity rather than student learning" (p. 12). We might find, for example, that participation in the LCs resulted in improved retention for the participants. But, suppose if when all the costs are tallied in our case study, what was found was that the program cost $8,990 per student. In the case study, it is important to note that the resources of MCU are modest, and with 40 students proposed to participate in the programs (20 in the education LC and 20 in the business LC), if the aggregate cost was $359,600, this amount is likely to be far more than could be sustained by the university's budget. So, while the goal of the program (increased retention) was met, the costs were prohibitive. Strictly speaking, the data suggested that the program was a success (retention was improved), so from an assessment point of view it should be continued, but from an evaluation perspective, it should not (the program was cost prohibitive).

Research

Our experience is that student affairs educators can be worried by the thought of undertaking assessments because they think what they are contemplating is conducting a research study, similar to writing a dissertation as part of completing a doctoral degree or conducting a study that would form the basis for a manuscript that would be submitted to an international journal with rigorous acceptance rates. We submit that such is not the case with assessment. Rather, we assert that while research methods are used in the process of conducting an assessment, we are not advocating a level of rigor that would be required to complete a doctoral dissertation. Suskie (2009), again, is informative on this point: "Assessment ... is disciplined and systematic and uses many of the methodologies of traditional research" (p. 14). She adds, "If you take the time and effort to design assessments reasonably carefully and collect corroborating evidence, your assessment results may be imperfect but will nevertheless give you information that you will be able to use with confidence to make decisions ... " (p. 15).

We would like to identify several distinctions between assessment and research that further illustrate the point. First, assessments are guided by theory but research frequently is conducted to test theories. So, in our LC example, the theory of student engagement (Astin, 1984) could guide an assessment of the LC but a research study of Astin's theory of student engagement might look at a number of ways that students are involved in the life of the campus outside the classroom and determine the potency of each of them.

Second, research often is not time bound to the extent that assessments are time bound. For the LCs to be continued beyond a trial period, say two years, the inquiry will need to be completed in time to make a decision about the efficacy of the LC program. If one is conducting a research study, it is completed when all aspects of it have been finished at the highest level of sophistication possible. If an extra month is needed for further data analysis, then the extra month is taken. In our example, a decision needs to be made so that space in the residence hall can be reserved for the LC, staff need to be hired, budgets need to be prepared, and so on.

Third, it is common for assessments to have a public or political dimension to them. Participants will want to know if the program is going to be continued and if so, in what form. Residence hall leaders may have an interest in supporting the program or opposing it strictly on budgetary grounds. Senior institutional leaders might find the program useful as a talking point in meeting with prospective students, their parents, and legislators. Research in many cases will not attract much interest beyond those who have a disciplinary interest in it. This is not always the case, but we would submit that assessments of student programs typically engender broader interest than research projects in many disciplines on campus.

Fourth, assessments typically are funded out of unit or divisional budgets, which can put something of a strain on providing support for all of the activities planned by the unit, especially if resources are not designated for assessment in organizational base budgets. Research often is financed through special support such as a grant or contract secured specifically to support the project. In developing a proposal the investigator will prepare a budget to address the costs of the project. It is quite common for faculty, in particular, to seek funding from a source external to the institution to underwrite the research project.

Reasons for Assessment

Why Should We Be Concerned about Assessment?

In looking through our case study, it is clear that the reasons for assessment are varied depending on one's point of view. Sean's staff wanted to know if students needed the program. Sami was concerned about how the program might be improved from one year to the next. The fiscal officer wanted evidence that the expenditures for the learning communities were wise and prudent. Casey, the director, wanted to know about the time spent on the program, and how its value might be communicated to senior administrators. All of these questions were legitimate in the eyes of the persons asking them. In many respects the questions reflected their responsibilities at MCU and what they were responsible for at the university.

As we pointed out in the first edition of this volume, there are many reasons for conducting assessments, even more than those illustrated by our case. But our view is that perhaps the most central reasons for conducting assessment are identified by Ewell (2009): accountability and improvement. Ewell analyzes

why do assessment

the reasons behind accountability and improvement in his paper and in the end concludes that both are important.

In our case study, we find a number of questions being raised about the proposal, but in the end the concerns essentially deal with accountability or improvement or both. In this section we provide reasons for why student affairs educators should be concerned about assessment and use the term *program* interchangeably with the terms *initiative, learning experience,* or *activity.*

Assessment for Accountability

Ewell (2009) characterizes assessment for accountability as "Accountability requires the entity held accountable to demonstrate, with evidence, conformity with an established standard of process or outcome" (p. 7). Volkwein (2011) offers this question, which illustrates the accountability dimension of assessment: "Is the student or program or institution meeting educational goals?" (p. 11). With accountability come such features as answerability to stakeholders, shared governance, organizational transparency, and so on. Let's unpack these a bit in the context of the case study.

Sean wants to implement learning communities because she knows from her personal experiences and from the literature that learning communities lead to student growth and improved retention rates for first year students, the results of which are beneficial to students and the institution. But those who are responsible for approving her decision are either not familiar with the literature or are skeptical that the results she asserts will occur at MCU. Sean knows that learning communities are a common feature of residential living on many campuses, though not at MCU, and her experiences with them elsewhere have been very positive. So, as an element of her proposal, she will have to agree that she will conduct an assessment that will determine, to the greatest extent possible, that the learning communities achieved their goals. In short, she needs to make sure that the implementation of learning communities will result in the outcomes she has asserted will occur.

This element of planning underscores another difference between assessment and research. Typically assessments are conducted for local, that is, campus-based, purposes such as to determine if a program or other initiative meets its goals. While there may be some individuals beyond the campus who are interested in whether or not a program works, such as others in the field, the generalizability of the findings are limited. In research projects, particularly those that employ quantitative methods, generalizing to a broader population could very well be a purpose of the project. Note that in describing the circumstance for Sean, the individuals with whom she consulted appeared to want to know very specifically about the value of the LC experience at MCU. Whether they are aware of the research literature focused on LCs is beside the point. They are narrowly focused on MCU, which typically is a difference between assessment and research. Sean needs to address their questions with data from MCU.

Sean has asserted that participation in learning communities will result in improved retention for the participants and increased learning for them. Improved retention is an outcome that would be hard to argue with, but traditionally the residence halls at MCU have been seen as places to which students can escape from the pressures of class and enjoy the social aspects of their collegiate experience. Now, Sean is indicating that student learning such as increased self-awareness (see Kennedy-Phillips & Uhrig, 2013) will occur for those who participate in the learning communities. Casey wonders if self-awareness really should be an outcome that the department should care about or even see as desirable. Casey puts it this way: "We've been providing good quality service for students for years, and messing around with learning outcomes that are hard to measure and really are not part of our mission might be a distraction from what we are trying to accomplish in our residence halls." So, this element of the program and potential assessment underscores a basic tenet of assessment: Is the assessment measuring an outcome that is consistent with the unit's mission? Sean might have to retreat from the student learning outcome element of the proposal because the residence life department has not established learning outcomes and simply focus on increasing retention as the central reason for establishing learning communities.

Students who will live in the learning communities are central to the proposal. Since living in a learning community will be on a voluntary basis, students will need to be recruited to the learning communities. Since MCU has no tradition of offering these experiences, explaining how students will benefit from the experience will be a challenge. Fortunately, Sean has been working with a student advisory group in developing the proposal. Sean realized the challenges in establishing the learning communities and recruiting students to live in them, so an advisory group was formed from the start and the members of the group have agreed that they will help recruit participants and they will be serving as community advisors (CAs) in the learning communities. Sean knows that establishing a program as complex as this one will be a challenge, so she has borrowed from the concepts of Weick (1984) that she read about in graduate school, which essentially are to start small and try to build on successes if she expands that program in the future. Weick concluded, "Changing the scale of a problem can change the quality of resources that are directed at it" (p. 48).

An aspect of accountability is the extent to which resources are expended on behalf of a program. This was the concern of the fiscal officer. So, the matter of assessment to determine efficiency and affordability is captured under our accountability dimension. In the case of the LC proposal, which was not going to cost lots of money, the issue had more to do with staff time. Casey, the senior leader, was concerned about that. Wellman (2010) points out that "Ideally, to look at cost-effectiveness, one would look at the role of funds in producing educational value added, or the translation of inputs into outputs" (p. 6). If we find that students are more likely to persist by participating in the learning communities, there is a direct benefit to the institution through increased revenues that students contribute through tuition payments, room and board, books, and so on. There is also the benefit to the students themselves. If they are more likely to complete their college degrees, they will benefit economically but their families also are likely to benefit (see Hamrick, Evans, & Schuh, 2002). Since Sean finally decided that what the assessment would try to measure is the extent to which students who participate in LCs were more likely to persist than students who did not participate, then it would be fairly easy to determine if the program were cost effective.

It is important to note that the assessment process also has costs associated with it. But, Swing and Coogan (2010) remind us "What ultimately matters most is not the amount spent on assessment but the amount gained compared to the amount spent" (p. 18). This expenditure of resources is a little more difficult to measure. Certainly direct costs such as purchasing survey instruments or paying someone to transcribe a tape of a focus group is a direct cost that is fairly easy to measure, but what about costs associated with an administrative staff person reserving a room and arranging for snacks to be served at a focus group? The person's time has value but if the activities are conducted randomly, meaning that snacks were ordered one day and beverages the next, it becomes difficult to calculate the cost of the person's time.

One of the questions that needs to be raised under the umbrella of assessment for accountability is this: Accountable to whom? The simple answer: stakeholders. In the case of this program, stakeholders include the student participants, those who provide oversight for the residence organization, the division of student affairs, faculty who teach undergraduate courses, parents, governing board members, and so on. Essentially what Sean would be trying to accomplish through conducting an assessment is to determine if the program did, in fact, increase retention. This outcome is fairly simple and direct, but extremely necessary as part of a program initiative.

Assessment for Improvement

The other reason for assessment attributed to Ewell had to with improvement. In a general sense, assessment for improvement asks the basic question: How do we get better? Volkwein's question (2011) related to improvement is this: "Is the student or program or institution improving?" (p. 12). As will be pointed out elsewhere in this book, institutions of higher education typically are getting better or worse. That is, rarely do they remain static with respect to the quality of their programs and activities, so an important general aim of assessment is to learn how to get better.

More specifically, assessment for improvement can include several more specific goals. One would be to conduct an assessment to measure student satisfaction. In previous years this might have meant gathering data to answer this question: Did the participants enjoy the experience? Those conducting the assessment would conclude that the program was successful if the students indicated that they were satisfied with the experience. More contemporary thinking would be to get at this question: Were the students' goals for participating met? Having a good time might be a goal for some, but others might have had such goals as achieving learning objectives, receiving support for their academic goals, learning about how to deal with those who are different, and so on. These goals suggest a more sophisticated, nuanced approach to conducting an assessment than simply trying to measure the extent to which students had a good time.

Assessment for improvement also suggests gathering data of a formative nature. That is, the data can be used to make decisions about continuing the program and if so, what changes are necessary to make it more effective. At times the data may suggest easy changes such as the timing of events as related to the academic calendar (for example, scheduling an LC field trip when mid term exams are scheduled), how they are presented, and where they are held. In other cases, however, participant problems may not have been anticipated, such as students having to enroll in general education courses that made it impossible for them to achieve the goal of enrolling in the same sections of three courses. That matter can be resolved in subsequent years but creates a challenge for the first year of the operation of the LC.

Suppose the goal of improving retention rates from one year to the next is not met at the conclusion of the first year of operation. What then? The data generated by an assessment of the program will be crucial in determining whether or not the program should be continued. Maybe the data reveal that a reorganization of the program is indicated. If so, then maybe that will be key to continuing the effort. But what if the assessment reveals that students never really understood the purpose of the LC, and did not participate fully over the course of the year? What if they enrolled in the program simply because it was situated in a very popular residence hall and the desirability of the living space was the real motivation of the students?

Selected Historical Documents Related to Assessment Practice in Student Affairs

The beginning of the assessment movement in student affairs is difficult to identify but one way of thinking about assessment is that it began when one student asked another, "How was your course session this morning?" It is similarly difficult to identify when professional practice began in student affairs, but two commonly used markers are the adoption of *The Student Personnel Point of View, 1937*, and the *Student Personnel Point of View, 1949* (NASPA, 1989). While professional organizations for deans had been founded years before (see Dungy & Gordon, 2011) and literature had been introduced (for example, Lloyd-Jones, 1929), very little attention was paid to assessment for decades after the first deans were appointed, just before and after the turn of the twentieth century (Rhatigan, 2009).

Mueller's text (1961), which was used for much of the 1960s in the professional education of student affairs practitioners, referred to evaluation, but a volume with a specific focus on assessment would not be written until 15 years later when Aulepp and Delworth developed a monograph on environmental assessment in the 1970s, published under the auspices of the Western Interstate Commission for Higher Education. This monograph was designed to provide information on how campus environments could be developed to enhance the student experience. Assessment, however, was not widely discussed in the literature for another decade.

The work of the Study Group on the Conditions of Excellence in American Higher Education (1984) that resulted in the report *Involvement in Learning* can be used as a marker for the beginning of the contemporary assessment movement in higher education. In the report the authors identified assessment and feedback as conditions of excellence in higher education. They asserted that "The use of assessment information to redirect effort is an essential ingredient in effective learning and serves as a powerful lever for involvement" (p. 21). They also suggested five recommendations for assessment and feedback in their report, one of which is as follows, "In changing current systems of assessment, academic administrators and faculty should ensure that appropriate instruments and methods used are appropriate for (1) the knowledge, capacities, and skills addressed; and (2) the stated objectives of undergraduate education at their institutions" (p. 57).

Astin, a member of the study group, added to this report by publishing his volume *Achieving Educational Excellence* (1985), which included his view of the centrality of involvement and engagement in enhancing the student experience. Talent development was a central focus of his view of providing high quality experiences for students. Professor Astin observed "Assessing its (the institution's) success in developing the talents of its students is a more difficult task, one that requires information on change or improvements in students' performance over time" (p. 61). He added, "I believe that any good college or university assessment program must satisfy two fundamental criteria: it must be consistent with a clearly articulated philosophy of institutional mission and it should be consistent with *some* (italics in original) theory of pedagogy or learning" (p. 167).

Ewell, a highly regarded expert on higher education assessment, marks the beginning of widespread interest in assessment as occurring in the early 1980s, which confirms the work of the Study Group and that of Professor Astin. He concluded (2009): "In 1987 the so-called 'assessment movement' in U.S. higher education was less than five years old. It had, in part, been stimulated by a combination of curriculum reform reports that called for greater curricular coherence, the use of powerful pedagogies known to be associated with high learning gains (citing Chickering & Gamson, 1987) and knowledge about student outcomes and experiences (citing Ewell, 2002)" (p. 5).

The American College Personnel Association released *The Student Learning Imperative* (1996) in a special issue of the *Journal of College Student Development*. This step was another important development in that the process of assessment became a central activity of student affairs practice. This document included a recommendation about the centrality of assessment in measuring student learning. The document recommended " ... the outcomes associated with college attendance must be assessed systematically and the impact of various policies and programs on learning and personal development periodically evaluated" (1996, no page). The document continued, "They (student affairs professionals) should routinely collect information to redesign institutional policies and practices and rigorously evaluate their programs and services to determine the extent to which they contribute to the desired outcomes of undergraduate education" (no page).

The National Association of Student Personnel Administrators and the American College Personnel Association published "Learning Reconsidered" (2004), a document whose purpose was "to re-examine some widely accepted ideas about conventional teaching and learning, and to question whether current organizational patterns in higher education support student learning and development in today's environment" (p. 1). In this document the authors asserted, "Student affairs must lead broad, collaborative institutional efforts to assess overall student learning and to track, document, and evaluate the role of diverse learning experiences in achieving comprehensive college learning outcomes" (p. 26). They also recommended, "Student affairs and academic affairs educators must work in teams to evaluate and understand the actual outcomes. These data provide invaluable information not only on what students are learning but also on how programs, classroom instruction, activities, and services should be improved" (p. 28).

The document was updated in 2006 (Keeling, 2006) and includes a heavy emphasis on assessment. Bonfiglio, Hanson, Fried, Roberts, and Skinner (2006) assert that "A transition from a teaching-oriented to a student-centered learning environment requires institutional or divisional self-analysis or assessment; turning the results of that analysis into strategies; creating student learning experiences (that is, not just experiences unaligned with learning); and measuring the intended learning outcomes to determine whether the delivered experiences actually contribute to transformative learning in the context of institutional mission" (p. 43).

Project DEEP (Documenting Effective Educational Practices), a study of 20 institutions with higher than predicted graduation rates and higher than predicted scores on the National Survey of Student Engagement, found that assessment played a central role in the life of these institutions (Kuh, Kinzie, Schuh, Whitt, & Associates, 2010). The institutions were committed, according to the study, to continuous improvement. The authors concluded "Most DEEP schools systematically collect information about various aspects of student performance and use it to inform policy and decision making" (p. 156).

More recently, the National Institute for Learning Outcomes Assessment (NILOA) was established at the University of Illinois in 2008. The institute publishes occasional papers, reports, and examples of good assessment practices, all designed to "... discover and disseminate ways that academic programs and institutions can productively use assessment data internally to inform and strengthen undergraduate education, and externally to communicate with policy makers, families and other stakeholders" (2014, no page). The publications of this organization, as the name suggests, focus on learning outcomes, and some of the monographs have direct application to assessment in student affairs (for example, Blaich & Wise, 2011; Schuh & Gansemer-Topf, 2010). NILOA is a valuable resource for those who are interested in cutting edge approaches to assessment. The development of the Institute and its attendant publications reflects on the contemporary importance of assessment on college campuses. It is moving in the direction of being an essential practice.

Assessment in Contemporary Student Affairs Practice

Of course it is difficult to describe the importance of assessment in contemporary student affairs practice with absolute precision, because the role of assessment will vary from institution to institution. That being acknowledged, it is clear from our brief history of assessment that this practice has become increasingly important on our campuses, and is likely to become even more important over the next few years. What evidence points to this conclusion? Several developments support our conclusion. We will discuss them in the next section of this chapter.

Accreditation

We start with the importance of assessment in the accreditation. It is safe to assert that virtually no institution of higher education could exist without being accredited. Without accreditation students are not eligible for federal financial aid, credits are not transferable, and degrees typically will not qualify the graduate for eligibility for admission to graduate or professional school degree programs.

The role of assessment is articulated or implied in the guiding documents of our regional accrediting bodies, those that accredit entire institutions. For example, the Southern Association of Colleges and Schools (2011), in its fundamental characteristics of accreditation, asserts, "Accreditation requires institutional commitment to the concept of quality enhancement through continuous assessment and improvement" (p. 3). Another example is provided by the New England Association of Schools and College (2011) offers this observation about assessment of student learning: "The institution implements and provides support for systematic and broad-based assessment of what and how students are learning through their academic program and experiences outside the classroom" (no page). Other examples (WASC, 2013; Northwest Commission on Colleges and Universities, 2010) abound of regional accrediting bodies asserting that assessment is an important part of the process by which accreditation is offered or renewed. Being accredited is not an option in higher education; it is a requirement.

Student Affairs Administration

Student affairs education has evolved to the point where assessment is an expected activity. Sandeen and Barr (2006), two leaders of the student affairs field for more than four decades, observed: "Assessment is now the most powerful movement in

American higher education. It is not a passing fad, but a reality, and it will continue to have a major impact on how colleges and universities are funded, how they teach, and what students learn" (p. 154). Accordingly, professionals in student affairs are holding each other responsible for comprehensive assessment programs. This means that when programs are reviewed in student affairs divisions, or regional accrediting bodies come to campus to determine whether accreditation ought to be renewed, professionals in student affairs will expect of each other to have comprehensive assessment programs in place. Anything less will be regarded as substandard administrative practice, potentially resulting in inferior learning experiences for students.

While the Council for the Advancement of Standards (CAS) in Higher Education's standards for student affairs will be discussed in greater detail elsewhere in this volume, it is important to note that assessment is integrated into the standards for various programs and services covered by the standards. In short, an institution cannot comply with the standards unless it has a robust program of assessment. In addition, an important general standard for CAS (2011) indicates that "Programs and services must have a clearly articulated assessment plan to document achievement of stated goals and learning outcomes, demonstrate accountability, provide evidence of improvement, and describe resulting changes in programs and services" (p. 14).

Student Affairs Graduate Preparation Programs

Finally, the CAS standards also assert that the professional preparation of student affairs practitioners also includes a course in assessment. The standards are used by graduate program faculty to develop their curriculum, and in this case CAS makes it clear that graduate education without a significant understanding of assessment, ranging from why to conduct studies to how to conduct studies to how to use the results. When subject matter is included in the educational program of future practitioners, a milestone has been reached. That is, the subject matter, in this case assessment, is being introduced as a crucial element of the education of practitioners of the future.

The Politics of Assessment

Though referenced in the previous discussion on reasons for improvement, we want to emphasize the political nature of assessment. While those responsible for academic programs will debate the extent to which assessment activities infringes on academic freedom (see Cain, 2014), student affairs educators do not have the luxury of resisting assessment using the argument of academic freedom. Rather, they have an obligation to demonstrate that their programs and experiences contribute to student learning or risk that their budgets may be cut dramatically. Indeed, we return to the advice of Sandeen and Barr (2006), two highly influential student affairs leaders, who observe: "Assessment may be the best way to ensure a strong educational and ethical commitment to quality services and programs in student affairs" (p. 144).

Whether assessment activities on a given campus demonstrate a sufficient level of accountability and lead to sufficient improvement of specific programs is likely to be campus-specific. That is, what is acceptable at one institution may or may not be adequate at others. We are certain of this: Failure to conduct assessments in student affairs on any campus is a risky proposition that could lead to a dramatic restructuring of student affairs. Consider Blimling's (2013) recommendation: "To answer these questions, student affairs administrators need to make assessment a routine part of what they do. Even if the demand for this data has not occurred for a particular student affairs organization, it is only a matter of time until the current climate of accountability in higher education turns more of its attention to student affairs" (p. 12). Is this a risk worth taking?

Returning to Learning Communities at Mid-Central University

This chapter began with a case study that described the challenges Sean faced with implementing a pilot learning communities program at Mid-Central University (MCU). Sean was asked by a variety of administrators in the department of residence life to demonstrate the efficacy of learning communities on the student experience, but in each case the administrator had a view of accountability from his or her perspective. For example, the financial officer wanted to know if the program would be administered in a fiscally responsible manner. Others wanted to know how success would be measured, if there were a need for the program, and so on. All of these questions led to an inescapable conclusion: A number of questions need to be answered as this project is developed.

Assume that Sean is given permission to implement the pilot project and wishes you to be a consultant to an assessment process. Then, provide the answers to the following questions:

1. Would it be possible to design this pilot project without an assessment element? Why or why not?

2. How would you measure the process if the program was a success? What would be the elements of this strategy?

3. What could you learn from the brief history of assessment in student affairs that you might implement in this pilot project?

4. Given that you have multiple questions that have been asked about this project, how might you design a strategy to answer them?

5. Differentiate between an assessment of the LC and an evaluation of it. How can the assessment be used to inform the evaluation? Under what circumstances might the assessment achieve its goals but the evaluation would lead to discontinuing the project?

Discussion Questions

1. Other than fiscal measures, are there other yardsticks that can be used to evaluate a student affairs program? What are some of these? How might they be used?

2. Several aspects in the chapter were identified that differentiate a research study from an assessment project. Are there other aspects that distinguish research studies from assessment projects? What are these and why are they different?

3. Several reasons were identified in the chapter that emphasize the importance of assessment, among them accreditation, contemporary practice, and the CAS standards. Are there other reasons that underscore why assessment is important in contemporary higher education? What strategies can be employed to address these additional reasons?

4. Are there common themes that can be found in the historical documents that introduced and stressed the importance of assessment? How might these themes be addressed in contemporary assessment projects? Can any be ignored?

References

American College Personnel Association. (1996). The student learning imperative: Implications for student affairs. *Journal of College Student Development, 37*, 118–122. Retrieved from http://www.acpa .nche.edu/sites/default/files/ACPA%27s%20Student%20Learning %20Imperative.pdf

Astin, A. W. (1984). Student involvement: A developmental theory for higher education. *Journal of College Student Personnel, 25*, 297–308.

Astin, A. W. (1985). *Achieving educational excellence.* San Francisco, CA: Jossey-Bass.

Aulepp, L., & Delworth, U. (1976). *Training manual for an ecosystem model.* Boulder, CO: WICHE.

Benjamin, M. (Ed.). (2015). *Learning communities from start to finish.* New Directions for Student Services no. 149. San Francisco, CA: Jossey-Bass.

Blaich, C., & Wise, K. (2011). *From gathering to using assessment results.* Champaign, IL: National Institute for Learning Outcomes Assessment.

Blimling, G. S. (2013). Challenges of assessment in student affairs. In J. H. Schuh (Ed.), *Selected contemporary assessment issues* (pp. 5–14). New Directions for Student Services no. 142. San Francisco, CA: Jossey-Bass.

Bonfiglio, R., Hanson, G. S., Fried, J., Roberts, G., & Skinner, J. (2006). Assessing internal environments. In R. P. Keeling (Ed.), *Learning reconsidered 2: Implementing a campus-wide focus on the student experience* (pp. 43–51). Washington, DC: ACPA, ACUHO-I, ACU-I, NACADA, NACA, NASPA, & NIRSA.

Council for the Advancement of Standards. (2011). *General standards: CAS standards and guidelines*. Washington, DC: Author. Retrieved from http://standards.cas.edu/getpdf.cfm?PDF=E868395C-F784-2293-129ED7842334B22A

Dungy, G., & Gordon, S. A. (2011). The development of student affairs. In J. H. Schuh, S. R. Jones, S. R. Harper, & Associates, *Student services: A handbook for the profession* (5th ed., pp. 61–79). San Francisco, CA: Jossey-Bass.

Ewell, P. T. (2009). *Assessment, accountability and improvement: Revisiting the tension*. Champaign, IL: National Institute for Learning Outcomes Assessment.

Hamrick, F. A., Evans, N. J., & Schuh, J. H. (2002). *Foundations of student affairs practice*. San Francisco, CA: Jossey-Bass.

Keeling, R. P. (Ed.). (2006). *Learning reconsidered 2*. Washington, DC: American College Personnel Association (ACPA), Association of College and University Housing Officers–International (ACUHO-I), Association of College Unions–International (ACUI), National Academic Advising Association (NACADA), National Association for Campus Activities (NACA), National Association of Student Personnel Administrators (NASPA), and National Intramural-Recreational Sports Association (NIRSA).

Kennedy-Phillips, L., & Uhrig, K. (2013). Measuring the second-year transformational experience program (STEP) at The Ohio State University. In J. H. Schuh (Ed.), *Selected contemporary assessment issues* (pp. 83–88). New Directions for Student Services no. 142. San Francisco, CA: Jossey-Bass.

Kinzie, J. (2009). Foreword. In T. W. Banta, M. Griffin, T. J. Flateby, & S. Kahn, *Three promising alternatives for assessing college students' knowledge and skills* (p. 4). Champaign, IL: National Institute for Learning Outcomes Assessment.

Kuh, G. D., Kinzie, J., Schuh, J. H., Whitt, E. J., & Associates. (2010). *Student success in college*. San Francisco, CA: Jossey-Bass.

Livingston, C. H., & Zerulik, J. D. (2013). The role of the assessment coordinator in a division of student affairs. In J. H. Schuh (Ed.), *Selected contemporary assessment issues* (pp. 13–24). New Directions for Student Services no. 142. San Francisco, CA: Jossey-Bass.

Lloyd-Jones, E. (1929). *Student personnel work at Northwestern University.* New York: Columbia University, Teacher's College, doctoral dissertation submitted in partial fulfillment of the doctoral degree.

Mueller, K. H. (1961). *Student personnel work in higher education.* Boston, MA: Houghton Mifflin.

National Association of Student Personnel Administrators (1989). *Points of view.* Washington, DC: Author.

National Association of Student Personnel Administrators and American College Personnel Association. (2004). *Learning reconsidered.* Washington, DC: Authors. Retrieved from https://www.naspa.org/images/uploads/main/Learning_Reconsidered_Report.pdf

National Institute for Learning Outcomes Assessment. (2014). *About us: Our mission and vision.* Champaign, IL: Author. Retrieved from http://www.learningoutcomesassessment.org/AboutUs.html

New England Association of Colleges and Schools. (2011). *2011 standards for accreditation.* Burlington, MA: Author. Retrieved from https://cihe.neasc.org/downloads/Standards/Standards_for_Accreditation.pdf

Northwest Commission on Colleges and Universities. (2010). *Standards for accreditation.* Redmond, WA: Author. Retrieved from http://www.nwccu.org/Pubs%20Forms%20and%20Updates/Publications/Standards%20for%20Accreditation.pdf

Rhatigan, J. J. (2009). From the people up. In G. S. McClellan, J. Stringer, & Associates, *The handbook of student affairs administration* (3rd ed., pp. 3–18). San Francisco, CA: Jossey-Bass.

Sandeen, A., & Barr, M. J. (2006). *Critical issues for student affairs.* San Francisco, CA: Jossey-Bass.

Schuh, J. H., & Gansemer-Topf, A. M. (2010). *The role of student affairs in student learning assessment.* Urbana, IL: National Institute for Learning Outcomes Assessment.

Southern Association of Colleges and Schools. (2014). *The principles of accreditation.* Decatur, GA: Author. Retrieved from http://www.sacscoc.org/pdf/2012PrinciplesOfAcreditation.pdf

Study Group on the Conditions of Excellence in American Higher Education. (1984). *Involvement in learning: Realizing the potential of American higher education.* Washington, DC: National Institute of Education.

Suskie, L. A. (2009). *Assessing student learning: A common sense guide* (2nd ed.). San Francisco, CA: Jossey-Bass.

Swing, R. L., & Coogan, C. S. (2010). *Valuing assessment: Cost-benefit considerations.* Urbana, IL: National Institute for Learning Outcomes Assessment.

Upcraft, M. L., & Schuh, J. H. (1996). *Assessment in student affairs.* San Francisco, CA: Jossey-Bass.

Volkwein, J. F. (2011). *Gaining ground: The role of institutional research in assessing student outcomes and demonstrating institutional effectiveness.* Champaign, IL: National Institute for Learning Outcomes Assessment.

WASC. (2013). *2013 handbook of accreditation.* Alameda, CA: Western Association of Schools and Colleges Senior College and University Commission.

Weick, K. E. (1984). Small wins. *American Psychologist, 39*(1), 40–49.

Wellman, J. V. (2010). *Connecting the dots between learning and resources.* Champaign, IL: National Institute for Learning Outcomes Assessment.

2

DESIGNING AND PLANNING AN ASSESSMENT PROJECT

We looked at the foundations of assessment, defined terms, and described a potential assessment project as it applies to learning communities in Chapter 1. Now we move on to planning an assessment project, looking at salient questions to be considered in developing a plan to conduct an assessment project.

In this chapter we examine how a person who has never conducted an assessment might develop a plan to determine to what extent a new initiative has been successful. First, the chapter examines principles of good assessments. Then we will move on to a general discussion of crafting learning outcomes for assessment projects. Next we will look at questions that can be used to develop an assessment plan. Finally, we return to the hypothetical assessment project to examine approaches that our staff can take in developing the assessment of the initiative.

A First Assessment Project for Mike

Mike is the newly appointed Greek Advisor at Hawthorne University (HU), a regional university in the northwest corner of the state. Mike just finished the master's degree at the State University (SU) in student affairs and this is his first professional position. He was active in his fraternity as an undergraduate at South Central College (SCC), and decided as a junior that he would like to become a student affairs professional. As a consequence he pursued his master's

(Continued)

degree while he was a graduate assistant in Greek Affairs at State University. While a graduate student he assisted the Associate Dean of Students and worked with Greek letter organizations in leadership development. In part as a consequence of his work in leadership development, he was hired as Greek advisor at HU, with the charge that he will provide oversight for the fraternities and sororities at HU and begin to explore the possibility of offering a leadership development program for the officers of the Greek letter organizations.

There are six fraternities and four sororities at HU. The average size of each Greek letter organization is 40, with a range from 30 to 50. The overall health of the organizations is good. Leaders of a couple of the smaller Greek letter organizations are a bit concerned about the size of their memberships, but to date all of the organizations are current on their mortgage obligation, the houses are able to pay their bills on time, and support from the alumni and alumnae is quite robust. The individual houses are in good repair though several of them are going to need major renovations in the next decade.

Altogether, Mike inherited a good working situation with no pressing problems. His job is to develop programs to add value to the Greek letter experience of the students. The year before he began his work, Amy, his predecessor, conducted a needs assessment with the leaders of the fraternities and sororities and learned that they wanted in-depth experiences that would help them hone their leadership skills.

Mike began to develop a plan for the leadership development program, which he conceptualized as beginning with a retreat in the early fall, followed up by monthly seminars in fall, two seminars in the spring, and a celebratory reception two weeks before spring break. He decided to invite a combination of campus experts on leadership development, alumni and alumnae from some of the Greek letter organizations to make presentations and he identified, with the help of the HU Foundation, several businesses that would be willing to sponsor the program. Mike was very enthusiastic about what he was able to organize in a few short months. But one element of the activities was of concern to him: How would he measure the extent to which the leadership development program would be successful? He knew he would need help with developing an assessment designed to measure what he hoped to achieve but he did not know how to proceed. He decided that his next step would be to contact Cindy, who worked as the assessment coordinator for the division of student affairs. He was confident she could help him figure out how to plan and implement an assessment project.

Principles of Good Practice in Assessment

The American Association for Higher Education (1992) developed one the most important contributions to the literature of assessment related to assessing student learning two decades ago. We cited this work in our first volume (Upcraft & Schuh, 1996) and believe that the principles continue to provide an excellent foundation for those who seek to learn about planning assessments in student affairs. Accordingly, we revisit this work with additional commentary by Hutchings, Ewell, and Banta (2013), who were members of the original team that produced this work. The AAHE team's principles, as modified (Upcraft & Schuh, 1996), are as follows:

1. The assessment of student affairs programs, activities, and learning experiences begins with identifying educational values. Typically, educational values can be found in an institution's mission and values statements, and also are included in the mission and values statements for the division of student affairs. Also important, individual units should try to identify the learning outcomes that potentially will result from a student's participating in various activities, learning experiences, and so on. For example, what will a student learn from living in a residence hall? What learning will be the result of volunteering at a community service agency? If students participate in a leadership development program

such as the one being developed at HU, what will they learn and incorporate into their leadership style?

2. Assessment is most effective when it reflects an understanding of organizational performance as multidimensional, integrated, and revealed in performance over time. It is very difficult to deconstruct the student experience. So many factors are involved: For example, critical thinking skills can be enhanced through coursework, out of class experiences, part-time employment, and so on. Nor is it easy to measure growth from one day of a student's experience in a typical college student's career. That is, one would hope that students learn and grow a little bit each day and over the course of a semester or a year they will be able to demonstrate significant growth, but the student experience in a routine week is not likely to yield much in the way of measurable growth. In short, growth occurs a little at a time but should be measurable over the course of a semester or academic year.

   Similarly, institutions rarely experience demonstrable growth from one day to the next or even one month to the next. Certainly it is possible that a faculty member will receive a significant award or the institution may receive a transformative gift, but these events are comparatively rare. Rather, institutions tend to grow over time, meaning that they get a little better from one year to the next. This growth may be through a carefully crafted strategy to improve the undergraduate experience or it may be a consequence of a reorganization that yields a more efficient organization. So, the point of this principle is that institutions may not "get better" over the course of a week, a month, or even a semester. Through using comprehensive data and carefully making changes that yield improvement in the academic program or the out of class student experience, institutions can get better over time. An example of this was found in Project DEEP (Kuh, Kinzie, Schuh, & Whitt, 2005/2010) when the president of an institution noted that many of the university's students left campus for part time jobs. The president used some of her contingency funds to improve compensation for student jobs on campus in an effort to retain students. The strategy worked and students became more engaged in the life of the institution through their employment on campus.

In the case of the proposed program at HU, Mike is proposing a series of activities that are designed to help the student participants strengthen their leadership skills. But they might also strengthen their skills as a consequence of their participation in out of class activities other than their involvement with their Greek letter organizations, course work, and perhaps even from work experiences, such as serving as paid paraprofessionals on campus (Lillis & Schuh, 1982).

3. Assessment works best when it has clear, explicitly stated goals. This principle suggests that doing assessment simply to do assessment has the potential to yield disappointing results. Rather, the assessment should have a specific goal, such as, according to our case study, learning if and how students' leadership skills improved as a consequence of participating in the program that Mike was developing. The learning outcomes will have to be more precise, but in this case Mike will have a very specific purpose—did the experience help the participants develop improved leadership skills, or not? Might the participants have participated in other experiences that also contributed to their growth as leaders?

4. Assessment requires attention to outcomes but also, and just as important, to the processes that lead to them. The previous principle makes it clear that assessment ought to have goals, meaning that those conducting the assessment will need to have a clear goal or goals in mind when they are conducting the assessment. But it is also important to understand that a great deal can be learned from the process of conducting the

assessment. If students are involved in the process potentially they will learn a great deal by constructing items and analyzing data, or sitting in on focus groups and analyzing the resulting data. Those conducting the assessment also can learn about the steps required in planning a complex process. Assessments are not easy to conduct and much can be learned from developing a plan that leads from identifying the purpose of the assessment to sharing the results and potentially making changes as a result of what was learned. So, it is important to remember that the process of assessment can be instructive and valuable.

5. Assessment works best when it is ongoing, not episodic. There will be times when conducting an assessment is necessary or may appear to be simply a response to external expectations that one be conducted. Ewell (2009) speaks to the accountability dimension of assessment as a necessary feature in a campus's assessment plan. In our case study, Mike is going to have to figure out how to respond to questions related to the leadership development program's efficacy, particularly if asked about that by the benefactors of the program or those who have served as session presenters. To not have an assessment in place to respond to such queries would be a significant mistake. But in addition, simply responding to questions by providing data, without thinking about how the assessment information can be used to sharpen and improve the program in the future, assuming it will be repeated from one year to the next, is short-sighted, and in some respects a waste of an important opportunity.

For those who are engaged in accreditation work or program review, it is all too obvious when assessments are conducted just in advance of the visit of external evaluators or accreditors. Quite, simply, this example of "just-in-time assessment" illustrates the concept of conducting assessments to keep external reviewers happy without a real commitment to getting better over time. Ongoing assessments can be used to meet accountability issues without question, but they also can be used for improvement, as Ewell (2009) points out. Episodic assessments are better than not conducting assessments at all, but their potency does not begin to measure up to the value of conducting ongoing assessments.

6. Assessment is most effective when representatives from across student affairs and the institution are involved. We think that an element of the value of assessment is that the process, as well as the results, can be used to inform important constituents and stakeholders about the value of the programs, activities, and experiences that are found in the portfolio of student affairs. Faculty members, in particular, often are not well informed about student affairs. The involvement of faculty in the assessment process can be a very useful experience for them as well as for the division of student affairs. Involvement of faculty in an assessment process, for example, can lead to faculty members accepting assignments as student organization advisors or program or unit advisory board members. They may also, as a consequence of learning more about the student experience, be active supporters of student affairs as members of campus governance units, such as the faculty senate or various advisory committees on campus.

7. Assessment makes a difference when it begins with issues of use and illuminates questions that people really care about. Clearly, programs, services, and activities that are developed by student affairs units are designed for students. The illustration is that students will not grow if they do not engage in learning opportunities. But it is also important to note that simply recording the number of participants in a learning opportunity does not provide the depth that is necessary when one conducts an assessment. For example, beyond identifying the number of participants in a specific activity, assessments are designed to determine what the participants learned and how that learning may affect their future activities. It would

be good to know that a leadership development experience was well attended, to use the previous example, or that the program was well organized and enthusiastically received, but it would be very important to learn that the participants enhanced their leadership skills through learning about leadership theory, meeting management, membership recruitment, and financial supervision.

8. Assessment should be part of a larger set of conditions that promote change. While we defined assessment as, in effect, a process by which program or department effectiveness was determined, but we also pointed out that assessment can lead to improvement. The purposes of assessment have been sharpened over the years and as Ewell (2009) has concluded, assessment increasingly is thought of as a mechanism to demonstrate accountability to stakeholders, or a process that leads to improvement, or both. As we demonstrate in Chapter 14, establishing an ongoing program of assessment is an important element in establishing a culture of evidence in our colleges and universities and a key dimension of the improvement process.

9. Through assessment student affairs professionals meet responsibilities to students, the institution, and the public. This final principle is something of an umbrella principle in that it addresses the concept that assessment is a means by which obligations to stakeholders can be met. This principle assumes that assessments are conducted with transparency and that results are shared widely. Moreover, it assumes that the results lead to organizational or program improvement. Failure to conduct assessments with openness or to use the result to inform organizational change is to obviate the potential potency of the process. In this case, Mike will need to conduct an assessment to meet his obligations to the program participants, the advisory group, the benefactors of the program and others who may have an interest in its effectiveness.

Developing an Assessment Plan

Mike plans to initiate a leadership development program for students at HU but has been advised to develop an assessment plan as an element in the program. He has not taken on an assessment project in his professional experience, so he will be starting from scratch. Before we move into a list of questions that he can use to guide his inquiry he needs to think about developing learning outcomes for the assessment.

Student learning is a central focus of institutions of higher education along with inquiry and public service. In the eyes of some (see, for example, King & Magolda, 2011; U.S. Department of Education, 2006), student learning must be placed at the heart of the collegiate experience with an ever-increasing emphasis on outcomes. Regardless of one's perspective on this issue, there is no question that many organizations, including accrediting bodies, have an interest in student learning and measuring the extent to which institutions actually measure what students learn (Association of American Universities, 2013; National Commission on Accountability in Higher Education, 2005; Provezis, 2010).

In reviewing the current status of the importance of learning outcomes on campus, Kuh, Jankowski, Ikenberry, and Kinzie (2014) offer a number of conclusions, among which are the following:

- Stated learning outcomes for students are now the norm in American higher education. In 2013, about 84% of all colleges and universities had adopted stated learning outcomes for all their undergraduates, an increase of 10% from 2009.

- The prime driver of assessment remains the same: expectations of regional and program or specialized accrediting agencies.

- There is significantly more assessment activity now than a few years ago.

- "The range of tools and measures to assess student learning has expanded significantly. National surveys remain popular (85% of all schools use them), but there has been a large increase in the use of rubrics, portfolios, and other classroom-based assessments as well. . . ." (p. 3)

Kuh and his colleagues add that in the final analysis institutions must "complete the transition from a culture of compliance to a culture of evidence-based decision-making" (2014, p. 36).

Student Learning and Development Outcomes

The Council for the Advancement of Standards in Higher Education (CAS) can be viewed as providing commonly accepted standards for various aspects of student affairs practice and will be discussed later in this volume. The CAS standards include standards for 43 higher education programs and services (CAS, 2012) including academic advising programs. Six broad learning and development outcomes, known as domains, have been established for each of the 43 programs under the CAS umbrella and are as follows:

1. Knowledge acquisition, construction, integration, and application
2. Cognitive complexity
3. Intrapersonal development
4. Interpersonal competence
5. Humanitarianism and civic engagement
6. Practical competence

These learning and development outcomes can be traced to various seminal documents in student affairs practice, including *The Student Personnel Point of View, 1937, 1949* and *A Perspective on Student Affairs* (National Association of Student Personnel Administrators, 1989). Whether or not all of these outcomes would be appropriate for all institutions of higher education is not entirely clear because institutions have such a wide range of missions and approaches to student learning (see Association of American Universities, 2013), but most would be appropriate at many institutions. The challenge to student affairs professionals, of course, is to align these domains with the educational purposes of their institutions, make them practical, and apply them in their daily interaction with students. Further discussion of learning and program outcomes is provided in Chapters 4 and 5.

The potential learning outcomes previously identified provide an extensive list for the college student experience. The program that Mike is planning to organize has excellent potential to advance a number of the learning outcomes identified in the previous section. For example, students who assume a leadership role in an organization very well may improve their leadership skills, their oral and written communications skills, and their skills at long-range planning, and, as a consequence, may gain enhanced self-esteem. In crafting his leadership development program, Mike should identify potential learning outcomes that may result from students' participating in the program.

Questions That Guide the Assessment Process

In our 2009 book (Schuh & Associates, 2009), we posited a number of questions that can be used to guide the assessment process. These questions may not fit with all assessment processes, but they form an excellent basis for planning most assessments. In the case of our example, Mike needs to develop his assessment plan to measure the learning that results from the leadership development program. He needs to consider some questions that will help shape the assessment aspect of his project.

What Are the Issues at Hand (Step 1)?

This question, which has to do with framing the purpose of the assessment, is direct in Mike's case. He will need to determine if the leadership development program was successful. In that respect, then he needs to provide information to the various stakeholders who have supported the program, and participated in it, that the program achieved its goals. Secondarily, the assessment will need to determine how the program can be improved in the future, should it be offered again.

There are other issues that may frame the purpose of the assessment. These can be everything from proving the efficacy of that which is being assessed to demonstrating that the initiative and/or experience was worth the cost (in dollars) and effort (in staff members' time). An example of an assessment of this type could result in changes in staffing a facility or program such as shifting from professional staff to paraprofessional staff, adding an initiative to the student affairs portfolio, such as a learning community, or developing a partnership with another institution in the area, such as shared recruitment fairs with another college in the same town. All of these examples suggest that an assessment is imperative to determine the value and provide an empirical basis for continuing the program, modifying the program dramatically, and not renewing it.

We pointed out in our 1996 book (Upcraft & Schuh, 1996) that it is nearly impossible to extricate assessment activities from the political environment in which they are conducted. Someone would like to have the resources devoted to the object of the assessment assigned to that person's unit, but someone else does not think the initiative should be undertaken in the first place, and still others question whether or not student affairs has a place on the campus. Certainly other issues also may be at hand. So, it is important to note the political environment and heed any special challenges that will need to be addressed. In the case of Mike's program, if someone believes that leaders are born, not made, and as a consequence there is no reason to undertake a complex leadership development program, that issue, which is part of the political environment, will need to be addressed.

What Is the Purpose of the Assessment (Step 2)?

Mike will need to measure what students have learned from participating in the leadership development program. Very specifically, the assessment will help determine if the program's goals have been met and the learning outcomes achieved—partially, fully, or not at all. Determining the purpose of the assessment, in effect, narrows the thinking that spins out of the first question (determining the issues at hand) and begins to bring focus to the assessment activity. The purpose of this assessment for Mike is to determine if the students who participated in the leadership development program enhanced their leadership skills. In short, Mike is attempting to determine if the program worked; this is an example of assessment for accountability, as discussed in Chapter 1.

Who Should Be Studied (Step 3)?

Mike's program was designed for the executive officers of the various Greek letter organizations at HU. Each of the fraternities and sororities could nominate as many as three participants for the program, so the maximum number of students who will participate is 30. Some organizations may not nominate three participants and a few may drop out, but for planning purposes, the maximum number will be 30.

What Is the Preferred Assessment Method (Step 4)?

Given the number of participants, Mike decided that qualitative methods will be used to assess the program. With just 30 participants, it would be difficult to conduct a quantitative study, so the approach that seems to make the most sense is to employ qualitative methods. It is important to note that the methods used in the assessment project will be driven by the guiding questions of the study and the nature of the data that will be collected for the project. We believe that those conducting an assessment will be making a mistake if they use their personal preference to guide the assessment method they select. For example, if the project leaders selected a quantitative method because they are more comfortable with numbers rather than words, even if the project is focused on how students make meaning of their experiences, we believe that is an error. On the other hand, if a qualitative method is selected because the assessors prefer working with words rather than numbers, that, too, would be a mistake in our view. We believe that the purpose and nature of the assessment should guide the selection of the method that is most appropriate for the project. Chapter 7 of this volume provides more information about selecting and applying qualitative methods to assessment projects.

How Should We Collect Our Data (Step 5)?

Several different approaches could be used to conduct data. Before the retreat in the Fall, several focus groups could be conducted to gather baseline information on what the participants thought about their leadership skills, how they thought the leadership development program might help them, and what they could do to assist their organizations in the upcoming year. Cindy agreed to help Mike develop an interview protocol for the focus groups.

After each leadership development experience, the participants could complete an activity described by Suskie (2009) as a "minute paper." The paper is designed to elicit information from participants that focuses on two outcomes: the most important thing the participants learned in the program and what important questions related to the topic of the day remained unanswered. Suskie recommends that the participants who are answering each question provide no more than a sentence. These answers to the questions help those leading the workshop to determine if the learning outcomes as identified by the participants were consistent with the learning outcomes that were planned for the activity, and they also help identify what needs to be covered in succeeding activities in the series.

A third assessment activity would be to ask the participants to keep journals. They would not necessarily need to contribute entries on a daily basis, but instead would be asked to contribute their reflections after they served as leaders of their organizations, such as when the organizations had meetings, events, or other activities in which they applied their leadership skills.

Another potential aspect of the assessment process would be for Mike, with some help, to occasionally observe the participants as they led various activities for their organizations. Mike would need some help because with the number of participants (potentially 30), it would not be possible to observe all of them in leadership roles. He and Cindy decided to develop a plan where some graduate students from an evaluation course might be able to assist in this activity.

Finally, focus groups could be held at the end of the academic year. These would be designed to have the participants reflect on their activities as leaders, how (or if) the leadership development activities helped them develop their skills, how they applied their learning to their organizations, and other thoughts they might have about their experiences as leaders. This would be a summative activity, meaning that it would be designed to provide a final evaluation of the leadership development series to determine its effectiveness and to determine if it should be repeated in succeeding years. If it is to be repeated, how might it be modified so that it could be more potent from the standpoint of the student participants?

What Instrument Should We Use (Step 6)?

The nature of the study will determine the type of instrument that the assessor will use. If we were going to conduct a quantitative study, we would need to select an instrument that we would administer to our participants. So, if we were interested in student experiences in their first year of college, we might use the "Your First College Year Survey" (Higher Education Research Institute, 2015). The instrument has been administered for over a decade and can be tailored to meet specific institutional needs. Our view is that using a standardized instrument with strong psychometric properties is preferable to developing one's own instrument, although it may be that a specific project is unique and a commercially developed instrument may not be available. In that case, an instrument may have to be developed for the project. Palomba and Banta (1999) provide a further discussion of commercially available instruments compared with locally developed instruments.

But in the case of Mike's study, with a small number of potential participants, the preferred method of collecting data will be a combination of qualitative techniques including focus groups, minute papers and even participant observation. Chapter 9 discusses developing instruments for qualitative studies.

How Should We Analyze Our Data (Step 7)?

Data analysis techniques will be determined by the nature of the information that is collected. For example, if numerical data are collected, a statistical analysis is the most likely method. In this project, we are using a combination of qualitative methods, looking for themes, patterns, and trends in the data. Cooper and Shelley (2009) provide a step-by-step approach to analyzing qualitative data that includes strategies for insuring rigor in a quantitative data analysis. In this book, Chapter 7 provides a detailed discussion on the use of qualitative techniques and Chapter 8 includes detail on conducting quantitative assessments.

How Should We Report the Results (Step 8)?

Without question, assessment results need to be reported, regardless of what is learned from the project. Even if the results are discouraging, or the findings indicate that the student experience was negative (for example, the students did not learn anything from participating in a specific experience), the results need to be reported to interested stakeholders. Stakeholders include the student participants, those responsible for developing and implementing the program, those providing oversight for the unit offering the program, and other members of the institution's family.

The exact method of reporting will vary depending on the nature of the project and the number of people who need to be informed of the results. Senior institutional leaders such as the dean of students, vice president for student affairs, and so on probably should receive an abstract with information about how to access more details. Senior leaders typically are very busy people who receive a tremendous amount of reading material and there very well may be an inverse relationship between the length of reports sent to senior administrators and the likelihood that these reports will be read: That's why we recommend that an abstract of the information be sent to them.

Those who participate in the study should be notified that results are available. An efficient means of doing so is to send them an e-mail with a link to a website where the complete report is available. Other electronic means of notifying the participants as well as members of the campus community include the use of Facebook and Twitter. These means can be used to notify potential readers that the report is available and where to find it electronically. It may also make sense to provide a link to the report on the homepage of the department or unit conducting the assessment. If the unit or program has an advisory board, members should receive a special notice that the report is available for their review. For Mike's assessment, an announcement of the availability of the report could be placed on the homepage from the Greek affairs program at HU with a link to the report itself. He also ought to notify those who helped him develop the program and the program's benefactors that the report is available. Chapter 13 of this volume provides additional ideas and details about reporting results.

Should the local media be informed that the results are available? Our view is that it is best to provide information about the availability of a report. If the results are newsworthy it is likely that the media will find out what has been learned anyway, so it is better to let the media know about the report and then take questions as they are asked by media representatives.

How Can We Use the Data for Improvement (Step 9)?

Finally, we think a guiding question has to do with using the information from the assessment for improvement purposes. This is a fundamental aspect of assessment according to Ewell (2009), and we agree that it is central to the assessment process. The data can point to changes and modifications in the project. The assessment should shed light on the efficacy of the project being assessed. Did the project yield the desired results? In the case of Mike's leadership development program, did the skills of the leaders improve? The answer could range from yes to no to partially. For example, maybe the participants' meeting management skills improved but their communications skills did not. A careful analysis of the results coupled with strategies to address deficiencies should be part of this aspect of the assessment. And, there may be other aspects of the assessment that should be considered. Perhaps the assessment indicated that the program was effective, but it was so time consuming that the participants reported that while they learned a lot, which was confirmed by the assessment, it took so much of their time that they recommended that it should be scaled back for future participants. Mike will need to confer with interested stakeholders to determine whether to continue with the leadership development program in the future and, if so, what modifications should be considered for future iterations. Bringing about change through assessment is addressed in Chapter 13.

Questions about Assessing Leadership Development at HU

This chapter's contents are illustrated by an assessment plan that Mike, the Greek letter organization advisor at Hawthorne University, should consider in developing an assessment of a new leadership development program. Since the program Mike was developing had not been offered before at Hawthorne, he did not have a blueprint to follow in developing his plan. Based on your reading of this chapter and the challenges Mike faces in developing his assessment plan, please consider these additional questions for discussion:

1. What are the most difficult challenges Mike faces in developing his assessment plan?

2. What educational values from Hawthorne University would guide the development of an assessment plan?

3. What learning outcomes might result from students' participating in this leadership development program? How might Mike determine if these outcomes are realized?

4. Mike consulted with Cindy, the student affairs assessment coordinator, in developing his assessment plan. Are there other people on campus who could be helpful in developing an assessment plan?

5. If Mike had decided to conduct a quantitative assessment, how would that decision have affected the assessment plan?

6. Besides the stakeholders identified in the dissemination plan, are there other people who should have been notified that the assessment had been completed?

Discussion Questions

1. Why is identifying educational values important as a principle of good practice in assessment? If educational values are not identified, will that make a difference in the potency of an assessment project? Why or why not? How would you identify educational values that can be used to frame assessment projects?

2. Why should assessment be conducted on a routine basis? What message is implied if assessments are conducted primarily in the two years before an institution is accredited? What barriers exist to conducting assessments on a routine basis? How might these be overcome?

3. Among the principles of good assessment practice is the assertion that assessment illuminates questions that people really care about. What are the questions people really care about? How are these identified? Does a person's role in a college or university affect what he or she cares about? Are there questions that should be universal no matter what one's role is in an institution?

4. The chapter asserted that assessment is a way of meeting obligations to various stakeholders. Identify three or four stakeholders and explain how assessment can be used to meet their expectations. Why might they have different expectations for programs in student affairs?

References

American Association for Higher Education. (1992). *Principles of good practice for assessing student learning*. Washington, DC: Author.

Association of American Universities. (2013). *Survey on undergraduate student objectives and assessment*. Washington, DC: Author.

Cooper, R. M., & Shelley, M. C., II. (2009). Data analysis. In J. H. Schuh & Associates, *Assessment methods for student affairs* (pp. 141–170). San Francisco, CA: Jossey-Bass.

Council for the Advancement of Standards in Higher Education. (2012). *CAS professional standards for higher education* (8th ed.). Washington, DC: Author. Retrieved from http://www.cas.edu/standards

Ewell, P. T. (2009). *Assessment, accountability and improvement: Revisiting the tension.* Champaign, IL: National Institute for Learning Outcomes Assessment.

Higher Education Research Institute. (2015). *Your First College Year Survey.* Los Angeles, CA: UCLA Higher Education Institute. Retrieved from http://www.heri.ucla.edu/yfcyoverview.php

Hutchings, P., Ewell, P, & Banta, T. (2013). *AAHE Principles of good practice: Aging nicely.* Champaign, IL: NILOA. Retrieved from http://www .learningoutcomeassessment.org/PrinciplesofAssessment.html

King, P. M., & Baxter Magolda, M. B. (2011). Student learning. In J. H. Schuh, S. R. Harper, S. R. Jones, & Associates, *Student services: A handbook for the profession* (5th ed., pp. 207–225). San Francisco, CA: Jossey-Bass.

Kuh, G. D., Jankowski, N., Ikenberry, S. O., & Kinzie, J. (2014, January). *Knowing what students know and can do: The current state of student learning outcomes assessment in U.S. colleges and universities.* Champaign: University of Illinois at Urbana-Champaign, National Institute for Learning Outcomes Assessment.

Kuh, G. D., Kinzie, J., Schuh, J. H., & Whitt, E. J. (2010). *Student success in college.* San Francisco, CA: Jossey-Bass. (Original work published 2005)

Lillis, C. J., & Schuh, J. H. (1982). The perceived long-term benefits of holding a resident assistant position. *The Journal of College and University Student Housing, 12*(1), 36–39.

National Association of Student Personnel Administrators. (1989). *Points of view.* Washington, DC: Author.

National Commission on Accountability in Higher Education. (2005). *Accountability for better results: A national imperative for higher education.* Denver, CO: State Higher Education Executive Officers.

Palomba, C. A., & Banta, T. W. (1999). *Assessment essentials.* San Francisco, CA: Jossey-Bass.

Provezis, S. (2010). *Regional accrediting and student learning outcomes: Mapping the territory.* Urbana, IL: National Institute for Learning Outcomes Assessment.

Schuh, J. H., & Associates. (2009). *Assessment methods for student affairs.* San Francisco, CA: Jossey-Bass.

Suskie, L. A. (2009). *Assessing student learning: A common sense guide* (2nd ed.). San Francisco, CA: Jossey-Bass.

Upcraft, M. L., & Schuh, J. H. (1996). *Assessment in student affairs.* San Francisco, CA: Jossey-Bass.

U.S. Department of Education. (2006). *A test of leadership: Charting the future of US higher education.* Washington, DC: Author.

3

FRAMING ASSESSMENT WITH
THE HIGHEST ETHICAL STANDARDS

Ethics are often thought of contextually. Student affairs practitioners may regard ethics in terms of professional practice, while graduate students and faculty tend to view ethics as linked with research. The purposes of this chapter are to introduce the basic principles of ethical research, to establish the need for ethical practice in assessment, to apply ethical standards to assessment projects, and to provide recommendations for ensuring the highest ethical standards are met in assessment work. Primarily, we want to be sure that assessment projects are consistent with what is required for the protection of participants and their records. This chapter will provide details about how to make sure that assessment is conducted using the most rigorous ethical principles consistent with contemporary practices and federal guidelines.

The basic types of institutional review board (IRB) approval are not covered in this chapter. There were two reasons for this omission. First, there has been considerable ongoing federal debate regarding the basic classifications of research approval and whether or not federal standards should apply to particular methodologies (for example, historical research). Second, according to general application of federal policy, student affairs assessment work is often not reviewable by the IRB. However, we believe the basic principles of respect for others, beneficence, and justice as outlined in *The Belmont Report* (U.S. Dept. of Health, Education and Welfare, 1979) should be considered irrespective of the need for institutional approval. This chapter provides recommendations for applying these principles with the goal of framing assessment work in the highest ethical standards. We believe ethical consideration should be a foundational and fundamental component of any assessment project.

Definition and Use of Ethics in Assessment

Federal guidelines distinguish between research and assessment activities based on audience. Research is conducted with external audiences in mind while assessment is completed for internal audiences. Although individual campus policies may vary, few student affairs assessment projects meet this definition of research and therefore do not fall under the jurisdiction of the IRB. A misconception, however, is that because assessment activities generally are not IRB-reviewed, federally provisioned ethical principles do not apply and, as a result, can be overlooked. This is not to suggest those conducting assessment work intentionally ignore the rights and protections afforded to participants in their projects. However, we often talk with practitioners who have not considered basic ethical principles prior to choosing a sample, administering an instrument, protecting sensitive data, or engaging in assessment activities involving human participants or their records. We contend that aside from the intended audience, there are few differences with regard to how research or assessment data are collected and analyzed. Because of this similarity, we view ethical principles as applying to both external research and internal assessment efforts. To illustrate how ethical principles can be applied to assessment projects, this chapter includes two case studies, using different data collection methods.

The Welcome Week Leader Experience at Metropolitan University

Erika is the director of new student programs at Metropolitan University (MU). Her primary areas of responsibility include student orientation, welcome week, and first year student experiences.

MU is a large institution located in a major city. Each year, the institution admits approximately 4,000 new undergraduate students; most are 18 to 20 years of age. As part of her work, Erika selects and supervises a large student staff of orientation and welcome week leaders to help new students acclimate to college. Other members of her office staff include two assistant directors, two graduate assistants, and several student workers. Each year, the staff selects 22 student orientation leaders who will participate in a spring course as well as summer training before implementing orientation sessions for new students. Also, during the spring she selects a group of approximately 200 upperclass students to serve as fall welcome week leaders who attend a day of training in spring as well as several days of training in early fall before implementing welcome week activities for approximately 20 new students each in the week prior to the beginning of classes in the fall.

According to the assessment results from new student and parent satisfaction surveys, orientation and welcome week participants have been pleased with their experiences. Erika is curious about the experiences of the student leaders who organize and offer these events. Specifically, she wants to know more about the welcome week leader experience, as the time she spends with them is considerably less than with orientation leaders. As part of their training, welcome week leaders receive instruction ranging from institutional procedures and policies to helping strategies for aiding new students in their transition to college life. Erika wants to know more about the experiences these students have, with the hope of refining the training and support program. Most of her orientation leaders are selected from the welcome week leader pool and many of the student leaders across campus at one time also served as welcome week leaders. As a result, there is some interest among her colleagues in other offices about how students view their welcome week leader experience.

Thinking back to her assessment course, Erika decides the best way to learn about student experiences is through qualitative data.

(*Continued*)

Limitations she has to contend with will be the time and resources required to conduct the study, but she is fortunate to have office staff who can help. From mid to late fall, staff from new student programs will complete focus groups with welcome leaders from the prior year. They plan to develop a common, semistructured instrument (see Chapter 9), hold group sessions with six to eight leaders at a time, and provide pizza during the interview as an incentive to participate. Questions during the session will focus on the overall experience of being a welcome week leader, including perceptions about their preparation, interactions with new student programs staff, and general satisfaction with participation. There will be some focus on learning outcomes, but this is a lower priority because the office uses a separate pre/post survey to evaluate student learning. All 200 welcome week leaders will be asked to participate in the focus group sessions and Erika hopes to gain perspectives from at least 30 members of the group. After developing the interview questions, her two graduate students will recruit and conduct all interviews.

Living in Fraternity/Sorority Housing at Eastern Wesleyan College

Frank is the assistant dean of students for fraternity/sorority involvement at Eastern Wesleyan College (EWC). His primary responsibilities involve facilitating fraternity/sorority recruitment, advising the three fraternity/sorority governing councils, facilitating leadership training and student development, working with chapter advisors and alumni, and overseeing the occupancy, maintenance, and upkeep of fraternity/sorority housing. He has two coordinators that aid in these responsibilities. EWC is a mid/large-sized university located in a mid-sized city about an hour from a major metropolitan area. Approximately 20 percent of the 14,000 undergraduate students belong to one of the 25 internationally and nationally affiliated fraternities or sororities and membership in each group ranges from 6 to 120. Fourteen of the organizations (eight fraternities, six sororities) are housed on campus. Occupancy ranges from 40 to 60 members per facility.

Frank is interested in assessing the living environment in fraternity/sorority housing. Specifically, he wants to know resident member perceptions about the academic environment, safety and security, brother/sisterhood activities, and risk-taking behaviors related to the living environment. He worked with a faculty member in psychology to develop the survey, which incorporates items (with permission) from existing instruments. To ensure he has the broadest possible representation, Frank wants to survey all members of organizations with houses, inclusive of residents and nonresidents. He is hoping for at least an 80 percent return rate from each group. Initially, he and his staff planned to visit each house during a chapter meeting to distribute paper-based surveys, but time limitations as well as concern about entering and analyzing data led him to choose an online service to distribute the survey. To ensure groups will respond, Frank announced that groups who do not have at least an 80 percent return rate would not be eligible for homecoming awards.

A Historical Overview of Research Ethics

In 1991, the Department of Health and Human Services (DHHS) as part of its Code of Federal Regulations (CFR) developed 45 CFR 46, a federal policy outlining the basic guidelines for the protection of human subjects in research. The guidelines were heavily influenced by *The Belmont Report* (U.S. Dept. of Health, Education and Welfare, 1979), a document jointly developed by the National Commission for the Protection of Human Subjects of Biomedical and Behavioral Research that outlines basic ethical principles in research involving human subjects.

Most federal agencies that sponsor or conduct research follow 45 CFR 46. Recently updated in 2009, 45 CFR 46 includes four subparts:

1. Subpart A describes the Federal Policy or the "Common Rule"
2. Subpart B adds additional protections for pregnant women, human fetuses, and neonates
3. Subpart C adds additional protections for prisoners
4. Subpart D adds additional protections for children

In the context of educational research or assessment, many of the provisions seem not to apply, as few studies involve possibly harmful treatments or vulnerable research subjects. However, potential harm to participants extends beyond what may seem easily recognizable. For example, interviewing a student about her experiences in class as part of an assessment on classroom environment may seem harmless, but questions probing her perceptions of the faculty member's grading policies have the potential to affect her grade if her identity is revealed.

In our experience, practitioners seldom consider the potential effects assessment design, conduct, and reporting may have for participants. There also seems to be some misunderstanding regarding whether the campus IRB should review an assessment project. This chapter focuses on Subpart A ("The Common Rule"), which outlines the form and functions of the IRB, the informed consent process, and compliance with a focus on relevance for assessment projects. There are few definitive "rules" for when an assessment project falls under the jurisdiction of 45 CFR 46, especially when conducted in common educational settings. Rather than provide a litmus test for whether an assessment project should be reviewed by an IRB, we focus on how the basic principles for ethical research should be considered for data projects involving students, faculty, staff, or other institutional stakeholders or their records.

Two terms used in the federal guidelines for research are important to know: human subjects and minimal risk.

Understanding what is meant by these terms can help you to interpret campus-policies as well as to decipher institutional requirements for review. Human subjects is a term used to describe people who participate in research or research-based studies. Secondary subjects is a term often used to describe indirect participation, such as individual records. Unless we are directly quoting or referring to specific policy, we use participants to mean human subjects and participant data to refer to secondary subjects. Minimal risk is a term used to describe the least possible harm or discomfort a researcher anticipates will result from participation in a study. Minimal risk generally is thought of as not greater than ordinary situations or circumstances encountered in daily life or during the performance of physical or physiological tests.

What Is Considered Research?

In Chapter 1, we distinguished between research, assessment, and evaluation for the purpose of defining the scope of this book. The ethical conduct of research (broadly defined) involving human subjects requires some additional clarification. From the federal perspective (45 CFR 46.102d), research is defined as a systematic investigation including research development, testing, and evaluation, which is designed to develop or contribute to "generalizable knowledge." In subsection f, DHHS defines a human subject as "a living individual about whom an investigator (whether professional or student) conducting research obtains (1) data through intervention or interaction with the individual or (2) identifiable private information." Finally, the Code provisions the creation and conduct of a campus IRB, a group established to make determinations as to the ethical conduct of campus research. The IRB reviews research and grants approval for investigators to conduct studies within the guidelines of federal policy.

Because the guidelines can be somewhat vague, the composition of the IRB can influence what is or is not considered research (that is, what is reviewable). For example, an IRB that strictly defines research as any investigation involving human subjects or records might consider assessment projects to fall under its jurisdiction. Conversely, an IRB may choose to determine what is reviewable based on the "generalizable knowledge" provision and choose to not review assessment projects. As a first step in beginning assessment work, we advise anyone who is contemplating an assessment project to consult with the institution's IRB resources to determine if there are provisions for what the IRB reviews. For example, in its IRB Guide for faculty, staff, and students, the University of Tennessee, Knoxville (UTK) IRB provided the federal definition of research as outlined in 45 CFR 46.102d, but clarified by noting.

"In other words, research is systematic observation and data collection which

1. Is intended for research to the scientific community as a contribution to knowledge

2. Is portrayed (explicitly or implicitly) as research or experimental investigation, and/or

3. Is intended to fulfill requirements for a master's thesis, doctoral dissertation, or other research requirements at the University."

Activities that cannot be defined as "research" by one or more of the criteria do not have to be reviewed by the UTK IRB. These include the following:

1. Data collection for internal departmental or other university purposes (for example, teaching evaluations, student evaluations, and staff evaluations).

2. Program evaluation carried out under independent contract for an external organization that is for their internal purposes only. Examples of program evaluation include: personnel studies, staff effectiveness studies, human cost benefit analysis, treatment effectiveness studies, or human engineering studies.

One more consideration is approval for partnerships with large-scale surveys, such as the National Study of Student Engagement (NSSE). This case can vary considerably by institution. Some IRBs want to review all research-based efforts conducted on campus personnel external to the university, even if they are funded or otherwise sponsored by a campus department and intended for internal use. Often, this is because some large-scale data services, while marketed and administrated specifically for internal use, also maintain the rights to deidentified student data. For example, large-scale datasets created from multi-institution participation often are mined by researchers and published for external audiences. Our advice when partnering with external agencies is to seek IRB guidance. While data collection and reporting may be intended to inform campus practice, the aggregated data may be made available to off campus researchers. A campus IRB or even legal counsel can help review the contract to determine whether the project needs to be submitted for review. Following a review process, we advise seeking exemption for future administrations of the specific surveys, as some IRBs maintain lists of survey providers and databases whose administration or use does not require repeated review.

Basic Ethical Principles

The authors of *The Belmont Report* (U.S. Dept. of Health, Education and Welfare, 1979) defined three basic criteria for the ethical conduct of research: respect for persons, beneficence, and justice. The authors referred to these as "basic ethical principles" and noted they are "among those generally accepted in our cultural tradition." IRB members use these criteria when making determinations about research approval. Kitchener (1984) expanded these three principles into five considerations, introducing a conceptual framework that Schuh and Associates (2009) also used to describe norms for the ethical conduct of research. In 2011, Kitchener and Anderson reemphasized these principles within the framework of psychology and counseling practice, arguing that whether codified or not, they constituted "common norms" for both research and professional practice. For consistency with federal language and to promote common terminology between assessment practitioners, faculty, and the IRB, we describe and apply only the three core principles. A discussion of each follows.

Respect for Persons

The "respect for persons" principle has two aspects, the right to act as a free agent and freedom of thought or choice. The authors of *The Belmont Report* (U.S. Dept. of Health, Education and Welfare, 1979) considered these aspects as affording autonomy in research. Specifically, participants should be treated as individuals (for example, autonomous agents) and individuals with limited ability to deliberate (that is, diminished autonomy) are entitled to protection. In other words, participants should be made aware of activities and possible adverse circumstances related to participating in a study and have the freedom and judgment ability to choose whether to join. Applying this principle to ethical practice in student affairs, Kitchener (1984) extended this concept to (1) the right of self-determination (that is, individuals have the right to free choice), (2) the right to privacy or confidentiality, and (3) informed consent (the right to full information when making a choice).

Applied to assessment, respect for persons is related to how participants are recruited, to confidentiality of their participation (if ensured), and whether they are given adequate information about the project to make an informed decision about participating. Schuh and Associates (2009) also applied the respect for persons principle to situations when participants feel pressured or coerced to participate, intentionally or not. For example, new student union employees might be required to complete and submit a survey about their training as a condition for signing off on their final employment paperwork. The staff member's intent may be to ensure a high response rate and perhaps make improvements to the next training based on feedback; however, the requirement creates a situation that takes away the employee's choice. The "respect for persons" principle also serves as the basis for informed consent, which will be discussed in a subsequent section.

Beneficence

The "beneficence" principle also has two aspects: to do no harm, and to maximize possible benefits and minimize potential harms. The authors of *The Belmont Report* (U.S. Dept. of Health, Education and Welfare, 1979) specifically chose the word for its connotation to kindness or charity, but emphasized its meaning as an obligation. This principle is clearer when applied to medical research, where exposure to a treatment is weighed in terms of potential harm or risk versus the possible reward of a more effective treatment. Kitchener and Anderson (2011) connoted the "do no harm" aspect of this principle with nonmaleficence, a legal term having to do with negligence (that is, risking or causing harm to others by not conducting work responsibly or acting carelessly). It is important to note that harm can be physical or psychological, as in the case of the Stanford Prison Experiment (Zimbardo, 2016). For example, adherence to the beneficence principle often applies to determinations about potential psychological risk in deception studies. Applying this principle to ethical practice in student affairs, Kitchener (1984) synonymized beneficence with "benefiting others," and regarded this principle as being "an acknowledged goal of student services professionals" (p. 22). Further, Kitchener (1984) noted that because higher education is dedicated to the service of society, student affairs as agents of the institution have an ethical obligation to benefit others.

Applied to assessment, beneficence ensures participant decisions are respected, efforts have been made to ensure participants are protected from harm, and overall that efforts have been made to secure participant well-being. For example, a problem might ensue if a focus group participant initially agreed to take part in a local assessment about controversial speakers on campus, but did not agree to let their data be used as part of an external study on student issue awareness.

While assessment projects involving potential physical harm are not typical, emotional or psychological distress can be much more common when studying college student experience, perceptions, and behaviors. For example, women on college campuses tend to experience a higher rate of assault than their male peers; therefore, a wellness survey asking about campus safety could cause significant distress for participants. A final and, in our experience, more common example is the overuse of demographic reporting in survey and focus group assessment. While it is important to be as specific as possible when reporting results, if there is only one or just a few responses to a demographic category or combination of categories, the consequence is that individual responses can be identifiable. For example, let's say only one sophomore student participated in a recent focus group on campus dining. Participants were drawn from a residence hall with only two sophomore residents. If the assessment report revealed themes or specific comments by class standing, the sophomore participant could be identified easily.

Justice

The "justice" principle is concerned with fairness, or equal treatment. The authors of *The Belmont Report* (U.S. Dept. of Health, Education and Welfare, 1979) evaluated justice by posing the hypothetical question, "who ought to receive the benefits of research and bear its burdens?" This concept might be best understood when considering injustice, or the case when a benefit is denied without good reason or when a burden is unduly imposed. One application of this aspect has to do with participant selection. This ethical evaluation considers whether participants were selected fairly, without bias toward any trait or characteristics, unless the study is specifically and with good reason delimited to certain groups. Kitchener (1984) considered justice as having two aspects: being just and being faithful. Being just has to do with impartiality, equality, and reciprocity (that is, adhering to the golden rule). Being faithful means not denying access to information that would allow an individual to make an informed decision about participating. Failing to honor a pledge or agreement such as an assurance of confidentiality is a related issue. Kitchener (1984) considered this to be a contractual obligation for student affairs. As members of a helping profession, practitioners agree not to exploit, lie to, or otherwise deceive those in their professional care.

Applied to assessment, Schuh and Associates (2009) simplified the concept as "being absolutely true to what is promised" (p. 196). A less egregious example is providing an accurate estimate of the time needed to participate; respondents should not be told a survey will take 15 minutes, when it really takes 30. Also, incentives as well as results from studies should be delivered as promised. Schuh and Associates (2009) also discussed these aspects under the notion of being faithful. A participant's investment in a project (that is, time, experiences, perceptions) should constitute an agreement that anything implied or otherwise promised should be provided. This can range from compensation to protecting anonymity. Further, the authors noted that when participants know a program or service is being assessed, they might worry about their job, what will happen, and/or whether the program will be eliminated, especially in cases where the institution or division does not have a culture of assessment. Finally, an ethical assessment practitioner should be faithful to the data by not slanting the wording or highlighting certain findings while concealing others. Such practices can affect implications and results from the findings. For example, if students seeking study abroad opportunities consistently mention challenges they experience when working with a particular staff member, this finding should be reported, but specific feedback be reserved for a private conversation outside the assessment process. While results should be reported faithfully, they need not cause embarrassment or be related in a way that exacerbates existing problems. Care should be taken to ensure that data are related professionally and to the appropriate personnel. In the case in which the problematic staff member is the person who receives the report, it is particularly important to be honest about the results.

Informed Consent

Informed consent is the most common means of ensuring that the "respect for persons" principle is met. An informed consent document (ICD) is a description of the activities, potential risks, and data management plan involved in a study. Participants may sign an ICD or be provided a copy after giving verbal assent, depending on the nature of the study and confidentiality procedures. Informed consent is most often obtained in research when conducting individual or focus group interviews and used less often in observation or quantitative studies. For surveys in particular, informed consent may be replaced with a study information sheet that contains many of the basic elements of an ICD, but does not require a signature.

Informed consent may be among the least understood and underused procedures in assessment work; however, Schuh and Associates (2009) suggested informed consent should be obtained when working with human subjects. We view the ICD process as more nuanced in assessment practice and recognize that requirements to obtain consent can be highly influenced by campus IRB policies and preferences. While there are no definitive rules about whether or not to obtain consent in this context, several best practices should be followed to ensure the federal regulations are met. Obtaining written consent for participation in an assessment project is most appropriate in cases where participants are put at more than minimal risk. Consent not only makes participants aware of this risk but also can help safeguard the person collecting data against noncompliance issues or legal ramifications stemming from participant harm or risk.

The OHRP (46.117c) provides for the alteration or waiver of consent in some circumstances, in particular when the project "is designed to study, evaluate, or otherwise examine: (i) public benefit or service programs; (ii) procedures for obtaining benefits or services under those programs; (iii) possible changes in or alternatives to those programs or procedures; or (iv) possible changes in methods or levels of payment for benefits or services under those programs." In most cases, assessment work would seem to meet these considerations and informed consent is not needed; however, some basic requirements still should be followed. Those most relevant to assessment, outlined in 46.117d, include that the research involves no more than minimal risk and that waiver of or alteration does not adversely affect the rights or welfare of participants.

A final, but important consideration to note is that minors are considered a vulnerable population in human subjects research. This would include college students under the age of 18. If some potential participants may be minors, the investigator should consult with the IRB to determine whether or not a waiver of consent is applicable. Studies including minors must undergo IRB review. In cases where there is even a slight chance that participants under age 18 may be included in a sample, using a prescreening procedure and not including those students in the project may be sufficient.

The Project Information Sheet

Although informed consent may not be required for assessment practice, we strongly recommend that all assessment work involving direct interaction with participants, such as interviews, observations, and surveys, include a project information sheet. An information sheet can be formatted to fit the needs of the project and should be tailored to the audience. For example, the information might be presented as a fact sheet or as a listing of frequently asked questions (FAQ) that can be handed to participants. In the case of electronic data collection, the information sheet might be a statement on the initial page of the instrument that is also printable. Regardless of format, the following information, derived from 46.116, should be minimally included:

- An explanation of the purposes of the project
- The expected duration of the subject's participation
- A description of the study procedures
- A description of any reasonably foreseeable risks or discomforts to the subject
- A description of any benefits to the subject or to others which may reasonably be expected from the research
- A statement describing the extent, if any, to which confidentiality of records identifying the subject will be maintained
- A listing of whom to contact for answers to questions about the project
- A statement that participation is voluntary, refusal to participate will involve no penalty or loss of benefits to which the subject is otherwise entitled, and the participant may discontinue participation at any time without penalty or loss of benefits

Risk Considerations

This section relates instances where seemingly minimal risk assessment projects can become problematic. Often, concerns involving risk for participating in assessment involve data confidentially and issues that could arise if participant identities were linked to their records. Certainly, there are cases where a data leak would not be an issue, such as when participants agree to be identified or when analysis does not require linked participant records. Researchers and assessment practitioners are frequently unaware of the many ways confidentiality might be compromised. Several examples are offered, with suggestions for safeguarding data. In addition, during the course of collecting assessment data, an interviewer or observer may learn about behavior that is potentially harmful to the participant, another group or individual, or the institution. Some considerations for handling these types of situations are presented in the following.

Participant Confidentiality

The primary question that confidentiality poses is whether or not a person's participation in the project, if known, could put them at risk in some way. Another way confidentiality could become problematic is if a participant's responses could be linked to their identity. Many believe that simply not collecting names is a way to ensure that confidentially can be maintained; however, (1) the manner in which the data is collected, (2) the number of participants and nature of data collection, as well as (3) the extent of demographic questions are instances in which individuals may be identified and are all potential areas of concern when collecting, storing, and reporting confidential participant data. Following are three examples demonstrating often and easily overlooked problems.

1. With regard to how data is collected, unless the feature is disabled, online survey programs record Internet protocol (IP) addresses that can be linked to individual computers. Further, online surveys that require identification for accessing the questions or that request contact information also permit the ability to link responses to identities. Most contemporary survey software can be configured to mask IP addresses and to send individual participant confirmation or contact

information to a different database than the data, although this provision can be easily overlooked. Student government elections, for example, require a unique login to track whether a person has voted, but the login should be used only to grant access and then not linked to the responses. More recently, one of the authors was asked to complete a survey about well being, including questions about stress, personal fitness habits, and the work environment. A unique link to the survey was provided, but no information about the confidentiality of the responses was given.

2. With regard to the number of participants and nature of data collection, one potential area of risk arises with small sample size, such as in a project utilizing interviews. For example, if the study is about admissions tour guides and only 3 of the staff of 12 participate, the risk of knowing who those individuals were is high. A similar issue can arise with surveys when the sample is very small. Additionally, an often-overlooked potential breach relates to participant recruitment. For example, if students are asked to sign up for interview times on a sheet kept in a public place or accessible by personnel other than those collecting data, or asked to respond to e-mails to set up an interview, it would not be difficult to determine who participated based on the interview times.

3. With regard to the extent of demographic questions, a potential breach can occur based on how data are reported. This can be challenging in assessment as well as research projects, particularly in studies that either include small samples or when certain demographics or combinations of characteristics makes individuals identifiable. Often and for good reason, we want to include every possible demographic question, generally in the interest of gathering a representative voice. However, caution must be taken when reporting results, particularly in cases in which an

individual can be identified when the person was told results were confidential. For example, in a recent project involving advising experiences, students were asked to identify by gender, race/ethnicity, and major. Of the 12 kinesiology majors, only one identified as male and African American. While it is important to attribute quotations or statistic data by demographic, in this case reporting that level of detail would distinguish the student. Another example is the use of titles. In many cases, there is only one vice president of a campus organization, so using her title in a study would reveal her identity. An effective safeguard against this risk is to ask two questions:

1. When designing an instrument or observation protocol, are all demographic characteristics necessary?

2. When reporting results, would the combination of demographic variables make an individual identifiable?

Witnessing Harmful Behaviors

Professional counselors have codes of ethics that allow for a breach of client confidentiality in the case of harm to self or others. Assessment data collection involving interaction (direct or indirect) with others can create ethical concerns that should be considered prior to beginning research. For example, an interview participant during an assessment of study practices in residence halls may reveal detrimental behaviors such as nonprescription drug use or unsafe roommate behaviors that could be extremely harmful if unreported. Specific to observation, you may witness actions that violate university policies or place others at risk. For example, if during an observation at the campus bookstore focusing on customer-staff interactions, you witness a student place a book into her backpack without paying, how will you react? Is your obligation to remain focused on the assessment or should you inform someone immediately and perhaps exposing your study?

Rhoads (1995) recalled this dilemma in his study of fraternity culture:

> In the end, I was faced with one of those ethical decisions that ethnographic and qualitative researchers rarely seem to discuss: Should I out of obligation to my research participants ignore the serious implications of their interactions with women and focus on other cultural issues (and there were many), or should I put a concern for advancing understanding of fraternity exploitation of women first? (p. 312)

Practitioners gathering interaction data should consider how they might handle these situations. We advise discussing possibilities with supervisors and especially with an IRB representative prior to data collection, in particular if data collection has the potential to yield findings incongruent with university policy or involves detrimental or harmful behaviors.

The Use of Incentives

Participation is essential to data collection; one way to encourage participation is to offer incentives or rewards. Coupled with a perception that receiving more data generally is favorable, a common practice in assessment projects that involve students has been to offer incentives. Incentives gained prominence when representativeness became more important; requiring the inclusion of a broader diversity of participants to ensure the sample was reflective of the overall population (Grant & Sugarman, 2004). Statisticians often use incentives as a way to increase survey response rates, just as qualitative researchers frequently incentivize participation in interviews and focus groups. Generally, incentives for completing a survey or interview are given following completion of the instrument. Examples include monetary compensation, gift cards, entry into prize drawings, or extra credit for a course. Incentives for participating in focus groups may be similar, but often involve providing food to participants during or after the session. Other examples include providing small prizes to all participants (for example, a $5 gift card) or entering all participants into a drawing for a larger prize (for example, a $50 gift card).

According to Grant and Sugarman (2004), an incentive is most often used as a means to motivate individuals to participate. In this way, incentives function as prompts to which participants respond. However, this can create ethical concerns. Essentially, incentives are a way to get someone to do what you want them to do. Cast this way, Grant (2014) described an incentive as a form of power, distinct from persuasion and coercion. Grant and Sugarman (2004) noted, "in general, then, while incentives are always employed to induce someone to do what they otherwise might not, the ethically suspect situation is one in which an incentive is used to induce someone to do something to which they are averse" (p. 728). The appropriateness of an incentive is another consideration. Conceptually, an incentive makes the choice to participate more attractive than not, creating a situation in which both parties stand to gain. Issues occur when the incentive is attractive enough to tempt individuals to participate against their better judgment.

The three basic ethical principles can be applied when considering the use of incentives: (1) "Respect for persons" would prompt the researcher to ask whether the incentive could be considered coercive or manipulative, ensuring individuals are recruited without undue influence. This is particularly problematic with valuable incentives such as monetary rewards or gifts as well as situations in which the incentive is not equivalent to an alternative. For example, a person might be asked to participate in a 15-minute survey for extra credit compared with writing a long essay. (2) "Beneficence" would raise the question whether the incentive influences a person's determination of risk. A contemplation of potential risk is always advisable when working with participants in any form of research. For example, would knowing someone participated in a study have an effect on his or her employability or academic standing? If the confidentiality of data were somehow breached, would the responses put individuals at risk and, if so, is that potential for risk explained in sufficient detail so that a potential participant can make an informed decision about participating? (3) "Justice" can be applied to fairness and honoring the incentive. For example, were all potential participants given equal opportunity to receive the incentive? Also, can the incentive be provided as promised and in a timely manner?

Many practitioners believe participants must be enticed to participate, fearing that participation rates will suffer without the offer of compensation. Incentives can come in many forms; monetary incentives such as cash, gift cards, or valuable objects are common. An alternative method of increasing potential participation rates is by offering to share results, or by clearly explaining the benefits of participating in the study. We have found that students are much more interested in contributing when they believe their responses or opinions will be used to improve practice or can contribute meaningfully to the welfare of others or campus in general.

Disseminating the Results

Generally, most assessment projects in student affairs are intended for institutional purposes or program evaluation for internal purposes only, classifying them as not research (that is, not reviewable) by IRB standards. We occasionally are asked what happens when someone decides to publish the results of a project that was previously not reviewed or would like to present the results at a professional association meeting. Essentially, this shifts the intent of the study from internal use to publically distributing results. Very likely, the campus IRB has a policy or perspective covering this case, as the federal guidelines leave this up to campus jurisdiction. In many cases, the essential consideration relates to participant consent. If participants were assured that data would be used only internally, then it is not appropriate to use data for broader scholarly works unless their consent can be obtained. If this is not possible, such as a case where data are older and participants are no longer easily reachable, there may be a provision to consider the data as an archival database. In this case, the potential researcher would submit the appropriate protocol for IRB review of archival data.

Final Considerations

As Reybold, Halx, and Jimenez (2008) noted, individuals interpret ethical principles according to the contexts and choices available. In other words, what makes sense in one context can be different the next time or in a similar situation.

> The transitory nature of organizational and societal ethical standards leaves only an individual's personal view as a constant in professional reasoning. Organizational rules and societal standards serve only as a guide; therefore, professional ethics are ultimately defined and put into practice by the individual based on personal values. (Reybold, Halx, & Jimenez, 2008, p. 112)

Regardless of your decision whether to seek IRB approval and/or gather written or verbal consent from participants, we recommend the following for every project (1) providing participants with sufficient information about the study (respect for persons), (2) ensuring the study is conducted safely and that participant data is safeguarded as promised (beneficence), (3) ensuring participants are fairly selected and being truthful about the project with participants (justice), and (4) providing an information sheet and/or obtaining informed consent.

Returning to the Case Studies

This chapter began with two case studies describing assessment projects that Erika and Frank planned to implement. In the following, we offer some potential ethical concerns that arise. Some might not view the issues as problematic, while others might easily identify additional concerns. Application of ethics and evaluation of potential concerns, while guided by basic criteria for the ethical conduct of research, can be highly subjective. When considering potential issues that could arise from a project, it is always advisable to discuss your thoughts with colleagues. If you feel the project presents risks that you cannot minimize or resolve, contact your IRB representative for advice. It is always preferable to err on the side of caution when considering participant risk.

In the first case study, Erika wants to know more about the experiences of welcome week leaders at Metropolitan University (MU). She hopes to use the results to refine the training and support program. Four aspects of her project design raise potential ethical concerns.

- Most of the future orientation staff will be selected from the welcome week leader pool

- Questions include perceptions about preparation, interactions with staff, and general satisfaction with participation

- The sign-up sheet for focus groups is displayed in a public location

- Staff members (two graduate students) will conduct all interviews

In the second case study, Frank wants to know about the living and learning environment in the fraternity/sorority houses at Eastern Wesleyan College (EWC). He hopes to identify issues that could lead to positive changes for residents. Two aspects of his project design raise potential ethical concerns.

- To ensure a high (80 percent) return rate, participation is a condition of eligibility for homecoming awards
- Some questions focus on risk taking, including alcohol and other drug use and sexual behaviors

We ask that you provide the answers to the following questions.

1. Why are the issues identified problematic?
2. How do the issues relate to the three basic criteria for the ethical conduct of research?
3. How should the issues be addressed and resolved?
4. What other issues not listed here raise concerns?

Discussion Questions

1. What is the purpose of an ethical review of research?
2. What are the three basic ethical principles? Provide an example of how each relates to assessment practice.
3. What are the differences between an informed consent document and a project information sheet? Provide an example of when you would use each.
4. What are some potential ethical concerns when using incentives? Name some incentives along with alternatives for increasing participation.
5. If you decide to present or publish your assessment results beyond campus, what steps should you take related to the ethical conduct of research?

References

Grant, R. W. (2014). *Strings attached: Untangling the ethics of incentives*. Princetown, NJ: Princeton University Press.

Grant, R. W., & Sugarman, J. (2004). Ethics in human subjects research: Do incentives matter? *Journal of Medicine and Philosophy*, *29*(6), 717–738.

Human Subjects Research Act, 45 U.S.C.A. § 46101 *et seq.* (2009).

Kitchener, K. S. (1984). Intuition, critical evaluation and ethical principles: The foundation for ethical decisions in counseling psychology. *Counseling Psychologist*, *12*(3), 43–55.

Kitchener, K. S., & Anderson, S. K. (2011). *Foundations of ethical practice, research, and teaching in psychology and counseling* (2nd ed.). New York, NY: Routledge.

Reybold, L. E., Halx, M. D., & Jimenez, A. L. (2008). Professional integrity in higher education: A study of administrative staff ethics in student affairs. *Journal of College Student Development*, *49*(2), 110–124.

Rhoads, R. (1995). Whales tales, dog piles, and beer goggles: An ethnographic case study of fraternity life. *Anthropology & Education Quarterly*, *26*(3), 306–323.

Schuh, J. H., & Associates. (2009). *Assessment methods for student affairs*. San Francisco, CA: Jossey-Bass.

U.S. Department of Health, Education, and Welfare. (1979). *The Belmont Report*. U.S. Department of Health and Human Services. Retrieved from http://www.hhs.gov/ohrp/humansubjects/guidance/belmont .html

Zimbardo, P. (2016). *Stanford prison experiment*. Retrieved from http://www .prisonexp.org/

4

MEASURING INDIVIDUAL STUDENT LEARNING AND GROWTH

Institutions generally have broad goals for the qualities and characteristics of the students they graduate. Ideally, their curricula, programs, services, and environments are designed to support the development of these attributes. However, focusing on assessing the learning and development of individual students is a relatively recent emphasis across higher education. This chapter begins with a case study that frames multiple levels of outcomes assessment. It then explores the identification of intended learning and developmental outcomes, reviews published outcomes statements, discusses interventions that facilitate achievement of outcomes, and examines approaches to assessment of individual outcomes.

Service-Learning Outcomes at Acorn College

Acorn College, a small liberal arts college, has as part of its mission statement that it seeks to graduate students who have the competence and commitment to be effective leaders, citizens, and agents of change in the world. The intended outcomes for graduates, drawn from the AAC&U LEAP project (AAC&U, n.d.), focus on critical thinking, teamwork, civic knowledge and engagement, and global learning. These outcomes are designed to be used for planning and assessment across all parts of the student experience. The college's newly developed strategic plan calls for increases in

(Continued)

retention, student engagement, and service to both the local and global communities.

Acorn has long prided itself on experiential learning and a high level of volunteerism, but the efforts have been separate and siloed. In response to the strategic plan, the vice presidents for Academic Affairs and Student Affairs have jointly charged a committee to develop a formalized service-learning proposal.

The resulting cross-divisional initiative, called Mighty Oaks, uses the institutional mission and intended outcomes as the foundation for a set of integrated institutional programs (some existing and others to be developed):

- Designated service-learning courses in both general education and classes required for majors

- A policy regarding the number of service-learning courses required for graduation

- A service-learning certificate option, which includes both coursework and cocurricular experiences

- A living-learning community focused on service-learning

- International service-learning alternative break trips

- Formal partnerships with community agencies to create long-term service projects

The Office of Institutional Effectiveness has requested that, prior to implementation, the responsible units develop an assessment plan, mapped to the institutional mission and intended outcomes, that identifies specific intended learning and developmental outcomes for each program and describes strategies for measuring them.

Shift from Inputs to Outcomes

Higher education in the United States has multiple purposes; historically, these include the creation of an informed citizenry for democracy, the generation of knowledge, and the development of solutions for problems of varying kinds (Thelin, 2011).

Ultimately, however, the purpose for which our institutions were created is student learning and development, characterized in the *Student Personnel Point of View* (American Council on Education, 1949) as a "full and balanced maturity" (p. 2). This end goal is now defined differently by different kinds of institutions and includes a range of missions from professional preparation and technical training to education in the liberal arts tradition.

Forsyth Technical Community College: "provides students with flexible educational pathways to a competitive workforce for the community and global economy." (Forsyth Technical Community College, 2007–2014)

Harvard Business School: "We educate leaders who make a difference in the world." (Harvard Business School, n.d.)

Massachusetts Institute of Technology: "We seek to develop in each member of the MIT community the ability and passion to work wisely, creatively, and effectively for the betterment of humankind." (MIT, 2015)

UCLA: "We seek to serve society through both teaching and scholarship, to educate successive generations of leaders, and to pass on to students a renewable set of skills and commitment to social engagement." (UCLA, n.d.)

Westminster College (PA): "The mission of Westminster College is to help men and women develop competencies, commitments, and characteristics which have distinguished human beings at their best . . . . The College sees the well-educated person as one whose skills are complemented by ever-developing values and ideals identified in the Judeo-Christian tradition." (Westminster College, n.d.)

Institutional missions conceptualize the end goal differently, but regardless of the mission, the intent is to teach students and, as a result, to have them learn and grow. This intended learning should be pervasive throughout the entire institution and the full student experience; assessment of individual student outcomes is one element of determining whether the institution is fulfilling its mission (Schuh & Gansemer-Topf, 2010). Institutional mission creates the larger context in which individual assessment occurs.

Historically, the focus of attention and assessment was on inputs (Kuh, Jankowski, Ikenberry, & Kinzie, 2014). The questions designed to assess the educational process looked at metrics like student-faculty ratios, volumes in the library, academic programs and support provided, and programs and services offered. Attention to outcomes tended to use indirect measures such as attendance, retention, grade point average, or graduation as proxies for learning and development (see Suskie, 2009). While logically one might assume that at least a correlation exists between learning and graduation, the latter is not a good measure of the former. With increasing expectations for accountability, as well as the growth and increased sophistication of the assessment movement, the emphasis has shifted from inputs (for example, the number of programs offered, the range of experiences available) to outcomes. The question has become not *what did you offer?*, but *how are students different as a result of engaging in it?* That shift in emphasis represents a sea change in assessment in student affairs. In a recent study, 84 percent of institutions reported having common learning outcomes for all students (Kuh et al., 2014). Learning and developmental outcomes are not all that needs to be measured, but assessment cannot create a clear, comprehensive picture of results without attending to the effect on individual students.

Intended and Actual Learning Outcomes

While the developmental growth of college students began to be a focus of student affairs literature beginning in the 1970s (for example, Brown, 1972; Miller & Prince, 1976), it was not until the publication of *The Student Learning Imperative* (SLI) (American College Personnel Association, 1996) that the attention of the field shifted to focus more broadly on learning. SLI argued that "[t]he concepts of 'learning,' 'personal development,' and 'student development' are inextricably intertwined and inseparable" (p. 2), and used the terms interchangeably. The concept of *learning* has come to represent a broader understanding of the ways that students change as a result of engaging with ideas, experiences, programs, and environments, or the outcomes of their engagement.

The term *outcome* is used in two ways, and distinguishing between them adds to clarity in describing assessment practice. "The word *outcome* itself can be confusing, since it is typically used to refer to both the desired effect and the resulting effect" (Barham & Dean, 2013, p. 5). In a literal sense, it is not possible to "write outcomes" for something that has not yet happened. It is helpful, then, to refer to *intended outcomes* as those that are the desired result of a planned intervention or experience and to reserve the term *outcomes*, or more specifically *measured outcomes* or *actual outcomes*, for those changes that are found to have occurred as a result of engagement. Learning outcomes (to include developmental growth) are those that describe change at the individual level; program and operational outcomes describe results at the aggregate or unit level and are discussed in Chapter 5.

Intended learning outcomes should be identified at every level of the student experience, ideally from the broadest institutional level down to the most specific and discrete outcomes intended to result from programs like one-time workshops. Aligning intentions throughout the institution contributes to a coherent, tightly coupled experience in which each of the pieces designed intentionally is crafted to contribute to the larger goals (Keeling, Underhile, & Wall, 2007). In the Acorn College case, the institutional intended learning outcomes of critical thinking, teamwork, civic knowledge and engagement, and global learning set the context for developing more specific intended outcomes for the various programmatic initiatives. The living-learning community (LLC), for example, may then shape its service-learning emphasis around the intended outcome of developing a sense of civic responsibility in its members and create opportunities for them to learn, reflect, and demonstrate their learning through activities in the LLC and in the community. In this way, each element of the LLC in which they are involved aligns with the larger institutional intent to develop civic knowledge and engagement in its students.

Learning and Developmental Outcomes Frameworks

Several professional organizations have developed frameworks to describe the broad domains in which intended learning and developmental outcomes can be situated. Some of these frameworks use the broader term *learning* to include development; others specifically refer to both. Some institutions, or the divisions within them, have developed sets of intended outcomes designed to frame the programs and services offered therein; these offer a beginning point from which practitioners can develop intended outcomes scaled to the level of their work. In others, however, practitioners are challenged to identify broad goals and intended outcomes that align with the stated mission. In those situations, it can be helpful to consider existing frameworks that reflect the field's best thinking about the appropriate outcomes of a higher education experience. Three sets of frameworks described in the following illustrate the resources available.

Learning Reconsidered (NASPA & ACPA, 2004) echoed the earlier *Student Personnel Point of View* statements (American Council on Education, 1937, 1949) with its emphasis on the education of the whole student. It argued for the integration of student development as an aspect of learning, defining

> *learning* as a comprehensive, holistic, transformative activity that integrates *academic learning* and *student development*, processes that have often been considered separate, and even independent of each other. When we say learning, then, we do not mean exclusively or primarily academic instruction, the acquisition of disciplinary content, or classroom learning—though the

rich definition of learning we use certainly incorporates and includes all of those things. We do *not* say *learning and development* because we do not want to suggest that learning and student development are fundamentally different things, or that one does, or could, occur without the other. Nor do we specify separate, distinct, or categorical learning (in the pure academic sense) and developmental objectives and outcomes. Here we work to bring our terminology, and our way of understanding what student affairs professionals contribute to student outcomes, in line with the findings of current learning research and with our own empirical observations about how learning (as a complex integrated process) occurs among today's students. (NASPA & ACPA, 2004, p. 2)

Grounded in the understanding that student learning is interconnected across academic, social, and institutional contexts, *Learning Reconsidered* described the "goals and outcomes of a transformative liberal education ... defining integrated, intertwined academic and developmental outcomes" (NASPA & ACPA, 2004, p. 19). Drawing on multiple sources in the field, the authors posited seven overarching outcome domains: cognitive complexity; knowledge acquisition, integration, and application; humanitarianism; civic engagement; interpersonal and intrapersonal competence; practical competence; and persistence and academic achievement (NASPA & ACPA, 2004, pp. 21–22). Within each of the student outcome domains, they further described more discrete dimensions, designed to help users identify how the outcomes might be expressed by students (for example, effective reasoning, career decidedness, cultural competency), and offered examples of developmental experiences that could lead to such learning.

The Council for the Advancement of Standards in Higher Education (CAS) is a consortium organization comprised of professional associations across higher education, primarily those concerned with student-focused programs and services. Using a collaborative, consensus-based model, CAS develops and promulgates professional standards of practice for more than 40 functional areas (CAS, 2015). Beginning with the earliest publication in 1986, the CAS standards specified that programmatic efforts should result in identifiable student outcomes; by the 2003 publication, that list had grown to 16 possible outcomes, offered as examples of desirable results of engaging in programs and services (for example, effective communication, clarified values, social responsibility, appreciation of diversity).

> However, in 2008 after the publication of *Learning Reconsidered 2* (2006), CAS reviewed the learning outcomes it had promoted and decided an integration of both learning outcome documents would enhance the profession's efforts in promoting student learning and development. Consequently, CAS hosted a "think tank" involving writers of *Learning Reconsidered 2*, CAS directors, and prominent practitioners and faculty members in student affairs to make recommendations for a revised learning outcomes document. (CAS, 2014, para. 1)

CAS used a similar framework as that of *Learning Reconsidered*, structuring the outcomes in six broad domains—knowledge acquisition, construction, integration, and application; cognitive complexity; intrapersonal development; interpersonal competence; humanitarianism and civic engagement; and practical competence—with accompanying dimensions. Instead of including examples of experiences that might lead to the outcomes, however, this framework offers examples of specific intended learning outcomes related to the various domains and dimensions (for example, makes connections between classroom and out-of-classroom learning, articulates rationale for personal behavior, engages in critical reflection and principled dissent). The CAS standards assert that assessment of learning outcomes is a necessary element in any program review or evaluation (CAS, 2015).

The work of the American Association of Colleges & Universities (AAC&U), an organization focused on undergraduate liberal education, concentrates on general education, but the Liberal Education and America's Promise (LEAP) initiative is organized around a set of essential learning outcomes that can apply to both curricular and cocurricular learning. These outcomes include knowledge of human cultures and the physical and natural world, intellectual and practical skills, personal and social responsibility, and integrative and applied learning, each with subareas like teamwork and problem solving, civic knowledge and engagement, and ethical reasoning and action (AAC&U, n.d.-a.). The VALUE rubrics that accompany these essential outcomes are designed to provide a means for authentic, direct assessment of student work and progress toward the outcomes (AAC&U, n.d.-b).

Regardless of whether specific intended outcomes are based on institutional-level statements or from an externally developed framework chosen by a division or other unit, it is crucial that practitioners consider the larger context as they develop the intended outcomes that will guide their planning and assessment.

Developing Intended Learning Outcomes

Once the broad domains and dimensions of desired learning have been identified, the fundamental question is *What do I want them to know, or how do I want them to be different, as a result of engaging in this experience?* The level of intended outcome should match the level of the experience, so that longer-term, more complex experiences (for example, year-long participation in a living-learning community focused on service-learning) will have more broadly stated intended outcomes, while shorter-term, more focused experiences (for example, participation in a one-time volunteer service project) will have more specific intended outcomes. Keeping intended outcomes aligned at all levels, or *mapped* to each other, enables practitioners to describe how programs and services throughout the institution are contributing to the accomplishment of the overall mission.

A popular model for framing intended learning outcomes follows the ABCD structure (Heinich, Molenda, Russell, & Smaldino, 2002). ABCD represents audience, behavior, condition, and degree of successful performance. The format, then, follows this structure (Carretta & Rice, 2010):

Audience: Students/stakeholders will ...

Behavior: ... know/be able to do/value/experience what ...

Condition: ... under these conditions/circumstances ...

Degree: ... to this level of competency/effectiveness/ satisfaction.

Typically, this level of specificity is most useful in situations where the outcomes are most tangible and immediately measurable, such as those stemming from a short-term experience. For example,

A: First-year students

B: will describe the problem of food insecurity in the local area

C: after volunteering at a community food pantry as part of a Saturday Service Series

D: by listing three target goals of the pantry.

(Note that the parts of the outcome statement can also be presented in a different order, for example: After volunteering ... , first-year students will describe ...). This intended outcome presumes that the students will not simply donate their time and energy to volunteering at the food pantry, but while there will also learn about the program and what it is designed to address. There are multiple ways that this learning could be accomplished, and multiple ways that the learning could be assessed. Developing useful and useable intended outcomes involves thinking carefully and critically about the nature of the learning that is expected to occur.

The intended outcomes of longer-term, more complex programs more often follow only the ABC elements of the model previously described; this kind of learning generally needs multiple points of assessment to generate understanding of the changes that have occurred, and so the intended outcome may be stated more broadly. For example, "as a result of participating in a living-learning community focused on service-learning, students will commit to integrating service into their lives." Since "commit" is not readily measurable, additional, more specific outcomes will be needed to operationalize the meaning of commitment in this context. Students might be asked to write a statement of their personal philosophy of service, set goals for engagement in future service activities, or articulate how they might integrate service with their career goals. Each of these could contribute to an overall understanding of a student's commitment to service.

Writing effective outcomes statements also requires careful attention to the kind of learning that will be produced, how that learning will be expressed, and the types of activities or experiences that will facilitate it. In particular, the verbs used should be precise and descriptive; terms like *understand* or *be aware of* are difficult to assess. To develop strong outcomes statements, it is helpful to consider resources like the frameworks described earlier, as well as others like Bloom's taxonomy.

Bloom's taxonomy (1956) describes levels of knowledge, skills, and abilities beginning with knowledge, or basic recall, and moving through increasingly complex processes including comprehension, application, analysis, synthesis, and evaluation. A revised version, *A Taxonomy for Learning, Teaching, and Assessing* (Anderson & Krathwohl, 2001) updated the original to offer both a taxonomy of types of knowledge (that is, factual, conceptual, procedural, metacognitive) and a revised set of descriptors of cognitive processes (that is, remember, understand, apply, analyze, evaluate, create) and associated behaviors (for example, recognizing, summarizing, implementing, differentiating, critiquing, generating). The intersection of the two frameworks (knowledge and process) offers a more nuanced description of the phenomenon (for example, understanding facts contrasted with understanding concepts). An Internet search will yield multiple graphics reflecting different representations of the taxonomy, as well as verbs associated with the various levels and examples of behaviors that reflect them.

When developing measureable intended outcomes, it is tempting to write them at the more basic levels represented on the taxonomy, since it is easy to think about how they might be assessed. There are times when asking students to "list" or "identify" is appropriate to the intended level of learning, but learning that involves more complex cognitive processes like evaluating or creating needs to be demonstrated through actions that require that level of complexity. Asking students to critique an existing process, or to use what they have learned to develop a new one, means that they will need to use higher levels of processing to accomplish that task.

Five questions can guide the development of well-constructed intended outcome statements:

1. Who is the target audience? What do I know about their characteristics, such as developmental levels, prior experiences, and current knowledge/skills?

2. What is the scale of the learning experience? Is it a one-time program, a year-long involvement, or an element of the environment?

3. What will the students do? Will they attend, actively participate, or have leadership responsibilities? What is their role?

4. What is the level of learning that I want them to achieve? Where on Bloom's taxonomy is it represented, and what words most clearly convey my intent? (Remember that there are likely to be multiple intended outcomes for one event or experience, and that they typically should reflect increasing levels of complexity.)

5. How will I know if they have achieved it? What will they say or do that will allow me to determine their success in reaching my goals for the experience? What level of achievement or performance will I define as necessary for success?

> Another example of an intended learning outcome for the service-learning program at Acorn College could be:
>
> 1. Students
> 2. who receive the service-learning certificate
> 3. by completing the requisite courses and cocurricular experiences
> 4. will produce a portfolio of their experiences, including components of reflection, a personal philosophy of service statement, and a plan for continued engagement in service
> 5. that is determined by the Mighty Oaks Steering Committee to be a successful representation of content mastery and engagement.

Taking the time to craft well-structured, purposeful intended learning outcomes can help to inform the creation of the experiences that are designed to achieve them.

Intentional Interventions

Interventions are any experiences, programs, services, or aspects of the environment that are intended to have an effect on the students involved. They may be structured, like a living-learning community or leadership training, or environmental, including the policies and procedures that teach implicit lessons to students and passive programming such as bulletin boards or informational flyers. Creating such experiences with the end in mind leads us to more carefully develop the ways that we engage students in their learning. When we design opportunities intended to facilitate learning, we intervene in students' lives with the intent of creating change.

Interventions are most effective when they reflect what we know about how students learn. We know that student learning is enhanced by involvement (Astin, 1984), engagement (Kuh, Kinzie, Schuh, Whitt, & Associates, 2010), attention to different learning styles (Kolb, 1984), and opportunities for reflection (Kolb, 1984; Liddell, Hubbard, & Werner, 2000; Suskie, 2009). Once we have identified what we want them to learn, and at what level, we can more thoughtfully design experiences to facilitate that learning. The remaining, crucial question, though, is how we can know that they have achieved it?

Measuring Learning Outcomes

Assessing the achievement of intended outcomes involves gathering the data defined in the outcome statement or, for broader statements without specific measures included, deciding what data are needed to support a conclusion about the outcomes. Data can reflect either *direct* or *indirect measures* of learning. Direct measures are those in which students demonstrate their knowledge or skill; indirect measures are those where they report on it (Suskie, 2009; Yousey-Elsener, 2013). For example, after orientation for an international service trip, students might be asked to list three tasks they need to complete prior to leaving as a direct measure of the knowledge gained. An indirect measure would be to ask them the extent to which they agree with the statement "I know the tasks I need to complete prior to leaving on the trip." Direct measures are most useful in situations where the learning results in knowledge or skills that are tangible and verifiable, while indirect measures are appropriate in areas that are more intrapersonal and subjective, such as attitudes and viewpoints. Direct measures have the added advantage of identifying gaps in knowledge and specific areas where students lack understanding so that interventions can be adjusted going forward (Tucker, 2014).

Direct Measures

The more direct the measure of learning, the more we can be confident that students have achieved the intended outcomes. As Tucker (2014) asserted, "Our ability to measure learning is limited by the caliber of the instrument we use. Out-of-classroom assessment should not continue to ask students to report whether they learned; it must ask them to demonstrate what they have learned" (p. 29). When using questionnaires, a simple shift in the structure of the questions, as previously described, can create a more direct measure of what students actually know. Other written formats include quizzes or tests where students identify or supply correct answers and those that provide an open-ended opportunity for students to describe what they know. In this format, students can demonstrate more complex levels of learning by being asked to summarize, critique, evaluate, analyze, or use information to create. Data analysis for more complex responses can be accomplished most effectively using rubrics that define the elements of the desired response.

Rubrics, reflecting both the criteria to be considered and levels of achievement (Bresciani, Zelna, & Anderson, 2004), also can be used to guide assessment through observations. Intended outcomes that fall in the domain of interpersonal competence, for example, include behaviors like demonstrating democratic principles as a leader, treating others with respect, and considering others' points of view. Working with a group of students over time, a practitioner could use a rubric that described these behaviors in detail to guide observations of the extent to which students demonstrated these actions and how they changed over the course of a semester or a year.

Rubrics also can be useful as a tool for helping students see what they are learning (Suskie, 2009), and what they are not learning, thereby helping them take more responsibility for their experience (Bresciani, Zelna, & Anderson, 2004).

Other sources of data for direct measures are the various kinds of documents generated in the course of working with students, as well as those created specifically for assessment. Students can be asked to write one-minute papers, keep journals, write reflections, develop proposals, create programs for others, or write position papers; all of these can yield insight into what they have learned and what they are able to do with their knowledge. Document analysis can be done informally, through reading for general content and reflection of learning, or more formally, using qualitative methods to code and analyze the data.

In the course of our work, we interact with students regularly, and these interactions themselves can be the source of direct measures of intended outcomes, if we prepare ourselves to listen for, recognize, and record the evidence of learning. While this can be done in informal interactions, it is more reliable if we purposefully structure specific opportunities in which we plan to gather data. For example, end-of-year individual meetings with outgoing student leaders can be structured to focus on the intended outcomes of their leadership experiences. Similarly, focus groups can be planned with intact student groups or representatives from targeted interventions, and the content of the discussion can be considered informally, or alternatively through the use of rubrics or more formal data analysis.

Finally, there are inventories and instruments designed to assess various factors such as individual development or moral reasoning (for example, SDTLA: Winston, Miller, & Cooper, 1999; DIT: Rest, Narvaez, Thoma, & Bebeau, 1999). Although more often used to collect data for analysis in the aggregate, these can be used to assess specific aspects of individuals that are of particular interest to an institution or program. It is essential that the selection of such instruments be based on the intended outcomes to be assessed, rather than permitting an instrument to dictate what will be measured. When an instrument is used because it is convenient and "close enough" to the intended outcome, the results obtained will not be a valid measure of achievement and so will not be useful in determining the success of the intervention.

Indirect Measures

Although direct measures are ideal and should be employed when possible, there are times that indirect measures are sufficient indicators of achievement of an intended outcome. As a broad indicator (for example, "I gained all the information I needed at the pre-trip orientation"), an indirect measure can gauge the extent to which students perceive that they have benefited and, in combination with other, more direct measures, can provide a useful overall measure of program effectiveness.

Other indirect measures are those that serve as proxies, or substitutes, for intended outcomes. Persistence and graduation are often cited as indicators of student success and academic achievement; at one level, this is reasonable, since attrition and failure to graduate may be related to academic difficulty. The problem is that students leave school without a degree for many reasons, academic and otherwise, and some persist to graduation without the attendant skills and abilities that we generally associate with a college education. Similarly, grade point averages (GPA) can vary by academic program and institution, so that two students with similar GPAs may in fact have very different levels of achievement. For example, if class attendance is factored into a student's grade, does that reflect course learning? Again, this kind of measure can be useful as one indicator used to judge the achievement of a broad intended outcome, but caution should be used in interpreting an indirect measure to be a clear gauge of attainment.

A popular assessment strategy that can be either direct or indirect is represented by the use of portfolios, developmental transcripts, and cocurricular transcripts. All of these offer a way

for students to show what they have done, by collecting artifacts or recording their involvement and out-of-class experiences.
When they are presented without commentary or elaboration,
they serve largely as indirect measures of learning, but when they
are accompanied by the student's reflection and description of the
resulting learning, they can provide valuable insight into what
the student has done and what impact it has had.

Final Considerations

The task of identifying, developing, and assessing learning outcomes can be overwhelming. When we strive to create learning
opportunities through all of the interactions, programs, and environments that our students experience, the outcomes that we
could choose to assess are limitless. It is important to prioritize
assessment activity in the context of an overall assessment plan
or strategic plan and the goals of the unit, division, or institution.
Finally, it is also helpful to evaluate the precision and rigor with
which any assessment activity needs to be conducted. Consider
the analogy of taking photographs. Some experiences are captured
in the moment, with pictures snapped on the go with a phone
camera. These quick shots are enough to depict the essence of the
moment and can convey to others something about the event.
Other experiences are best captured more formally, with a scheduled portrait session and professional photographer. These posed,
structured pictures reflect the significance of the moment and
the desire to preserve it more fully. Such decisions are driven by the
need for the picture, the scale of the experience, the resources
available, and the desired use of the resulting images. Assessment
activity can be considered in the same light. Some assessment
needs can be answered through means such as informal observations or short end-of-event surveys, while others require more
in-depth approaches like portfolios or validated instruments to
capture deeper, more complex learning. Decisions about the necessary level of assessment depend on the culture of assessment
present, the need for the data, the scale of the experience or the

question to be answered, the resources available, and the uses for the results. The most effective and complete understanding of a student experience is likely to be gained by using a combination of snapshots and formal portraits to capture the moment.

Back to Acorn College

The Mighty Oaks Steering Committee has met, at the request of the Office of Institutional Effectiveness, to develop the assessment plan for the initiative. While the overall plan will include a program review for the initiative itself and assessment of programmatic and aggregate outcomes, they have focused initially on developing individual intended learning outcomes and the strategies that will be used to assess them.

Given the institution's mission, the committee has affirmed the importance of focusing on the broad outcomes of leadership, citizenship, and civic engagement, with more specific attention to critical thinking, teamwork, civic knowledge and engagement, and global learning. The initial assessment of individual student outcomes will target those students who have indicated that they will pursue the service-learning certificate.

The broad programmatic intended learning outcome they developed is this:

Students who achieve the Mighty Oaks service-learning certificate will demonstrate skills in critical thinking, teamwork, civic knowledge and engagement, and global learning through mastery of academic content, creation of projects reflecting the requisite skills, participation in a minimum of six appropriate cocurricular experiences, and creation of a Mighty Oaks portfolio; skill attainment will be assessed by course instructors, cocurricular advisors, and the Mighty Oaks Steering Committee using the relevant VALUE rubrics (AAC&U, n.d.), and the certificate will be awarded upon achievement of ratings of 3 or 4 across all areas evaluated.

(Continued)

With this overarching intended outcome, the committee will next conduct a survey of academic courses and cocurricular experiences that may contribute to these goals. Instructors and advisors will be invited to submit descriptions of how their experiences result in the intended outcomes, as well as their specific intended outcomes and assessment strategies, and a list of approved experiences will be compiled for student use. Students will also be permitted to propose additional experiences to be used toward the certification.

In addition to the on-campus assessment plan, the committee is also partnering with Career Services to add questions to alumni and employer surveys to gather data about effects that persist beyond graduation.

Discussion Questions

1. In the example from Acorn College, what additional intended outcomes might be appropriate for the Mighty Oaks initiative overall? For its program components?

2. Choose one of the program components and develop two or three intended learning outcomes for it. How could those intended outcomes best be measured?

3. What are the practical challenges in assessing individual learning outcomes? How can these be mitigated to encourage assessment?

4. What are the advantages and potential disadvantages of tightly mapping intended outcomes across an institution?

5. When are assessment snapshots most useful, and when are more formal approaches needed? In the Acorn College example, where would you use snapshots, and what formal means of assessment would be most appropriate?

References

American College Personnel Association. (1996). *The student learning imperative: Implications for student affairs.* Washington, DC: Author. Retrieved from http://www2.bgsu.edu/sahp/pages/resources2.html

American Council on Education. (1937, June). *The student personnel point of view.* American Council on Education Studies, Series I, Vol. I, No. 3. Washington, DC: Author. Retrieved from http://www2.bgsu.edu /sahp/pages/1937STUDENTPERSONNELnew.pdf

American Council on Education. (1949, September). *The student personnel point of view.* American Council on Education Studies, Series VI, Vol. XIII, No. 13. Washington, DC: Author. Retrieved from http:// www2.bgsu.edu/sahp/pages/1949SPPVrev.pdf

Anderson, L. W., & Krathwohl, D. R. (2001). *A taxonomy for learning, teaching, and assessing: A revision of Bloom's taxonomy of educational objectives.* New York, NY: Longman.

Association of American Colleges & Universities. (n.d.-a). *Essential learning outcomes.* Washington, DC: Author. Retrieved from http://www.aacu .org/leap/essential-learning-outcomes

Association of American Colleges & Universities. (n.d.-b). *VALUE.* Washington, DC: Author. Retrieved from https://aacu.org/value

Association of American Colleges and Universities. (2002). *Greater expectations.* Washington, DC: Author.

Astin, A. W. (1984). Student involvement: A developmental theory for higher education. *Journal of College Student Personnel, 25*(4), 297–308.

Barham, J. D., & Dean, L. A. (2013). Introduction: The foundation. In D. M. Timm, J. D. Barham, K. McKinney, & A. R. Knerr (Eds.), *Assessment in practice: A companion guide to the ASK standards* (pp. 3–8). Washington, DC: ACPA. Retrieved from http://www.acpa.nche.edu /assessment-practice-companion-guide-ask-standards

Baxter Magolda, M. B. (1999). Defining and redefining student learning. In E. Whitt (Ed.) *Student learning as student affairs work.* NASPA Monograph Series no. 23, pp. 35–49. Washington, DC: National Association of Student Personnel Administrators.

Bloom, B. S. (1956). *Taxonomy of educational objectives: The classification of educational goals.* London, UK: Longmans, Green.

Bresciani, M. J., Zelna, C. L., & Anderson, J. A. (2004). *Assessing student learning and development: A handbook for practitioners.* Washington, DC: National Association of Student Personnel Administrators.

Brown, R. D. (1972). *Student development in tomorrow's higher education: A return to the academy.* Alexandria, VA: American College Personnel Association.

Carretta, P., & Rice, A. (2010, June). *CAS's new learning domains: Using them in your assessment work*. Presentation at the meeting of the NASPA International Assessment and Retention Conference, Baltimore, MD.

Council for the Advancement of Standards in Higher Education. (2003). *CAS professional standards for higher education* (5th ed.). Washington, DC: Author.

Council for the Advancement of Standards in Higher Education. (2009). CAS learning and development outcomes. In Council for the Advancement of Standards in Higher Education, *CAS professional standards for higher education* (7th ed.). Washington, DC: Author. Retrieved from http://standards.cas.edu/getpdf.cfm? PDF=D87A29DC-D1D6-D014-83AA8667902C480B

Council for the Advancement of Standards in Higher Education. (2014). *Learning and development outcomes*. Retrieved from http://www.cas .edu/learningoutcomes

Council for the Advancement of Standards in Higher Education. (2015). *CAS professional standards for higher education* (9th ed.). Washington, DC: Author.

Forsyth Technical Community College. (2007–2014). *Our mission and core values*. Retrieved from http://www.forsythtech.edu/about-us/mission/

Harvard Business School. (n.d.). *About: Our mission*. Retrieved from http:// www.hbs.edu/about/Pages/mission.aspx

Heinich, R., Molenda, M., Russell, J. D., & Smaldino, S. E. (2002). *Institutional media and technologies for learning* (7th ed.). Englewood Cliffs, NJ: Prentice Hall.

Keeling, R. P., Underhile, R., & Wall, A. F. (2007). Horizontal and vertical structures: The dynamics of organization in higher education. *Liberal Education, 93*(4), 22–31.

Kolb, D. A. (1984). The process of experiential learning. In *Experiential learning: Experience as the source of learning and development* (pp. 20–38). Englewood Cliffs, NJ: Prentice-Hall.

Kuh, G. D., Jankowski, N., Ikenberry, S. O., & Kinzie, J. (2014). *Knowing what students know and can do: The current state of student learning outcomes assessment in U.S. colleges and universities*. Champaign, IL: National Institute for Learning Outcomes Assessment. Retrieved from http:// learningoutcomesassessment.org/NILOAReports.htm

Kuh, G. D., Kinzie, J., Schuh, J. H., Whitt, E. J., & Associates. (2010). *Student success in college: Creating conditions that matter*. San Francisco, CA: Jossey-Bass.

Liddell, D. L., Hubbard, S., & Werner, R. (2000). Developing interventions that focus on learning. In D. L. Liddell & J. P. Lund (Eds.), *Powerful programming for student learning: Approaches that make a difference* (pp. 21–33). New Directions for Student Services no. 90. San Francisco, CA: Jossey-Bass.

Massachusetts Institute of Technology. (2015). *MIT facts: Mission*. Retrieved from http://web.mit.edu/facts/mission.html

Miller, T. K., & Prince, J. S. (1976). *The future of student affairs: A guide to student development for tomorrow's higher education*. San Francisco, CA: Jossey-Bass.

National Association of Student Personnel Administrators, American College Personnel Association. (2004). *Learning reconsidered: A campus-wide focus on the student experience*. Washington, DC: Author. Retrieved from https://www.naspa.org/images/uploads/main/Learning_Reconsidered_Report.pdf

Rest, J. R., Narvaez, D., Thoma, S. J., & Bebeau, M. J. (1999). DIT-2: Devising and testing a new instrument of moral judgment. *Journal of Educational Psychology, 91*(4), 644–659. doi:10.1037/0022–0663.91.4.644

Schuh, J. H., & Gansemer-Topf, A. M. (2010). *The role of student affairs in student learning assessment*. National Institute for Learning Outcomes Assessment, Occasional Paper #7. Champaign, IL: National Institute for Learning Outcomes Assessment. Retrieved from http://www.learningoutcomeassessment.org/documents/studentAffairsrole.pdf

Suskie, L. (2009). *Assessing student learning: A common sense guide* (2nd ed.). San Francisco, CA: Jossey-Bass.

Thelin, J. R. (2011). *A history of American higher education* (2nd ed.). Baltimore, MD: Johns Hopkins University Press.

Tucker, J. M. (2014). Assessment matters: Stop asking students to "strongly agree": Let's directly measure cocurricular learning. *About Campus, 19*(4), 29–32.

UCLA. (n.d.). *Mission and values*. Retrieved from http://www.ucla.edu/about/mission-and-values

Westminster College. (n.d.). *About: Mission*. Retrieved from http://www.westminster.edu/about/mission.cfm

Winston, R. B., Jr., Miller, T. K., & Cooper, D. L. (1999). *Student Developmental Task and Lifestyle Assessment*. Athens, GA: Student Development Associates.

Yousey-Elsener, K. (2013). Assessment fundamentals—The ABC's of assessment. In D. M. Timm, J. D. Barham, K. McKinney, & A. R. Knerr (Eds.), *Assessment in practice: A companion guide to the ASK standards* (Chapter 1, pp. 9–18). Washington, DC: ACPA. Retrieved from http://www.myacpa.org/assessment-practice-companion-guide-ask-standards

5

PROGRAM OUTCOMES
AND PROGRAM REVIEW

In student affairs, much of the focus of our work happens at the program level, with the term *program* in this context representing a functional area such as residence life, student activities, or orientation. These "functional hierarchical structures ... are essentially administrative and service-oriented in focus and mission" (Kuk, Banning, & Amey, 2010, p. 12). While the specific organizational structures vary from institution to institution, their missions reflect a focus on serving student needs by providing programs, services, and environments that support both academic success and student development (Kuk, 2009). These units often are organized in departments, with directors, staff, mission statements, goals, and subunits that focus on specific elements of the program. Because they represent the major functions of student affairs, they are the building blocks that comprise the overall division. As such, assessment at the program level is an important component of a comprehensive student affairs assessment plan.

Because program-level assessment is part of the larger context, program goals, intended outcomes, and evaluation strategies need to be aligned with institutional and divisional missions, goals, priorities, intended outcomes, and assessment cycles. However, it is also important that these elements of any subunits also are aligned so that each level maps tightly to the next. Terminology can present challenges here, since the subunits may also be called "programs." For example, the Residence Life program may contain a living-learning program, and its resident assistants may be required to plan educational programs for their residents. Bresciani, Zelna, and Anderson (2004) defined *program* as "that which delivers the end results of what you are assessing.... It is anything that has an autonomous set of outcomes" (p. 10). For the purposes of this chapter, however, *program* will be used to refer to a functional area unit as previously described.

Assessment at the program level has two major areas of focus: outcomes and operations. The relevant outcomes questions at this level involve not only individual student learning outcomes (as Chapter 4 describes), but also aggregate outcomes. What are the effects of programs and experiences on groups of students? More specifically, what are the effects of individual specific programmatic interventions (for example, what effect does a residence hall educational workshop have on participants?), and what are the effects of the program overall (for example, what are the effects of living in residence halls?)? In other words, how can we assess the outcomes of student engagement at the program level?

In addition to aggregate student learning outcomes, other types of outcomes are also relevant to an understanding of overall program functioning. *Program outcomes* reflect measures of programmatic goals (for example, increasing attendance), while *operational outcomes* represent elements of the program's functioning (for example, cost per student). Comprehensive program assessment includes assessment of intended outcomes of all three types—learning, program, and operational—to create a complete picture of the unit's overall effectiveness.

Program review, sometimes called program evaluation, describes the process of taking a look at all of a program's elements and how they work together. It includes examination of the administrative aspects of the program, as well as consideration of the multiple outcomes that result from various aspects of the program. Relevant questions include how the program is operating and whether it is effective in fulfilling its mission. Further, is it meeting its goals in terms of intended student outcomes, program outcomes, and operational outcomes? How do we know?

This chapter begins with a case study carried over from Chapter 4 that frames multiple levels of assessment. It then explores the multiple levels of intended outcomes and relevant assessment strategies. Finally, it offers a framework for program review and a discussion of related considerations in designing a comprehensive program evaluation.

Service-Learning Outcomes at Acorn College

Acorn College, a small liberal arts college, has as part of its mission statement that it seeks to graduate students who have the competence and commitment to be effective leaders, citizens, and agents of change in the world. The intended outcomes for graduates, drawn from the AAC&U LEAP project (AAC&U, n.d.-a), focus on critical thinking, teamwork, civic knowledge and engagement, and global learning. These outcomes are designed to be used for planning and assessment across all parts of the student experience. The College's newly developed strategic plan calls for increases in retention, student engagement, and service to both the local and global communities.

Acorn has long prided itself on experiential learning and a high level of volunteerism, but the efforts have been separate and siloed. In response to the strategic plan, the vice presidents for Academic Affairs and Student Affairs have jointly charged a committee to develop a formalized service-learning proposal.

The resulting cross-divisional initiative, called Mighty Oaks, uses the institutional mission and intended outcomes as the foundation for a set of integrated institutional programs (some existing and others to be developed):

- Designated service-learning courses in both general education and classes required for majors
- A policy regarding the number of service-learning courses required for graduation

(Continued)

- A service-learning certificate option, which includes both coursework and cocurricular experiences
- A living-learning community focused on service-learning
- International service-learning alternative break trips
- Formal partnerships with community agencies to create long-term service projects

The Office of Institutional Effectiveness has requested that, prior to implementation, the responsible units develop an assessment plan mapped to the institutional mission and intended outcomes that identifies specific intended learning and developmental outcomes for each program and describes strategies for measuring them.

Developing and Measuring Program-Level Outcomes

Evaluating program effectiveness is a matter of identifying the intended outcomes that represent successful achievement of mission and goals, carrying out program elements purposefully to meet those outcomes, and assessing the extent to which the outcomes have been achieved. Student learning outcomes are key in the determination of effectiveness, but relevant indicators include program and operational outcomes as well.

Aggregate Student Learning Outcomes

While students learn from discrete experiences, student learning overall is the cumulative result of many different kinds of experiences, both curricular and cocurricular (Schuh & Gansemer-Topf, 2010). However, to understand student learning at the broadest institutional level, professionals must not only collect data at that level but also identify those smaller assessment projects that can contribute to a larger understanding. At the simplest level, this can be done by compiling information about results of separate assessments and then examining the conclusions that can be drawn from considering them together.

The next level involves creating separate, parallel assessments to be used across different parts of the program. This may take the form of full instruments, such as rubrics, used in multiple situations, or a set of questions or items that can be included across multiple larger assessment projects. Whether used as whole instruments or elements embedded within others, consistent use of specific rubrics, with accompanying user training, facilitates looking at the ratings across groups (Suskie, 2015). In either approach, the results can then be aggregated, or "rolled up," to represent learning at a larger level, whether program, division, or institution (Kuh, Jankowski, Ikenberry, & Kinzie, 2014, p. 12). Suskie (2015) further suggested that a single rubric can be used to assess individuals and then revised to reflect aggregate goals and achievement. For example, in the Acorn College example, the Mighty Oaks steering committee might decide to use the AAC&U VALUE rubric for teamwork (AAC&U, n.d.-b) to assess students in several elements of the initiative: the living-learning community, an international service-learning alternative break trip, and course-based service-learning projects. Advisors or instructors could then use the rubric to assess their students, ideally at the beginning of their participation and again at the conclusion, and those final results could be aggregated to reflect teamwork outcomes for Mighty Oaks. Additionally, the committee could establish goals for each level of the four-point rubric, such as aspiring to have 30 percent of the students reach the fourth "Capstone" level and 50 percent reach the second or third "Milestone" levels, and acknowledging that 20 percent would be likely to be at the first "Benchmark" level. The actual aggregated achievement levels could then be compared to the goals as one measure of the effectiveness of the program in achieving the intended outcome of teamwork. The additional opportunity to compare initial ratings to final ratings for individual students and for all participants does not prove unequivocally that the Mighty Oaks experiences led to increases in teamwork, but it does offer insight into how the students changed during the time that they were involved, and this allows inferences to be made about the effects of the program. Follow-up focus groups or individual interviews could then be used to gain additional understanding.

At the broadest level, program outcomes can also be examined by using surveys or other program-wide approaches that are designed or chosen to gather data related to program-level intended learning outcomes. Typically, these are indirect measures of learning, since they depend on self-report, but used in combination with other measures, they can contribute to an overall understanding of program learning outcomes. It is important to choose an appropriate perspective or metric that can offer meaningful insight for comparison. Suskie (2015) identified several perspectives that can be relevant in developing an understanding of program-level outcomes (see Chapter 11 for further discussion of the use of comparisons). An historical perspective looks at trends over time (for example, has the percentage increased or decreased over the past five years?), and while it can provide valuable insight into longer-term effects, it is not relevant for a new or significantly redesigned program. A strengths/weaknesses perspective breaks results into subscores that can be compared; in this way, a broad measure of "learning" can be examined as its components of knowledge, skills, and personal growth. This approach requires the use of well-designed, complex instruments and the skills to analyze the data at this level. The value-added perspective compares scores over time, such as scores from students with longer exposure to the experience (for example, seniors) to scores from when they were first-year students. This approach necessitates careful planning and data management, and it may not be feasible for programs in which few students persist over time. Additionally, there is no control group and so any effects that are identified cannot be attributed specifically to the experience.

The peer perspective typically compares student responses from one institution to those from peer institutions (or peer programs at other institutions). However, as Suskie (2015) pointed out, this approach is popular, but it may not always be meaningful. Peer benchmarking may be better used to compare programs within an institution. It is likely to be more useful to know, for example, that GPAs for students in a particular residence area or program are below the institutional average than to know that the overall GPA of graduating students is 2 percent below the average at peer institutions (Suskie, 2015).

Comparisons between institutions can in some instances offer useful insights. However, this only works if other institutions are using common measures so that the data are truly comparable and if the institutions being compared have common characteristics. For example, comparing retention rate from an institution with an open admissions policy with the rate from an institution with a selective admission policy is likely to be a waste of time. There is increasing interest in and pressure to adopt this approach, as reflected in initiatives like the Voluntary System of Accountability (VSA), sponsored by the Association of Public and Land-Grant Universities and the American Association of State Colleges and Universities, with support from the Lumina Foundation and the Fund for the Improvement of Postsecondary Education (FIPSE), and contributions from an array of organizations including AAC&U, HERI, NSSE, NILOA, ACT, and the Educational Testing Service (VSA, 2011b). The VSA has as a primary objective to "support institutions in the measurement of educational outcomes and facilitate the identification and implementation of effective practices as part of institutional improvement efforts" (VSA, 2011a, para. 1). The goal is to provide a platform that facilitates use of comparable measures across institutions and also offers comparative information for prospective students and their families. The motivations and interests related to the creation of the VSA are complex and beyond the scope of this discussion, but the project reflects the growing interest in the use of data to provide insight into accountability, effectiveness, and cross-institution comparisons.

Each of the perspectives described by Suskie (2015) and previously outlined can be useful, but the use of multiple perspectives can provide deeper understanding of program outcomes. The same data, examined in various ways, will look different from different perspectives. For example, comparisons on the NSSE measure of "connected your learning to societal issues or problems" may show increases from first year to senior year, and from five years ago to now for both groups, but the data may also suggest that overall scores are lower than those at peer institutions. In that case, it is reasonable to conclude that local efforts are effective and improving, but that additional progress is needed if scores are to be comparable to those of peers.

Building on the case outlined at the beginning of the chapter, if Acorn administers the National Survey of Student Engagement (NSSE) (Center for Postsecondary Research, 2015), Acorn might look at student responses on items such as "connected your learning to societal problems or issues," amount of time spent doing "community service or volunteer work," and how much their experiences have contributed to their "working effectively with others" and "being an informed and active citizen" (Center for Postsecondary Research, 2015, pp. 1–4). Responses from Mighty Oaks students could be compared with those who did not participate in the initiative. Responses from first-year students to seniors also could be compared and, over time, responses from the first year of the initiative to those in successive years. All of these pieces of information contribute to an understanding of the larger impact of the program.

In a 2013 survey by the National Institute for Learning Outcomes Assessment (NILOA; Kuh, Jankowski, Ikenberry, & Kinzie, 2014), the top mechanisms reported for identifying aggregate outcomes included national student surveys, rubrics, classroom-based performance assessments, and alumni surveys. When compared to a 2009 survey, the approaches that had increased most were rubrics, portfolios, external performance assessment (such as internship and service-learning evaluations), and employer surveys. This suggests that assessment practice is shifting increasingly toward the use of more direct measures of learning. However, the widespread use of commercially available, national instruments such as the National Survey of Student Engagement (Center for Postsecondary Research, 2015) reflects the interest in and utility of comparing students to peers beyond the local context. Although there are limitations in using them to identify specific needed local changes, they can be useful in gaining program-relevant insight.

Program Outcomes

Program outcomes can be thought of simply as "what you want your program to accomplish" (Bresciani, Zelna, & Anderson, 2004, p. 11). In addition to student learning, whether individual or aggregated, programs have goals that reflect their intended effects on groups of students. The relevant question is *What do we want to have happen as a result of this program?* The answers describe the indications that the program is meeting its goals. These may include participation levels, involvement of targeted groups of students, student satisfaction with the program, or measures that are associated with student success, such as grade point average or retention. We often think of retention as a measure of continued student enrollment, or persistence, at the institution, but students are retained in other ways: in living-learning communities or specific residence halls, or as residential students; in student organizations; or in student paraprofessional positions. If maintaining or increasing student involvement is a goal of the program, then participation and relevant retention data will demonstrate, at least in part, whether that goal has been met. For example, if an institution is interested in student engagement in active learning, measures might include the proportion of students involved in field experiences like service-learning (Suskie, 2015).

"The experiences of students, as evidenced by their intellectual and social integration, cause them to continually modify their intentions and commitments" (Palomba & Banta, 1999, p. 285). The challenge of measuring program outcomes, then, is identifying when students change their behaviors and understanding the experiences that led them to do so. One way of doing this is to compare outcomes for different groups of students (for example, those who continue in a living-learning community and those who do not return). However, such comparisons do not address the reasons for the difference. Instead, a program might conduct exit interviews or survey students who do not return to gain an understanding of factors associated with their decisions. If institutional mechanisms provide access to data, survey responses can be combined with information from student databases, including their intentions at the point of enrollment, expectations, precollegiate characteristics, academic major and performance, programmatic involvements, and so forth. This analysis can provide insight into the patterns associated with various characteristics and experiences.

Institutional use of published instruments can yield useful information related to program outcomes. In addition to NSSE, Your First College Year addresses first-year programming and retention strategies (YFCY; HERI, 2015b), and the College Senior Survey "connects academic, civic, and diversity outcomes with a comprehensive set of college experiences to measure the impact of college. The CSS can be used as a stand-alone instrument or in conjunction with our other surveys to generate longitudinal data on students' cognitive and affective growth during college" (CSS; HERI, 2015a, CSS para. 1). Additionally the Diverse Learning Environments Survey (DLE) "captures student perceptions regarding the institutional climate, campus practices as experienced with faculty, staff, and peers, and student learning outcomes. Diverse student populations are at the center of the survey, and the instrument is based on studies of diverse student bodies and the complexity of issues that range from student mobility to intergroup relations" (HERI, 2015a, DLE para. 1). Data from instruments such as these can be a useful component of a comprehensive assessment plan; while typically used for institutional level data and for institutional comparisons, specific items or categories can be analyzed to provide insight for specific programs or groups of students. Such data do not represent direct measures of learning, but measures of engagement in areas associated with learning; since student engagement varies more within an institution than among institutions, we need to understand these differences, which can then be addressed, often at the program level (Kuh, 2003). For example, if the data indicate that transfer students are less engaged in service activities, or that first generation students are less likely to have a sense of belonging on campus, programmatic interventions can be developed to target these issues. Additional assessment, at the program level or through analysis of later administration of the broader instruments, can determine whether those interventions were successful.

Setting intended program outcomes is, like setting any intended outcomes, a matter of considering what targets are challenging but not impossible. Targets are essential as a way to focus intent, but they need to be tied to something meaningful. "Numbers have meaning only when they are compared against other numbers" (Suskie, 2015, p. 169). For example, if an assessment plan includes tracking participation, we may know that 100 people attended an event. What we cannot tell is whether that is good or bad, unless we know whether the attendance target was 25 or 500.

Suskie (2015) suggested setting a range of minimal and aspirational targets, as well as both milestone (formative) and destination (summative) targets, rather than a single definitive goal. Useful questions include *What is the critical, minimal level that is acceptable and does not necessitate change, and what is the optimal level that reflects success?* Targets should be justifiably rigorous, externally informed, historically informed, and consistent across venues, modalities, and course or program levels (Suskie, 2015).

Operational Outcomes

Finally, while learning and program outcomes are the best indicators of program effectiveness, operational outcomes are useful descriptors of the "how" that facilitates the "what." These may also be referred to as performance or service utilization outcomes, which "seek to set standards for the utilization of services and facilities" (Bresciani, Zelna, & Anderson, 2004, p. 11). Examples of such metrics include expenditure per student served, average wait time for appointments, or level of participation measured against capacity (for example, residence hall occupancy). These measures may be more associated with efficiency than effectiveness, but they do reflect relevant factors such as use of resources, stewardship of funds, and student usage of the program.

Cross-Functional Outcomes

Although discussion in this chapter focuses on assessment at the program level, student learning cannot be contained or described as the result of any one experience or set of unit initiatives. Since student learning happens across organizational structures, assessment should also be considered across institutional units. Collaborative initiatives, such as the one described in the Acorn College case, are intended to create seamless learning environments for students and to help them make connections across experiences. Creative approaches to assessment ask the questions *Where are all of the places across the program or institution that our students are learning this,* and *how can we gauge their learning across all of those places?* As Bresciani, Zelna, and Anderson (2004) pointed out, in using this collaborative approach, "The institution slowly moves away from individual audits of units, programs, divisions, departments, and so forth to an outcomes-based, information rich model of student learning and engagement" (p. 5).

> Assessment is, after all, a process of meaning making that should always include "reaching up," "reaching down," and "looking around." Assessment practice is directly informed by "reaching up"—that is, having an awareness of, and adapting to, the institution's mission purpose and values—but also by "reaching down," to appreciate the details of the institution's footing, or context—attending to the institution's geographic and cultural roots, where it is located, what the needs and values of that city or region are, as well as who its students are, and what their particular learning and development needs embrace. "Looking around" informs assessment by ensuring that the practice of assessment is integrated and coordinated within and beyond departments and divisions and that assessment work is intertwined with the primary educational activities of the institution. (Keeling, Wall, Underhile, & Dungy, 2008, pp. 85–86)

Comprehensive program assessment includes not only an examination of the aggregate student learning outcomes, as well as the program and operational outcomes, but also an understanding of the context of the program and where it is situated in the larger institution and environment.

Program Review

Program review, sometimes called program evaluation, is more than just a compilation of smaller assessment projects conducted within the unit. Assessment attention now tends to be focused on learning outcomes; for too long, we focused on inputs rather than outcomes, and so the shift is needed and appropriate. Banta, Lund, Black, and Oblander (1996), echoing the American Association for Higher Education's *Principles of Good Practice for*

Assessing Student Learning (1992), reminded us that "It's not only where they end up, but how they get there" (p. 23).

> Processes, in a sense, are the road maps that enable educators to retrace the college experiences of students. Paying attention to processes thus helps make improvement possible. Analyzing the pathways, detours, and conditions that improve the higher education journey provides invaluable material to educators as they attempt to chart richer and more potent educational experiences for students. (Banta, Lund, Black, & Oblander, 1996, pp. 23–24)

If we assess only learning outcomes, our insight is limited. If we always reach our intended outcomes, then we may not have the need to examine our program delivery closely. However, if we do not achieve the designated outcomes, and our assessment strategy has not included anything else, then how will we determine which elements of the program need to be changed? (Jacoby & Dean, 2010). Program review looks at the administration and effectiveness of the overall unit to assess strengths and identify areas for improvement.

Suskie (2015) argued that effectiveness involves more than just achieving purpose and meeting goals, but also includes "meeting stakeholder needs, serving the public good, ensuring ongoing health and well-being, and deploying resources effectively, prudently, and efficiently" (p. 148). Student learning is a vital part of this, but Suskie (2015) pointed out that stakeholders are also interested in measures such as proportion of students who achieve their goals, who achieve those goals in a timely fashion, and who are successful in finding relevant jobs, as well as various metrics related to costs and benefits (for example, ratio of debt to income, ratio of tuition to post-degree income). A comprehensive program review can construct a cohesive picture that combines all of the elements that comprise the program.

The reasons to conduct program review are varied. At many institutions, programs—academic and cocurricular—are required to conduct cyclical, structured program reviews as a part of institutional effectiveness efforts, particularly as related to institutional accreditation. Such required reviews can serve as a main driver for assessment activity in the unit (Kuh, Jankowski, Ikenberry, & Kinzie, 2014). Reviews also may be conducted for accountability, for information to influence restructuring, as a source of information for resource allocation, or as an evaluation of a new or redesigned program. Regardless of the impetus, program review offers an opportunity for a unit staff to examine the operation and to better understand how it is operating.

If the program review model is not dictated by institutional or division policy, deciding on the model to be used is a crucial first step in designing a productive and constructive process. Royse, Thyer, and Padgett (2010) noted that "program evaluation involves making comparisons ... Few programs can be evaluated without comparing them to something" (p. 13). The choice of the basis for comparison has implications for the findings, since various frameworks emphasize different priorities and values (Young, Dean, Franklin, & Tschepikow, 2014).

Identifying Frameworks and Considerations

Kuk, Banning, and Amey (2010) pointed out that there are at least three dominant epistemological perspectives for understanding organizations: positivism or postpositivism, social constructivism, and postmodernism. Many of the current approaches to assessment are grounded in an essentially positivist perspective, with the assumption that there are ways to measure and understand organizational effectiveness objectively. However, social constructivism is also reflected in the understanding that local context and experience shape the reality of an organization, which can be understood through qualitative approaches to assessment. A postmodern perspective would focus instead on the structures of hierarchy and power present in the organization and would be designed to deconstruct them. The most productive approach to assessment is to recognize the presence and benefits of each and to use them purposefully, depending on the nature and needs of the assessment to be conducted (Kuk, Banning, & Amey, 2010; Love & Estanek, 2004).

Another relevant consideration in program review is implementation fidelity (Fisher, Smith, Finney, & Pinder, 2014). It is important to consider not only how the program was designed, but also how it was implemented.

> Ensuring implementation of a program or curriculum is a basic idea; however, when student learning or development does not occur as expected, this outcome is often (mis)interpreted as the programming or curriculum not "working," resulting in its abandonment. We believe that this conclusion maybe invalid or, at a minimum, premature without data to assess whether the programming or curriculum was actually implemented as intended. (Fisher, Smith, Finney, & Pinder, 2014, p. 28)

Program review design should attend to program design, intended and actual outcomes, and implementation fidelity to create a comprehensive picture.

Elements of Program Review

Institutional requirements may dictate the program review process, but when that is not the case, professionals must identify or develop a structure and process by which to conduct program review. The Council for the Advancement of Standards (CAS) recommends an approach that is characterized by self-assessment, broad input, the importance of supporting evidence, and the use of professional standards of practice as the basis for comparison (CAS, 2015). "One of the many benefits of the CAS process is that there is a clearly outlined implementation process.... The process, while not without challenge, is straightforward and the end result is valuable feedback from a variety of constituents" (Bresciani, Zelna, & Anderson, 2004, p. 39). The CAS self-study process offers an established way to structure a thorough program review.

The CAS standards, discussed at more length in Chapter 11, are designed to provide a description of good practice at the functional area level that can be used as the basis for comparison and evaluation (CAS, 2015). The standards include both learning and development outcomes (and the expectation that they are assessed) and statements related to essential program components (for example, organization and leadership, human resources, institutional and external relations, assessment and evaluation). The main elements of program review as reflected in the CAS model include choosing the basis for comparison, collecting evidence to support judgments about compliance with the standards, assembling and training a team to review the evidence and rate the extent to which each standard is met, and finally reviewing the ratings to identify areas of strength and areas in need of improvement. That information can then be used to "close the loop," developing and implementing action plans to address the identified needs. Conceptualized this way, program review becomes part of an ongoing, comprehensive assessment plan in which each element of the program and the overall program itself are assessed in a continuous, purposeful cycle. The outcomes assessment strategies discussed earlier in this chapter generate the evidence that is compiled to evaluate effectiveness of the program, achievement of its goals, and accomplishment of its mission. Although the CAS standards are not designed specifically to reflect regional accreditation criteria, they do represent a systematic and comprehensive way to conduct program reviews for accreditation self-studies. In particular, the CAS emphasis on assessing both student learning outcomes and program-level effectiveness, and on demonstrating evidence-based improvement, ensures that using this approach will generate the data required to demonstrate compliance with accreditation standards.

Role of Assessment Industry Partners and Products

One of the challenges of program-level assessment activity is that it can generate a large amount of data to be managed and analyzed. Campuses are increasingly turning to assessment industry service providers and products for assistance in implementing and managing assessment projects, and program-level assessment can benefit from this as well. Some of these options simply provide platforms for data collection and management that use locally designed data collection strategies and instruments. Others offer sophisticated mechanisms to assist campuses with every part of a comprehensive assessment plan, from identification and measurement of learning outcomes to management of compliance with accreditation criteria. They may also include the capacity to customize around local contexts and to benchmark against peers nationally. While the investment of monetary and human resources can be substantial, these providers and products can expand campus assessment capacity significantly. As with any assessment-related strategy, it is imperative that the choices be considered critically and carefully to ensure that they meet the specific needs of the program or institution.

Program Review and Regional Accreditation

We also want to acknowledge the role of program review in the process by which institutions are accredited by their regional accrediting body, such as the Western Association of Schools and Colleges or the Southern Association of Colleges and Schools. Institutions undergo a review for accreditation purposes on a periodic basis, typically every 10 years. As part of the process, institutions conduct self-studies that are framed by the criteria of the regional accrediting body. It is common for the criteria to speak to expectations for student affairs units that need to be addressed by program reviews. For example, the Middle States Commission has published the following criterion for an accredited institution: "An accredited institution possesses and demonstrates the following attributes or activities ... periodic assessment of the effectiveness of programs supporting the student experience" (2015, p. 9). Clearly, this requirement means that program assessment is part of the accreditation process. Other regional accrediting bodies have similar requirements. Accordingly, student affairs units and programs need to provide this information as self-studies are being developed.

Final Considerations

Programs are the building blocks of student affairs divisions, and program-level assessment is an essential part of understanding the contributions of the division to the larger institution. Careful attention to program outcomes assessment and program review ensures that these building blocks are sturdy and create a strong foundation for student success. Assessment of separate programmatic efforts is important, but "assessment is, by nature, intersectional" (Keeling et al., 2008, p. 88), so careful planning across a functional area program permits data to be aggregated and therefore to contribute to a larger understanding of program effectiveness. Tracking student behavior and patterns is useful, but as Suskie (2009) pointed out, behaviors can tell us only the *what*, not the *why*. In conjunction with other data, however, we can begin to make meaningful inferences from them. Multiple measures, multiple perspectives, multiple points of assessment ... understanding program effectiveness is a matter of having a purposeful, comprehensive assessment plan that includes multiple forms of outcomes and consideration of the working of the unit as a whole. When all of the parts are taken together, the picture that emerges is one that conveys the impact and effectiveness of the program.

Back to Acorn College

At Acorn, evaluation of the Mighty Oaks initiative involves assessment at multiple levels. The steering committee has developed a comprehensive assessment plan that aligns with the mission element of *effective citizenship*, the institutional intended learning outcome of *civic knowledge and engagement*, and the strategic plan initiative of *increasing service to the local and global communities*. Each of the Mighty Oaks programmatic elements reflects these institutional priorities.

The subcommittee working to develop the international service-learning alternative break trips has developed intended learning outcomes and assessment strategies for the experience. Acknowledging that an alternative break trip is a one-time, short-term experience, they have determined that as a result of participating in an international service-learning alternative break trip, students will do the following:

- Increase their civic engagement competency by increasing at least one level on three areas of the AAC&U Civic Engagement VALUE rubric (AAC&U, n.d.a), as measured initially through advisor observation during the pre-trip orientation discussion and then during the post-trip reflection meeting. The areas to be assessed are Diversity of Communities and Cultures, Civic Communication, and Civic Contexts and Structures. (Individual learning outcome)

- Demonstrate their level of civic engagement competency through their responses in journal entries to designated prompts that reflect the following categories of the Civic Engagement rubric: Analysis of Knowledge, Civic Identity and Commitment, and Civic Action and Reflection. Advisors will review entries daily and will provide summative feedback based on the rubric prior to the post-trip reflection meeting. (Individual learning outcome)

- As a group, increase the level of civic engagement competency so that 80 percent of the group increases a level as previously described. (Aggregate learning outcome)

- Demonstrate their appreciation of the experience by affirming interest and intention to pursue additional service-learning opportunities, as indicated on the post-trip participant survey, with a goal of 75 percent indicating continued interest. (Program outcome)

In the inaugural year of Mighty Oaks, there will be two international service-learning alternative break trips offered, each with the capacity to involve up to 12 students. The goal is to add one trip per year until a total of eight trips are offered annually. Advisors will use the assessment strategies previously described to assess individual, aggregate, and program achievement of the intended outcomes. They will have individual meetings with students to discuss their experiences, as well as facilitating group reflection activities after the trip. Beyond the individual student and trip level, the results will also be aggregated into a program database so that data can be compiled across trips and, in successive years, can be used for comparison and for assessment across all participants. Additionally, specific elements of the Civic Engagement rubric are also used for learning outcomes assessment in the living-learning community and in service-learning courses so that the results can be "rolled up" to reflect learning across the program. Finally, the names of participants are given to Alumni Affairs so that questions regarding trip participation, learning, and lasting effects can be asked of participants through alumni surveys.

The subcommittees working to develop the other Mighty Oaks program components also develop assessment plans, with the steering committee working closely with them to ensure alignment with the mission and intended outcomes and also consistency of assessment strategies to permit aggregating of the data and inferences at the program level.

Discussion Questions

1. What assessment strategies other than those previously described might be developed to assess the Acorn College alternative spring break trips?

2. Choose one of the other Mighty Oaks program elements and design appropriate intended outcomes and assessment strategies. What is the rationale for your choices? What did you consider as priorities in what you developed?

3. Often we see assessment being done at the level of smaller program elements (for example, workshops, staff training) and at the institutional level (for example, NSSE), but not at the program level. What are the barriers to program-level assessment? How can these be mitigated or addressed?

4. Effective program-level assessment and program review depends on the collaboration of multiple people. Who are the key stakeholders in your program area? How can they be engaged effectively and productively in the process?

References

American Association for Higher Education. (1992). *Principles of good practice for assessing student learning.* Washington, DC: Author.

Association of American Colleges and Universities. (n.d.-a). *Civic engagement VALUE rubric.* Washington, DC: Author. Retrieved from https://www.aacu.org/sites/default/files/files/VALUE/CivicEngagementSample.pdf

Association of American Colleges & Universities. (n.d.-b). *Teamwork VALUE rubric.* Washington, DC: Author. Retrieved from https://aacu.org/sites/default/files/files/VALUE/Teamwork.pdf

Banta, T. W., Lund, J. P., Black, K. E., & Oblander, F. W. (1996). *Assessment in practice: Putting principles to work on college campuses.* San Francisco, CA: Jossey-Bass.

Bresciani, M. J., Zelna, C. L., & Anderson, J. A. (2004). *Assessing student learning and development: A handbook for practitioners.* Washington, DC: National Association of Student Personnel Administrators.

Center for Postsecondary Research. (2015). *National Survey of Student Engagement: Survey instrument.* Bloomington, IN: Center for Postsecondary Research, Indiana University School of Education. Retrieved from http://nsse.iub.edu/html/survey_instruments.cfm

Council for the Advancement of Standards in Higher Education. (2015). *CAS professional standards for higher education* (9th ed.). Washington, DC: Author.

Fisher, R., Smith, K., Finney, S., & Pinder, K. (2014). Assessment matters: The importance of implementation fidelity for evaluating program effectiveness. *About Campus, 19*(5), 28–32.

Higher Education Research Institute. (2015a). *College Senior Survey.* Retrieved from http://www.heri.ucla.edu/cssoverview.php

Higher Education Research Institute. (2015b). *Your First College Year (YFCY) Survey.* Retrieved from http://heri.ucla.edu/yfcyoverview.php

Jacoby, B., & Dean, L. A. (2010). What does "quality" look like? Why higher education should care about standards for student programs and services. *About Campus, 15*(3), 29–32.

Keeling, R. P., Underhile, R., Wall, A. F., & Dungy, G. J. (2008). *Assessment reconsidered: Institutional effectiveness for student success.* Washington, DC: NASPA.

Kuh, G. D. (2003, March/April). What we're learning about student engagement from NSSE. *Change,* 24–32.

Kuh, G. D., Jankowski, N., Ikenberry, S. O., & Kinzie, J. (2014). *Knowing what students know and can do: The current state of student learning outcomes assessment in U.S. colleges and universities.* Champaign, IL: National Institute for Learning Outcomes Assessment. Retrieved from http://www.learningoutcomesassessment.org/documents/2013%20Survey%20Report%20Final.pdf

Kuk, L. (2009). The dynamics of organizational models within student affairs. In G. S. McClennan & J. Stringer (Eds.), *The handbook of student affairs administration* (3rd ed., pp. 313–332). San Francisco, CA: Jossey-Bass.

Kuk, L., Banning, J. H., & Amey, M. (2010). *Positioning student affairs for sustainable change.* Sterling, VA: Stylus.

Love, P. G., & Estanek, S. M. (2004). *Re-thinking student affairs practice.* San Francisco, CA: Jossey-Bass.

Middle States Commission on Higher Education. (2015). *Standards for accreditation and requirements of affiliation* (13th ed.). Philadelphia, PA: Author. Retrieved from http://www.msche.org/publications/RevisedStandardsFINAL.pdf

Palomba, C. A., & Banta, T. W. (1999). *Assessment essentials: Planning, implementing, and improving assessment in higher education.* San Francisco, CA: Jossey-Bass.

Royse, D., Thyer, B. A., & Padgett, D. K. (2010). *Program evaluation: An introduction* (5th ed.). Belmont, CA: Wadsworth.

Schuh, J. H., & Gansemer-Topf, A. M. (2010). *The role of student affairs in student learning assessment.* National Institute for Learning Outcomes Assessment, Occasional Paper #7. Champaign, IL: National Institute for Learning Outcomes Assessment. Retrieved from http://www .learningoutcomeassessment.org/documents/studentAffairsrole.pdf

Suskie, L. (2009). *Assessing student learning: A common sense guide* (2nd ed.). San Francisco, CA: Jossey-Bass.

Suskie, L. A. (2015). *Five dimensions of quality: A common sense guide to accreditation and accountability.* San Francisco, CA: Jossey-Bass.

Voluntary System of Accountability. (2011a). *About VSA.* Retrieved from http://www.voluntarysystem.org/about

Voluntary System of Accountability. (2011b). *VSA partners.* Retrieved from http://www.voluntarysystem.org/partners

Young, D. G., Dean, L. A., Franklin, D. S., & Tschepikow, W. K. (2014). Effects of assessment on collegiate recreation programs. *Recreational Sports Journal, 38,* 82–95.

6

FACILITATING DATA COLLECTION AND MANAGEMENT

This chapter focuses on data collection and management procedures. Practices relatable to both qualitative and quantitative approaches are provided and a discussion of using existing datasets and external data collection services also is included. The chapter also incorporates a section on data management, an often-overlooked topic in assessment. Practitioners may have developed a thoughtful plan for a study, but neglected to consider how to manage the data it generates. A data management plan can significantly enhance, or limit, the efficiency of data analysis. Finally, in the previous edition, we included a separate section on the use of technology for various different functions related to data. The proliferation of choices, widespread use, and capabilities of tools available suggest a review of specific technologies could necessitate its own volume. As a result, we incorporate discussion of technology when relevant to specific sections of the chapter.

Definition and Use of Data Collection and Data Management

Data collection refers to the process of determining, gathering, and assembling data to support an assessment project. Data management is concerned with how to create a dataset, as well as how to organize, store, and maintain data effectively as it is collected to ensure it can be used in various forms of analysis. A case study follows to illustrate the importance of these three main themes.

Developing an Assessment Database at Tiger State University

Sadie is the director for Student Leadership and Service at Tiger State University (TSU). Her responsibilities involve facilitating leadership training and service opportunities for undergraduates. As part of her role, Sadie is responsible for implementing Stripes, a large-scale pre-orientation summer program for new TSU students.

The Stripes program offers incoming students opportunities to learn about involvement on campus while meeting their new peers and developing leadership skills and capabilities. The program has become a campus tradition at TSU, having been a pre-orientation option for incoming new students for over a decade. Two years ago, Stripes was expanded to three distinct programs (the three-day Stripes Summit, the five-day Stripes Serves, and the six-day Stripes Outdoors), each with multiple sessions, and now serves nearly one third of the over 4,000 first year students.

The impact and popularity of the Stripes program have not gone unnoticed. Having heard from parents about the positive experiences students have with Stripes, the chancellor offered to lead a fundraising effort to endow the program. To accomplish this goal, he needs data to inform talks and presentations to potential donors. Fortunately, Sadie has conducted regular assessments of the programs including both satisfaction and outcomes-based surveys (which include some open-ended items), but with the exception of a few questions, the surveys have been highly tailored to each program. Summary data from the external survey site Sadie uses to send out surveys has evidenced overall satisfaction with the program and suggested a few areas for improvement. Unfortunately, time and resource constraints have kept her from analyzing responses to the short-answer questions or attempting to make any program comparisons.

Data Collection

Data collection is a multi-stage process, which involves identifying a sample, ensuring the sample aligns with the goals of the study, determining how to access the sample, selecting or developing an instrument, and deciding who will collect data. This section highlights data collection strategies from both qualitative and quantitative techniques. Many texts have been written on these topics. This chapter provides an overview of several we find beneficial to student affairs assessment.

Sample and Sample Size

A sample is a part intended to approximate or characterize a whole. The sample generally should represent the best available source of data to address your project goals and intended outcomes. While a sample is conceptually the same for most assessment approaches, the type/s of available data and intended research method/s can offer some guidance as to the numbers of participants or records needed for analysis. For example, the researcher can determine minimum responses for descriptive samples while minimum responses for evaluating difference, relationships, and prediction are determined by statistical requirements. Overall, however, it is important to remember that while we can offer some guidance for selecting a sample, the ultimate decision rests with the person coordinating the assessment and responsible for offering recommendations based on the results.

Like many other aspects of assessment we have emphasized in this text, sample, sample size, and sampling strategy must be suitably aligned with the purpose, available resources, questions being asked, and any constraints. While an important component of research is rigor, an equally vital aspect is the ability to support, or defend, one's choices. Schuh and Upcraft (2000) reminded us of the distinction between perfect versus "good enough" assessment design—a consideration very much aligned with choosing a sample. A perfect sample is the full population or complete dataset; however, most practitioners (or even full-time researchers) don't have the time or resources to devote to ensuring every member of a population is included in a study. Cost also can be a major barrier. Therefore, it is important to identify compromises, caution the audience of concessions and limitations, and be ready to defend your decision with viable and rational reasoning. Some considerations follow to help guide your choices based on qualitative or quantitative data collection techniques.

Qualitative Samples The commitment of qualitative research to a constructivist viewpoint often influences the way participants (interview and observation), locations (observation), and documents (review) are selected for study. Where statistical power and inference depend on randomly selected samples to create generalizability, qualitative trustworthiness and transferability rely on purposively selected, information-rich, samples to build credibility (Patton, 2015). While qualitative methodology historically has undergone some criticism for the lack of commitment to generalizability, choosing a sample is no less difficult when collecting qualitative data.

The central consideration for qualitative researchers lies between breadth and depth. Breadth means focusing on a specific set of experiences drawing on a larger range of people or records. This can be especially beneficial for an exploratory study or when attempting to show variety or differences. Depth involves focusing on a more open range of experiences drawing on a smaller number of people or records. The optimal sample size should be dependent on the information-richness of the cases matched with the skills of the researcher. Patton (2015) recommended choosing a non-negotiable minimum sample size based on "expected reasonable coverage" while also considering the purpose and audience of the study. Yet, a primary feature of qualitative inquiry is emergent design, so one should be as flexible as study constraints permit.

Quantitative Samples After meeting minimum criteria for specific quantitative analyses, sample size decisions should depend more on representativeness for the group, as opposed to a particular number. The first major decision related to choosing whom to study is whether or not the intention is to describe a subset of students (for example, students who participated in a leadership-focused FYS course) or to generalize to a larger population (for example, all students who participated in FYS courses). Following, we offer some questions to consider when aiming for a representative sample.

1. What is the expected rate of return? This question is related to both the total population and what you want to say about it. If describing an aspect of the population is your goal, for example, you may need fewer responses than if you hope to make comparisons with subsets of the sample or to generalize from the sample to the population.

2. How much potential error can you accept (the difference between your findings and the true results if you were able to sample the entire population)? This has to do with a concept called sampling error. This consideration is more prevalent in studies where statistical generalization is a goal, in other words, when you want to say that your sample is statistically similar to the population.

3. How much data does the analysis require? Related to the previous consideration, this has to do with minimum numbers needed for the most statistical analyses beyond basic descriptive statistics. For inferential data analysis, particularly involving groups, a minimally acceptable number of responses for comparison or relation is about

30 in each group (for example, 30 men, 30 women). For predictive studies, 30 responses per data point is recommended (for example, 30 responses for gender; 30 more responses for question 1).

Among the most efficient ways of determining the minimum number of responses needed for a statistical sample is to use power analysis. Briefly, power analysis takes the total number of data points along with the sampling error you are willing to accept, and estimates the total sample size you need to ensure generalizability. Power analysis software is included with many statistical packages; however, freely available online versions are relatively simple to use and interpret, requiring little prior statistical knowledge.

Regardless of the sample or sample size, the audience is the definitive judge of the study's credibility. Fowler (2009) and Suskie (1992) noted the representativeness of the sample is more important than the percentage of people or records sampled, except for very small populations. For example, a smaller sample that is representative is more generalizable than a larger sample that is not. This leads to Patton's (2015) universal, certain, and sage advice as to "how many" one needs for a sample as "it depends." The most certain advice we can give is to provide details about the sample by fully describing and explaining participant, case, or record selection while acknowledging strengths and weaknesses associated with study decisions.

Choosing a Method

The most concise response we can offer to the question, "What is it the best assessment method?" is "The one that fits your project." Too often, practitioners (and researchers) favor a particular methodology without consideration of its fit and appropriateness for the project purpose and objectives. Not all projects should be addressed with a survey and conversely, a preference for interviewing does not mean it is the optimal approach. While available resources (for example, assistance, funding, time) and research skills are considerations for choosing a method, they should not be treated as wholly preventative influences any moreso than convenience should be a substitute for good assessment design. Following are some considerations for choosing the best method suited to your study.

1. Is there alignment between the goal/s of the projects, the questions you want to ask or address, and the sample?

2. If assessing the entire population or data sources is not feasible, how accessible is a sample or subset of data?

3. How many participants or data sources will you need to meet the goals of the analysis?

4. Applying the forms (Chapter 7) or keywords (Chapter 8) approach, which method/s seems to best fit your question?

5. If you do not have the expertise or are not fully confident in your ability to implement the method you chose, what additional resources do you have (for example, statistical consulting on campus or a staff member with focus group expertise)?

Sampling Strategies

This section details various strategies for selecting samples. Following are several that represent common and best practices as well as a few recommendations for strategies we seldom see used but that are worth considering. The list is by no means exhaustive, but should provide enough choices to fit most projects. You may notice the absence of convenience sampling, which involves simply selecting a sample based on the easiest available cases. Although this approach may be most efficient in terms of saving time and effort and is probably the most common, it also involves the poorest rationale and lowest credibility (Patton, 2015). Following are 10 alternative recommendations (six qualitative, four quantitative). We use the word *case* in the descriptions of each strategy broadly to mean individuals, records, or other sources of data.

Qualitative Sampling Strategies Qualitative sampling strategies often emphasize identifying the most information-rich source or sources. This can lead to the need for multiple informants, observations, and/or documents to meet the goals of a project or require only a few central but highly detailed, cases.

- **Intensity sampling** involves identifying cases that are important, but not extreme (that is, outliers) for understanding a phenomenon. This strategy seeks exceptional or particularly rich, but not unusual, cases. Identifying an intensity sample requires prior knowledge of the phenomenon to aid in choosing the examples.

- **Homogeneous sampling** involves selecting cases that have specific characteristics. This strategy trades a broader perspective for a specific emphasis. It is most commonly used for focus group interviewing, but is applicable to all qualitative forms. Identifying an intensity sample requires knowing which trait or subgroup to specify beforehand and deciding how to explain characteristics that are not shared.

- **Criterion sampling** involves choosing cases that meet a certain criterion. This can be the most expansive of qualitative techniques, depending on the phenomenon of interest. Identifying a criterion sample involves specifying the primary phenomenon, experience, or event of interest and working to involve cases that meet this criterion in the study.

- **Typical case sampling** involves illustrating or highlighting what is typical, normal, or average to those unfamiliar with a phenomenon. This strategy attempts to identify and to describe a normal or average experience, but not to make generalized statements about each person or experience involved. It is important to get a broad consensus on what is typical and to ignore extreme cases. Identifying a typical case sample requires the help of informed stakeholders who can agree about what is typical.

- **Snowball or chain sampling** involves choosing information-rich or otherwise interesting cases based on recommendations. A strong indicator of importance is when multiple people suggest the same case/s. Michael Patton (2015) noted samples converge as key names or events are mentioned repeatedly. Identifying a snowball or chain sample involves asking multiple initial informants for suggestions until commonly endorsed sources emerge.

- **Opportunistic sampling** involves following new leads during fieldwork and taking advantage of the unexpected. At times, this may involve immediate decisions. This is perhaps the most closely aligned technique to the constructivist perspective as it allows the sample to emerge during data collection. Identifying an opportunistic sample involves being open to new opportunities as they arise during the study.

Quantitative Sampling Strategies Quantitative sampling strategies often emphasize identifying the most representative or common sources when the population, or all data points, cannot be accessed. The strategies outlined in the following generally involve some variation of random sampling, which is an assumption for most types of statistics beyond simple description.

- **Simple random sampling** involves selecting a randomly drawn sample from all cases in a population. All individuals have an equal and independent chance of being selected. Effective ways to generate a simple random sample include using an online random number generator or a random number assignment feature in a spreadsheet program.

- **Systematic sampling** involves placing the total population of cases on a list and selecting every X case until the desired sample size is reached. Determine the total sample size before deciding on X to ensure adequate space between cases. For example, if the population were 2,000, an X of 10 (meaning every 10th person is selected) would result in a systemically selected sample of 200.

- **Stratified (random) sampling** involves ensuring certain subgroups in a population are represented in the sample proportional to their numbers in the population. This type of sample is appropriate in studies where comparisons between subgroups are important. For example, if the population is 1,000 sophomore men and subgroups are 10 percent work study, 15 percent on-campus jobs, 40 percent off campus jobs, and 35 percent no jobs, then a stratified sample of off-campus jobholders should include 160 sophomore men (.40 × 1,000 = 400, 40 percent of 400 = 160). Random is shown in parenthesis purposefully to indicate that a stratified sample can be random only when members of the subgroups are also randomly sampled.

- **Cluster sampling** involves the inclusion of all members of group. This type of sample emphasizes groups over individual cases. An example is taking a random sample of FYS classes and then including all students who are enrolled in the classes sampled.

Accessing Sources and Using Existing Data

Assessment data can be collected by interviewing individuals or groups, administering surveys in person or electronically, conducting observations, or accessing documents and existing datasets. We refer to these collectively as data sources. Chapters 7 and 8 discuss descriptions, strengths, and weaknesses of qualitative and quantitative methodological approaches in detail. This section provides guidance for accessing data sources.

Accessing Sources

After determining a sample and methodology, it is essential to consider the availability and accessibly of the sources. Because qualitative research can be more personal or even obtrusive, data collected from individuals or groups can necessitate additional steps. Ethnographers often refer to this as negotiating access to the field, and although few assessment projects involve deep and sustained fieldwork, the basic concepts of building trust and rapport by being honest and upfront about the goals of the project still apply to working in a college setting. When planning interviews, being introduced by an insider, being upfront and genuine (without leading), and ensuring participants that their time is valuable can be effective means of building rapport and establishing trust, which often leads to more genuine and in-depth answers.

Survey and existing data research is highly dependent on access to the sample, and often involves identifying who has access. The sample may be physically accessible, such as an existing student group, program, or class. Identifying a gatekeeper, or person/s who can provide access, is essential. In the case of a broader group, you may need contact information such as e-mail addresses for surveys or file access for database research. A good place to begin is the institutional research or registrar's office. Conversely, a starting point for defined groups such as fraternities and sororities is the office that works most closely with them. In the case of larger samples, unless you have developed a high level of trust with data providers, it can be helpful to have upper administration endorse the request or make it for you.

For observational research, we recommend informing participants that you are collecting data as opposed to attempting to conceal the activity. Unless the setting has a provision for hidden (for example, a two-way mirror) or obscured (for example, a second-story balcony overlooking the room) observation, you will be visible while collecting data. Researchers have noted any presence can produce changes in behavior, affecting the validity of the findings, although the effect can diminish over time. This is more pronounced when the observer is also a participant. Webb and colleagues (Webb, Campbell, Schwartz, & Sechrest, 2000) and later Russell and Kovacs (2003) distinguished between simple and contrived observation. In simple observation, the researcher does not alter the setting in any way. In contrived observation, the researcher alters the setting to see what changes the alteration creates. For example, you might leave free coffee in a study lounge to see if students begin using the space more often.

Negotiating access to documents, particularly those that can reveal phenomena that cannot be observed or are not immediately apparent, is similar to reaching interview participants. A major benefit of using documents is the possibility of discovering critical background materials that reveal how programs, processes, and actions developed. Patton (2015) noted that often program participants, who may not understand the origins underpinning conflict, agreement, or ongoing discussion about phenomenon, might not know this information. We recommend identifying a gatekeeper to help obtain materials. Building rapport and trust with document providers can facilitate access to the sources you need and also may lead to suggestions for sources you did not know existed.

Using Existing Data

College campuses collect, store, maintain, and license access to a variety of databases. Existing data can be a collection of internal data points from student records (for example, financial aid or registrar data), raw data compiled from internal surveys, or an external database derived from records or survey research on your students (for example, NSSE). Following are general descriptions of existing data sources that may be maintained and accessible for assessment purposes. Additional suggestions for gaining access to these forms of data are also included.

Using Institutional Records Colleges and universities collect a tremendous amount of information on students. Some datasets are created and maintained as directed by federal mandates for external reporting (for example, financial aid), while others are produced to meet campus needs (for example, volunteer service hours). While it has been our experience that rich data exists on campus, in most cases, the data are highly decentralized. Learning what types of data offices maintain can be challenging. Gaining access also may be problematic, as some data raise privacy concerns that must be considered. This drawback can be minimized, however, by proposing to use only institutionally assigned identification numbers or generating case numbers. Further, linking records across datasets requires moderate to high expertise as well as the involvement of several stakeholders. The ideal situation is if the institutional research office has the staff and capability to do this for you. Gaining access to and using institutional data can be unique to each campus situation, based on the culture of the institution for what is collected, shared, and maintained. Following are examples of institutional data you may be able to access that could be useful in your assessment work.

When a student applies to the institution, the admissions office creates a database entry. If the student applies for financial aid, FAFSA information is entered into a record maintained by the financial aid office. When students register for classes, the registrar's office enters the information into a database. Sometimes, additional data points such as student group or athletic participation are also collected. For example, the volunteer office may log student participation hours and the fraternity/sorority involvement office maintains membership records. Student housing personnel may keep their own dataset for students who live (or have lived) on campus as well as facilities utilization information. On some campuses, the institutional research office links all this data, or has the capability of doing so. While not necessarily related to the broad spectrum of assessment goals, these records can be informative for needs-based and utilization efforts as well as informative for environmental assessment. Six questions to ask about institutional data include the following:

1. What data does your institution maintain?
2. What data can you use to inform your assessment?
3. If data are not centralized, can campus records be merged?
4. What political or other considerations must be addressed prior to gaining access to data?
5. Can the institutional research office aid in this process?
6. If you collect survey data, can it be merged or supplemented with an existing dataset?

Using External Databases Institutions often participate in large-scale external surveys. In most cases, data are collected by an external agency using a standardized survey. Examples include the pre/post designs of The Freshmen Survey (TFS), Your First College Year (YFCY), and College Senior Survey (CSS) as well as the first- and fourth-year National Study of Student Engagement (NSSE). Aside from these more prominent examples, your institution also may participate in Educause Center for Analysis and Research (ECAR), Pew Research, or Gallup Polling. Likely, some form of agreement exists between the institution and the external agency, and in many cases, the institution is paying for this service. It would be beneficial to learn more about these partnerships. Perhaps more so than institutional data, some external surveys may align with your assessment goals, and in the case of engagement surveys, they may have outcomes that can be linked to campus services.

A drawback to this approach is that you may not be able to link involvement with a specific office or program to outcomes.

For example, an existing survey may have an excellent leader-ship communication outcome, but you might not be able to link this with participation to the center for undergraduate leadership because there is no grouping variable for the office.

Another potential obstacle is that external datasets, even when funded by the institution, may not be accessible without additional permissions or funding. In many cases, reports from this data are made in aggregate and access to the data requires additional steps. Also, like internal institution datasets, the records may require additional expertise to collate and analyze.

One final consideration is that some external agencies allow for supplemental questions. This offers an excellent opportunity to add grouping variables such as participation in student govern-ment or other direct associations to services and programs such as attended freshmen orientation, allowing you to link existing data more precisely to campus services.

Five questions to ask about institutional data include the following:

1. What external data collection efforts does your institution participate in?

2. Do any of the data have responses that might be linked to your assessment goals?

3. What are the requirements for accessing this data?

4. What expertise is needed to analyze this data?

5. Are there others on campus that can assist with access or analysis?

Managing Assessment Data

As assessment data are collected, you will need to determine how it will be stored and organized. A first step is deciding how raw data will be kept as it is collected. Technology can enable this process, such as using an online survey program to gather data, an online file system to store audio files and transcriptions, or a text program for notes. If traditional methods to collect data are used, such as pen-and-paper surveys, or if you are using documents or images that have not been digitized, we recommend creating scans or images to promote access to all study files and implementing a back-up system to help ensure data are safeguarded. After determining the storage and organization methods that work best for the project and team, the next step is to create a central database to facilitate efficient data analysis both during and after the study closes.

Assessment data can accumulate quickly, even in small-scale projects, so developing and maintaining a data record is essential. User-friendliness, flexibility, and scalability have made spreadsheet programs the most common database tools. To create a database, raw data collected using traditional pencil and paper methods need to be entered into a file. Each survey should be assigned a case number and each question should be assigned a variable number. This allows for verifying or spot-checking data once entered. Many online survey platforms offer the advantage of storing data in a format that can be converted and downloaded into an offline spreadsheet program. Creating a database for questionnaire data, observations, and document review notes is not as straightforward. A two-step approach involves first creating a log for data collection that includes date, data form, and participants and/or locations. Second, preliminary notes such as early ideas for themes in the data collection log need to be stored and sorted.

In the short term, a well-structured and organized database can expedite data entry, enable data manipulation, simplify analysis, and aid in the creation of tables and figures. Additionally, keeping an updated record of numerical data or summary notes can reveal gaps that may need to be addressed. Further, a maintained and orderly database can be used to quickly produce preliminary reports of results, even during data collection. Longer term, storing data in a single location enables pre/post as well as longitudinal projects that utilize the same data or instruments multiple times. In instances where a few questions are commonly asked across several surveys or questionnaires, a searchable database can help locate responses for comparison.

A major capability afforded by a database is the power to link records. This can be accomplished in two ways. Nonidentifiable characteristic data might be connected across projects based on responses to specific questions. For example, some common questions such as specific areas of involvement might be asked on all divisional surveys. If these data were added to a master divisional dataset, general trends of involved students captured from a variety of instruments might be analyzed for an overall report. If a means to identify specific participants was collected as part of an assessment, data from other institutional records could be added to the database. For example, if participants provided a student identification number as part of a leadership training assessment, that number also might be linked with sorority membership and volunteer hours. As noted in Chapter 3, it is important to note that collecting identifiable information presents ethical considerations. An IRB representative should be consulted prior to collecting such data.

Our position is that it is never too late to create an assessment dataset. Whether you have to start with nothing, or if existing records can be reformatted to fit a dataset as you add new data, the benefits to continuity can be substantial. A well-maintained dataset can provide stability even as personnel, services, and office functions change. One of the challenges of creating a longitudinal dataset is that the same questions need to be asked of participants year after year. Changing the questions from one year to the next creates the risk of receiving responses that cannot be compared. One other dimension of developing a longitudinal dataset is that the characteristics of the student population can change over time. For example if the profile of the student body changes on the basis of student majors, gender, socioeconomic status, in- and out-of-state mix, or racial or ethnic background, even if the questions are the same, the results may not be compared easily. This is not to suggest that longitudinal datasets are not worthwhile. Rather, it is to offer caution about making comparisons if the characteristics of the institution's student body shift.

Working with Corporate Vendors

The past decade has seen a proliferation in external services to aid and facilitate campus assessment work. A corporate vendor is defined as a service provider offering tools to enable data collection, storage, and analysis, as opposed to an external research service that collects data and provides reports. The level of involvement a corporate vendor offers differs by provider, but most minimally have capabilities to create and store instruments, administer assessments digitally (online or using an external device), and perform basic data analysis and reporting. The functional ease and user support afforded by many vendors can be a major benefit to novice or unpracticed practitioners with assessment responsibilities. Basic descriptive and crosstabulation analyses are analytical functions many services provide alongside a variety of easily produced graphs and reports, removing much of the intimidation from statistical analysis.

Costs can vary significantly depending on the breadth and level of services, but should be evaluated in the context of the efficiency vendors provide and skills staff members have related to conducting assessments. In addition to basic analysis, most services also permit users to download raw data for more expansive analysis using statistical or qualitative analysis software. Some also offer the ability to upload instruments for subscriber use as well as the capability to search for and use instruments others have made available. A feature some services permit is the ability to store instruments and raw data. This service can help mitigate poor assessment database maintenance or lack of continuity resulting from staff changes. While partnering with corporate vendors can aid in data collection, management, basic analysis, and presentation of quantitative assessment data, beyond serving as a delivery system for open-ended questionnaires, similar services generally are unavailable for qualitative assessment data. Open-ended responses often will need to be downloaded and analyzed by hand or using a qualitative software program. Typically, observation or document review techniques also are not supported.

Returning to Tiger State University

This chapter began with a case study that described the challenges Sadie faced with implementing a data collection and management plan program at Tiger State University (TSU). The chancellor's request for summary outcomes data is a catalyst for Sadie, causing her to revisit her assessment plan. Fortunately, she can meet his immediate request using statistics, but she feels that not having a summary of the short answer data means that the assessment does not fully represent the impact of the program. Challenges revealed by her current data collection and management strategy include multiple and inconsistent survey instruments, the lack of a centralized multiyear database, and inadequate resources and expertise for analysis.

Sadie assembles a team made up of cross-campus stakeholders with varying areas of expertise and prioritizes the work. The team will review current instruments with the goal of creating a more standardized format, evaluate the data collection and storage plan to facilitate immediate and comprehensive reporting, create a format for internal longitudinal comparison, and align questions so that program outcomes can be compared to external benchmarks. She realizes these goals are lofty, but the team is enthusiastic and the work has the support of the dean of students. Sadie estimates having eight months to get the program finalized before the next summer's Stripes sessions. Assuming Sadie begins the work and has developed a standard survey and questionnaire, we ask that you consider the following four questions.

(Continued)

1. What are the primary considerations for selecting her sample?

2. How will she create a database that can be used to generate quick responses, facilitate in-depth analysis, and enable between and within program comparisons?

3. What other campus offices or personnel could she ask to assist in the work?

4. What are the ideal outcomes of creating and maintaining her database?

Discussion Questions

1. Using the case study as a basis, identify several other sampling strategies Sadie might use to collect data. What are the advantages and disadvantages of each?

2. Identify several offices on your campus that maintain datasets. How might you use that data for assessment purposes?

3. What are some steps you can take to ensure assessment data are effectively stored and easily accessible?

4. What are some ways data might be stored? What are some considerations for storing data using campus-based databases versus using datasets maintained by corporate vendors?

References

Fowler, F. J. (2009). *Survey research methods*. Thousand Oaks, CA: Sage.

Patton, M. Q. (2015). *Qualitative research & evaluation methods: Integrating theory and practice* (4th ed.). Thousand Oaks, CA: Sage.

Russell, R. V., & Kovacs, A. (2003). Unobtrusive measures. In F. K. Stage & K. Manning (Eds.), *Research in the college context: Approaches and methods* (pp. 63–80). New York, NY: Brunner-Routledge.

Suskie, L. A. (1992). *Questionnaire survey research*. Tallahassee, FL: Association for Institutional Research.

Webb, E. J., Campbell, D. T., Schwartz, R. D., & Sechrest, L. (2000). *Unobtrusive measures*. Thousand Oaks, CA: Sage.

7

USING QUALITATIVE TECHNIQUES IN CONDUCTING ASSESSMENTS

In the past few decades, qualitative techniques have gained a prominence in student affairs research and assessment, owing both to the philosophical alignment between the profession and constructivist epistemology (Manning, 1992) and the view that qualitative data "add a human dimension to an assessment effort" (Suskie, 2009, p. 33). Manning (1992) noted that "qualitative research methodology reflects and parallels the complexity and richness of the student affairs field itself" (p. 135). From the standpoint of assessing student needs relative to college adjustment, qualitative techniques have served as data collection tools since the earliest days of formalized student affairs practice (Certis, 2014). This disposition was likely enhanced with the proliferation of identity development theories following the popularity of Chickering's (1969) work, which continues to inform graduate preparation and student affairs practice related to the individual development and well-being of students.

A vice president in Green, Jones, and Aloi's (2008) study of high-quality assessment practices in student affairs commented, "it has been a challenge for folks to understand there are other ways [than surveys] to measure outcomes that are often more appropriate" (p. 146). The qualitative tradition, characterized by thick description and individual perception (Wolcott, 1987), can be perceived as misaligned with assessment's focus on groups, programs, and services. Assessment, broadly implemented, seems to be better matched with quantitative techniques emphasizing a reductionist approach (for example, Gasparatos, El-Haram, & Horner, 2008, 2009) to data reporting. The larger context of educational research and evaluation seems to favor this perspective. But the use of qualitative techniques can be very valuable in the assessment process. For example, Merriam (2002) pointed out that " ... qualitative research attempts to understand and make sense of phenomena from the participant's perspective" (p. 6). Suskie (2009) added, "Qualitative assessments allow us to explore possibilities that we haven't considered. They can give fresh insight and help discover problems—and solutions—that can't be found through quantitative assessments alone" (pp. 32–33).

Calls for accountability in P–12 education have centered on the concept of data-driven decision-making (DDDM), a largely quantitative approach calling for educators to sharpen their quantitative skillset to interpret student outcomes (Marsh, Pane, & Hamilton, 2006). Considering this emphasis on a quantitative demonstration of success in the postsecondary setting, Wagner and Ice (2012) recently observed that "higher education finds itself on the verge of diving deeply into the analytical end of the education transformation pool" (p. 25).

Rather than conclude that student affairs practitioners should exclusively focus on expanding their statistical skillsets, we believe the need to implement well-reasoned, rigorously conducted, and effectively reported qualitative assessment is more relevant than ever. Yet, our experience with graduate students and professionals indicates that they have a strong preference for qualitative techniques hindered by a faulty methodological understanding of how to design, conduct, and rationalize a qualitatively informed project. To address this deficiency, we review key concepts related to using qualitative techniques, emphasizing the rationale and importance of adding a constructivist perspective to assessment work. Further, we convey data analysis as a means of emphasizing the role of the researcher and the participants in coproducing answers to assessment questions.

Definition and Use of Qualitative Techniques

The term *qualitative* refers to qualities and meanings of a person, process, or setting that are not easily measured. Denzin and Lincoln (2011) offered a generic definition of qualitative inquiry, which emphasizes the role of the researcher as an observer and consists of interpretive practices "to make the world visible" (p. 3). Discerning and representing this distinct reality can be difficult. From a qualitative perspective, the world is different for each person and cannot be represented well with a generic or common description (Merriam, 2009). For example, while students may describe common aspects of what it is like living in a residence hall, the experience is unique for each resident. Representing this uniqueness while offering useful suggestions to enhance or improve practice is a challenging aspect of qualitative assessment (Patton, 1990).

It also can be challenging to distinguish between qualitative designs, owing to a "broad specificity" in the terminology. Researchers have developed a variety of terms to describe specific theoretical positions, forms of data collection, and types of data analysis that can be simultaneously daunting and confusing. Analogously, Denzin and Lincoln (2011) identified the two persistent barriers to defining qualitative methodology as: (1) a resistance to impose a single structure due to its open-ended nature (pp. xiii) and (2) a debate over complex terms, concepts, and assumptions (pp. 3–4). Fortunately, Stage and Manning (2003) simplified core concepts for application in the college context: "Qualitative research is an umbrella concept covering several forms of inquiry that help us understand and explain the meaning of social phenomenon" (p. 6).

For the purposes of assessment, Upcraft and Schuh (1996), drawing on Patton's (1990) characterization, pragmatically described qualitative techniques as "detailed descriptions of situations, events, people, interactions, and observed behaviors; use of direct quotations from people about their experiences, attitudes, beliefs, and thoughts; and analysis of excerpts of entire passages from documents, correspondence, records and case histories" (p. 53). Merriam (2009) elaborated that data tend to be collected from natural settings, tend to be more detailed and illustrative as opposed to summative, and tend to focus more on *how* something is experienced, rather than *what* occurred. Analysis is inductive (working from specific to general) rather than deductive (working from general to specific). As with any research approach, the form(s) of data collection and types of data that result can add specificity to these general points.

A major focus of this chapter is on promoting the interpretation and use of qualitative techniques for use in student affairs assessment. We begin by presenting a case study for undertaking a qualitative-focused assessment project. We introduce a forms approach for aligning assessment project goals with question selection and data analysis. Common techniques for analyzing qualitative assessment data are also included along with tips for effectively presenting results.

Common Spaces at College Town University

Brian is the assistant director of residence life at College Town University (CTU). His primary areas of responsibilities are to direct academic initiatives and assessment efforts, as well as to provide leadership and direction for the living and learning communities. As part of this work, he implements assessment projects and makes reports and/or leads discussions utilizing results to inform policy and practice for the department. CTU is considered a residential campus. Students who live more than 50 miles away are required to live on campus their first semester. CTU recently opened a new 400-bed residence hall (Green Hall) and revealed a five-year master plan provisioning for the major renovation of four other residence halls.

Brian stays up to date with current trends in campus housing by reading research, attending professional conferences, and making on-site visits at other campuses. One of the most recent developments he has noticed is the development of multifunctional learning and interaction in common spaces on resident hall floors. Different from the traditional model of building a central lounge in the lobby with smaller lounges on each floor and a study area or small recreation room in the basement, these newly envisioned spaces are not function-specific. With a main purpose to improve learning and foster student interaction, theses informal "hang-out" spaces blend aesthetics and comfort with mobile furniture and multifunction technological capabilities. Brian has seen the success of this model in the recently renovated ground floor of the library and hallways of the humanities building, where new seating, informal learning lounges, numerous wall boards and charging stations, LEED accent lighting, and individual and group work spaces provide students and faculty with new ways to work, collaborate, and socialize. While he has not seen empirical data for the effectiveness of these renovations in the two academic buildings, conversations with students, staff and faculty who work in the buildings, and his frequent walk-throughs of the very popular spaces, demonstrate the success of the design.

Green Hall, the newest residence hall on campus, incorporates many of these features, but integrates them with living space. The lobby resembles more of a high-end hotel with a grand staircase, two-story windows, and café dining options in addition to the flexible learning spaces with features reminiscent of the humanities and library renovations. The interior residential area floor plan also is organized very differently from the other residence halls on campus. While the bedrooms are suite-style, they are organized into units on each floor. The design committee, inclusive of administrators and students, refer to this organization as "pods." Instead of long extending hallways lined with room doors and a small common space near the elevators on each floor, the pod design organizes blocks of rooms around several central spaces. The aesthetic and equipment features

(Continued)

resemble those found in the humanities building and library, but serve a distinct population of those residents living in the corresponding pods.

Implementing the new design required some compromise on the building's capacity in the limited footprint Green Hall could take up on campus. Before plans are finalized for the renovations of four residence halls, administrators want to know if the reorganized pod design is being utilized as intended. Brian has been assigned to assess use of the space to inform recommendations to the committee.

Selecting Qualitative Techniques: A Forms Approach

Authors of educational research textbooks (for example, Creswell, 2014; Johnson & Christensen, 2014) offer a variety of suggestions for how to design a research study. While the capability of the researcher is a consideration, methodological choices should be based first on the purpose(s) of the project and the ability of the research approach to address project outcomes. As the next chapter discusses, quantitative techniques often can be linked to project goals with keywords. Qualitative research is not as clearly defined. Rather than offering distinct techniques that can be completed separately and matched to project purpose(s), qualitative techniques tend to be mutually reinforcing (Patton, 1990) and together enhance and enrich (Stage & Manning, 2003) other forms of qualitative data. Following Schuh and Associates (2009), we identify three primary forms of data collection for qualitative assessment: *interview, observe,* and *review.* Aligning the forms with the purpose(s) of the study can help practitioners meet intended outcomes. A brief overview of each appears in the following. Analytical strategies associated with the forms will be discussed in further detail later in the chapter.

Interviewing

Interviewing involves carefully selecting participants and working to build their trust, develop a suitable questionnaire, and facilitate natural, but intentional, conversation. Effective interviewing for assessment and research purposes requires considerable skill. An important concept to understand about interviewing is that the general purpose, as Seidman (2006) noted, "is not to get answers to questions" but instead to understand the "lived experience of other people and the meaning they make of that experience" (p. 9). This intention resonates with the philosophical tradition of student affairs, which values the needs and experiences of the individual student as a means of facilitating success. Interviewing, then, offers an opportunity to understand those experiences. Returning to Seidman (2006), "interviewing allows us to put behavior in context and provides access to understanding their action" (p. 10).

Interviews create records though interaction, which can occur with individuals or groups, and can happen face-to-face or be mediated by synchronous (for example, online video) or asynchronous (for example, e-mail) technologies. In addition, interviews can be formally structured by the researcher, informally or casually structured using an open-ended approach to allow the conversation to follow general themes, or semi-structured blending both prewritten questions and general talking points. The interviewer records data in some way, either verbatim or through real-time recording of conversations or keeping reflective field notes, which creates transcripts of text for later analysis.

While we acknowledge there are many variations of interviewing (for example, Seidman, 2006; Rubin & Rubin, 2012), we categorize three general types that serve assessment purposes: individual interviews, casual interviews, and focus groups. Individual interviews are more formal, generally scheduled interviews, which can take place a single time or multiple times as defined by the goals of the project. Casual interviews are less formal and generally are not scheduled ahead of time. Instead, the interviewer may choose a time and site and talk with participants who visit during that period. Focus groups involve several people at a time, can include formal or informal questions, and tend to be scheduled.

The primary advantage to interviewing is the capability it provides to build a rich understanding of a person, setting, or situation through the perspective of those experiencing it. Disadvantages include the time required in identifying participants and arranging interviews, the inductive and potentially more subjective nature of data analysis, and most often overlooked, the skills needed to interview effectively. Asking simplistic (for example, one word) response questions, failing to follow-up, rushing though questions, or guiding participants with leading questions can generate data that may not be valuable to the study and create disgruntled participants who may not participate in future studies. Moreover, in some cases the number of participants in a particular experience may be particularly small, such as students who are captains of athletic teams or hold elected leadership positions on campus.

When used for assessment, focus groups can be a highly effective way to get multiple perspectives in a relatively short time. Having multiple people involved also helps mitigate extreme or outlier views on a subject, as the group can act as its own control. Further, it is much easier to identify those views that are shared compared with those that are more singularly held. In addition to sharing the same disadvantages as interviewing previously outlined, organizing and facilitating focus groups can be very challenging. Also, Patton (2014) cautioned that a focus group session should be treated as an interview, not as a discussion or as a problem-solving or decision-making session.

Observing

Observing involves recording actions, events, and/or objects while participating in, viewing from within, or watching from outside, a social setting. Observation also requires a great deal of the researcher, who must manage a "relatively unobtrusive role" while "finely observing huge amounts of fast-moving and complex behavior" (Marshall & Rossman, 1995, p. 80). Patton (1990) noted, "training researchers to become astute and skilled observers is particularly difficult because so many people think that they are 'natural observers' and, therefore, have very little to learn" (p. 201). Methodologically, observational records can range from highly structured note taking (for example, completing a predetermined checklist) to unplanned holistic descriptions (for example, summarizing behaviors or events in a particular location).

In a reprint of a classic text on observation, Webb, Campbell, Schwartz, and Sechrest (2000) distinguished several types of observation: time-sampling, location-sampling, and time-and-location sampling. Time-sampling is used when a specific setting is the focus. Actions, events, and objects occurring in the place should be observed over multiple times and days. For example, if you wanted to know how students use the open study lounges in the library, you would want to make observations at various times of day on weekdays and weekends. Conversely, location-sampling is optimal when the focus is on individual behaviors in a setting and those individuals are relatively homogenous (that is, college students). Using this approach, the place should be considered the sample and varying locations should be used. For example, if you wanted to know about student organized games on the various intramural fields on campus, you would want to plan for observations at each location. Finally, time-and-location sampling is preferable when a phenomenon is the focus and both times and settings related to an experience need to be observed. For example, if you wanted to know how fraternity/sorority members prepare for the homecoming parade during the week prior to the competition, you would want to observe multiple groups, over multiple days and at varying times.

An advantage to using observation techniques is that they can offer rich data from a setting that otherwise would be difficult to obtain or influenced by participant interpretation. Observation also can complement additional methods. For example, watching people in a natural setting can aid in the selection of participants for follow-up interviews about their role(s) and behavior(s). Further, simply asking participants about their actions or behaviors in a setting informally (casual interviews) can lend insight into actions, events, and objects occurring in the place.

Observation has a number of limitations to consider. Over time and as fatigue sets in, the observer (as instrument) can become less thorough or inattentive. Further, the observer can be overwhelmed quickly by a large amount of extraneous information irrelevant to a focused assessment goal. Unfortunately, an observer often cannot predict when data related to specific actions, events, and objects will occur. Webb and others (2000) glibly referred to this as the necessity "to wait around, observe, and complain about the high dross rate of such a procedure" (p. 141). One of the simplest ways to mitigate many of the limitations is to plan additional observations. This strategy also can help refine coding and lessen overgeneralization based on limited data.

Reviewing

Reviewing involves appraisal of both documents and records, which most often take the form of text or images. In evaluative settings, Patton (1990) described document and record data as a "trail of paper that the evaluator can follow and use to increase knowledge and understanding about a program" (p. 233). Documents and records can serve the dual purposes of (1) providing direct information about programs, decisions, or activities and processes; and (2) suggesting additional questions to pursue through more direct interviews or observation by creating (Patton 1990). Love (2003) noted that documents in higher education are part of the context of institutional life, providing "an important avenue of voice, interpretation and meaning" (p. 83).

Cooper (2009) and Love (2003) categorized three general types of review data available on campus: institutional or official records, general records or public documents, and personal documents. Institutional or official records include budget and financial documents, policy manuals and handbooks, contracts, and annual reports. General records or public documents can suggest how events and decisions are linked, as well as show the history leading to the development of those associations. These can include meeting records, training materials, and strategic planning documents. Personal documents are specific records that can provide insight into individual thoughts or processes, such as personal meeting notes, e-mails, or written reflections. Boundaries between these categories can easily blur. For example, an incident report that a resident assistant completes about a policy violation could be considered a general document; however, it could be considered a personal document, depending on how it is written (for example, the write-up reflects personal beliefs about the incident). Merriam (1998) added the further distinction of documents already present (for example, public records, personal documents, and physical material) and researcher-generated documents (for example, asking someone to keep a log or diary, photographs produced by the investigator, or existing numerical data derived from surveys).

Advantages of using existing documents include low cost (often, access is free) and stability (documents rarely change). For Love (2003), document analysis provides background information leading to events that cannot be otherwise observed or that the researcher may not know to ask about during an interview. Also, documents can be more precise, containing names, references, and details of an event or policy that can serve as sources of descriptive information (Merriam, 1998). Aiding analysis, data mostly are already transcribed, saving considerable time when compared to working with interview recordings. Finally, documents can bound a study by suggesting observations, specific interview questions, and a means of validating results (that is, triangulation), particularly since the presence of the researcher is not altering what is studied.

Disadvantages of using existing documents include access issues in that some documents may be protected or access to them may be limited for other reasons, documents may be difficult to understand without insider knowledge, or records may be incomplete or inaccurate. For Love (2003), the most significant drawback to using documents is that they are noninteractive and nonreactive, which prevents member checking for context, meaning, or accuracy. Also, Merriam (1998) cautioned that because documents have been disconnected from their creation, it can be difficult to explore meaning. Further, documents can be unrepresentative or highly subjective, depending on the perspective and views of the author at the time of their creation (Merriam, 1998; Patton, 1990). For example, a specific discussion might have been left out of meeting minutes intentionally by the recorder or at the request of others in the meeting. Incomplete records are related to this issue and also a potential limitation. Finally, it can be difficult to determine the authenticity and accuracy of a record.

Using the Forms Approach

Choosing from among the three basic forms of qualitative data gathering does not have to be a decision of one over another. Each can work well separately or in combination. As Patton (1990) observed, qualitative techniques are not mutually exclusive. For example, under many definitions, informal interviews would fall under observation, as "participant observers gather a great deal of information through informal, naturally occurring conversation. Understanding that interviewing and observation are mutually reinforcing techniques is a bridge to understanding the fundamentally people-oriented nature of qualitative inquiry" (p. 32). Also, document analysis is rarely used alone outside of history-based research. Often, it is used as a complementary method to establish credibility (triangulation), to reveal gaps left by other forms of data collection, or to suggest additional or follow-up questions for interviews (Love, 2003). By utilizing more than one technique; however, researchers can find richer data (complementary and divergent), confirmable results (triangulation), and can add legitimacy (trustworthiness) to the study for external audiences.

Analyzing Qualitative Data

Qualitative data analysis is the process of creating meaning, or making sense, out of data. Miles and Huberman (1994) described three broad tasks for qualitative data analysis: (1) data reduction, (2) data display, and (3) conclusion drawing or verification. Unfortunately, there are no standard formulas, procedural strategies, rules, or straightforward validity tests for replicating the qualitative analytical process. Miles and Huberman (1994), Patton (1998), and Thomas (2006) offered a generalized form consisting of reviewing data, making notes that become codes, classifying these into categories, (sometimes) reading again/applying for accuracy across the data, describing categories and themes, and connecting them to assessment goals and/or theory.

For the purposes of this chapter, we define a code as a category or unit of analysis used to describe a singular aspect of data. This abbreviated definition represents a summary of Saldana's (2012) explanation that "a code in qualitative inquiry is most often a word or short phrase that symbolically assigns a summative, salient, essence-capturing, and/or evocative attribute for a portion of language-based or visual data" (p. 3). Coding refers to the process of grouping data according to a typology or category system. We use themes and subthemes as opposed to categories and subcategories to refer to central classifications of codes emerging from analysis. Four generalized characteristics of qualitative data analysis follow to introduce a basic procedure we recommend for coding data. This is followed by an overview of two common methods for coding data researchers use, along with considerations for analyzing specific forms.

Inductive Generally, data analysis can be categorized as either deductive or inductive (Thomas, 2006). A deductive approach often begins with hypotheses and sets out to test whether data are consistent with these beliefs. This form of analysis is more often associated with statistics. An inductive approach, conversely, allows findings to emerge from the data, ideally without predetermined assumptions. The basis of analysis is derived from frequent, dominant, or significant themes in raw data. Considered this way, inductive analysis can be described as emergent (for example, Strauss & Corbin, 1998). An inductive analysis process generally consists of condensing raw textual data into a brief, summary format; establishing clear links between project objectives and the summary findings to ensure that these links are both transparent (able to be demonstrated to others) and defensible (justifiable given the objectives of the research); and developing a model or theory about the underlying structure of experiences or processes in the data (Thomas, 2006).

Systematic Merriam's (1998) perspective is that qualitative analysis is both systematic and evolving. Throughout both data collection and analysis, the researcher is guided by questions, educated hunches, and emerging findings. The tasks of "tracking down leads, being open to new insights, and being sensitive to the data are the same whether the researcher is interviewing, observing, or analyzing documents" (Merriam, 1998, p. 120). Qualitative analysis commonly is not considered a formulaic procedure; however, several researchers have offered systemic processes for organizing and coding data. For the purposes of this chapter, systematic simply implies an ordered set of steps. While this may be problematic for researchers following a purely constructivist tradition, we have found having specific recommendations helpful when learning techniques for qualitative assessment efforts.

Reductionist Data reduction is the process of selecting, focusing, simplifying, abstracting, and transforming data. Merriam (1998) described the process as "consolidating, reducing, and interpreting what people have said and what the researcher has seen and read—it is the process of making meaning" (p. 178). By data reduction, we do not mean only quantification. A common misperception of working with qualitative data is that themes can simply be identified and counted from text and justified by frequencies. This amounts to descriptive statistics and is not consistent with what we consider to be qualitative data analysis. While relating word or page counts from transcripts or theme and subtheme frequencies generated from coding can provide insight as to quantity of data analyzed, such numbers are not intended to express meaning. Data can be reduced and/or transformed in many ways, including coding, narrative summary, grouping, or patterns. Miles and Huberman (1994) noted, "data reduction is not something separate from analysis. It is *part* of analysis.... Data reduction is a form of analysis that sharpens, sorts, focuses, discards, and organizes data in such a way that 'final' conclusions can be drawn an identified" (p. 11).

Ongoing Data collection and analysis often takes place simultaneously in qualitative research. While nearly all projects, especially assessment and evaluation efforts, have a point in which data are collated and reported, data analysis does not have to be relegated to the final phase. Keeping detailed notes about thoughts on data as they are collected, planning or adjusting data collection according to evolving findings, and questioning the data are actions that should be taken during data collection to facilitate and enhance analysis.

General Qualitative Data Coding

This section outlines a basic six-step model for qualitative data coding that can be applied to most forms of qualitative assessment data. An optional prestep for use with extensive records is also provided. Note that the term *data source* is used throughout the steps as a broad term to refer to an interview transcript, a set of observation notes, or a researcher-collected or created document.

Optional Prestep: Develop a Basic Description Prior to Analysis

Qualitative techniques can yield a tremendous amount of data—particularly if sources are rich or data are collected using a variety of methods. In the case of extensive data, Merriam (1998) recommended creating a basic description of the phenomenon as it is represented in the data prior to developing themes in data analysis. Keep in mind the importance of ensuring the project stays aligned with the study purpose(s) and objective(s). This approach can help focus the analysis process and allow you to make decisions about what should be included and left out of the analysis.

Step 1: Select and Review an Initial Data Source

Select and review a single data source. Ideally, this data source is important for some reason, such as being particularly rich and/or largely representative of other data in the study. As you review, make notes in the margin to indicate data that seem interesting, potentially relevant, or important to your study. Think of yourself as having a conversion with the data, asking questions, making comments, and so on. The goal is not to fully develop a coding scheme, but to get an initial sense of what to look for in the data.

Step 2: Identify Variation and "Recurring Regularities"

Reread the data source, this time taking notes on similarities, differences, or other interesting concepts that seem to come up repeatedly. These concept notes may represent variations or "recurring regularities" (that is, patterns) in the data that later can be sorted into categories. They should (1) reveal information relevant to the study, (2) stimulate you to think beyond the information, and (3) represent the smallest piece of information that can stand by itself (for example, be interpretable in the absence of associated information).

Reread the data source again, this time grouping similar notes and then giving those notes distinct names, or "codes." You will be grouping these later, so it is perfectly acceptable to have a variety of similar and dissimilar codes at this stage of the process.

Step 3: Review a Second Data Source, Checking for Congruence

Choose a second data source for review, keeping in mind the variation and recurring regularities you identified in the previous step and checking to see if they are present. This second data source can be another prominent example, or you may find it helpful to select a more general source. After completing this second review, examine both sets of notes and try to consolidate them into a general set of categories.

Step 4: Develop Major Themes and Subthemes

Starting with the general set of categories you developed in the previous step, distinguish themes and subthemes (that is, a taxonomy or classification system). These themes and subthemes should capture some of the recurring patterns that cut across the data. Themes are the major concepts in the data; subthemes fall underneath themes as related, but are sufficiently different to require separate labels. Devising themes and subthemes is largely intuitive, but should be systematic, informed by the study's purpose, grounded in what you learned while collecting data, and emerging from meanings made explicit by the participants.

Define themes and subthemes using names and/or labels that the participants or data sources used or concepts you derived from analysis. When naming based on participant labels, Patton (1998) specifically recommended using their words or specialized vocabulary (that is, *their categories and their frameworks*) to promote understandability and applicability for assessment feedback and reports. When naming themes you derived, be mindful that designations should emerge *from data* to the extent that this is possible, rather than from your own perspective. Present the categories to participants, if possible, for verification.

Review the number of themes and subthemes you developed and revise them, if needed. While there is no set rule on how many themes one should identify, in general, having too many themes often indicates a problem with the coding scheme. It is important to include examples, such as representative quotations or images, to illustrate the themes. Further, clarifying each theme at this point in the process and providing examples will aid evaluation and data reporting later on.

Step 5: Code the Remaining Data Sources and Evaluate the Themes

Analyze the remaining data by marking examples of the themes and subthemes. Focus on data sources that contribute to the purpose(s) of the study, as well as to the general themes. When coding, you may encounter a few outliers. Note these as you see them. If several of the same type (recurring regularities) become prominent, consider adding a new theme. If the outliers are few and cannot be connected to existing themes, you may note them in the final report. Generally, however, your themes and subthemes should fit the data at this point. If not, it is advisable to identify a third data source and recode again for themes and subthemes. When you think you have your codes set, complete the following:

Evaluate the Themes for Completeness The themes should be reasonably inclusive of the data and information collected. They should appear to be consistent and seem to comprise a whole picture. The themes should be reproducible by another competent judge such as a member of your research team, or otherwise make sense in terms of how data have been arranged.

Evaluate the Themes for Congruence The themes can be conceptually valued based on how they fit or hold together in a meaningful way. The themes should be representative in the data (for example, frequency should be mentioned), identifiable by outsiders, and be conceptually congruent.

Evaluate the Themes for Relevance The themes should reflect the purpose(s) of the study. Ideally, themes can reveal issues not otherwise identifiable by participants or stakeholders or that provide unique perspectives on an otherwise common problem. The themes also should be credible; this can be verified by asking the persons who provided the information.

Evaluate the Themes for Uniqueness While the themes should be compatible and correspond to the study purpose(s), the distinctions between them should be clear (that is, mutually exclusive and unique). In other words, themes should interrelate, but not intersect. Overlapping themes may suggest a fault in the classification system.

Step 6: Connect Themes to Objectives

Align the final themes to the project objectives or research questions. This process ensures that the assessment has addressed the purpose(s) of the project. If the goals of the study have more applications than just your campus or include a benchmarking component, it can be beneficial to consider these findings within the published body of knowledge on the issue.

Other Coding Systems

There are many ways to analyze qualitative data. We presented a generalized approach that can work for most assessment purposes, though two traditional forms of coding are often used: systematic design and the constant comparative method. Both are derived from grounded theory (see Merriam, 2002), a method used to generate theory explaining a process, action, or interaction.

Systematic design is the more formulaic of the two methods. It involves the three-step process of (1) open coding (initially categorizing data), (2) axial coding (selecting one of the open coding categories and relating all other categories to it), and (3) selective coding (writing a theory or explanation based on the interrelationships of categories from axial coding). Describing this process in detail is beyond the scope of this text, so we refer readers to Strauss and Corbin (2014) for guidance. For assessment purposes, systematic design can be particularly advantageous when looking for factors that influence certain phenomenon of interest.

The constant comparative method, as outlined by Glaser and Strauss (1967), is a means of deriving categories, properties, and hypotheses to inform conceptual links in the data. Merriam (1998) reasoned that this technique is more widely adopted because the basic strategy is consistent with the concept-building process common in qualitative analysis. As the name suggests, the basic procedure is to "constantly compare" codes and categories from data. This approach begins by coding a single data source and comparing those codes to codes derived from another single data source. These codes lead to tentative categories that are compared to other instances in the data. Comparisons are constantly made within and between the data until a theory, explanation, or set of themes can be developed. For assessment purposes, we have found the constant comparative method helpful when working with groups or teaching novice researchers data analysis. However, we have found it less valuable when there are few data sources or when data are not rich (for example, open-ended questions with just a few word responses).

Interview Data Analysis

In addition to basic coding for generalized themes, a common approach to analyzing interview data is to treat transcripts as case studies, particularly when variation in individuals or groups is the primary focus of the analysis. Patton (1990) suggested that the investigators should decide if a single case or cross-case analysis is better when using this approach. A single case analysis approach considers each person, group, or event participant as an individual unit. Writing case studies for each unit becomes part of the analysis. Conversely, a cross-case approach clusters answers from individuals to common questions, focusing on different perspectives on central issues. Patton (1990) noted these two forms are not mutually exclusive. A study often includes both types of analysis as a way to view issues as they are perceived by individuals as well as more generally by groups.

Interview data results include the themes and subthemes derived during analysis and frequently are displayed in a summary table. Because context is important, we recommend including an introduction that describes the setting(s) as well as explanatory text about the themes and how they were developed. It is customary to include representative quotations to illustrate themes and subthemes, though some authors prefer using a more generalized narrative or story approach to present results.

Observation Data Analysis

Emerson (2011) noted that writing field notes during observation is "an interpretive process: it is the very first act of textualizing" (p. 20). Field notes from observation data can be organized a number of ways for analysis. Organizing data should be determined in large part by how it will be most helpful to present answers. This approach can aid in analysis and in writing the final report. Following are a few of the suggestions Patton (1990, p. 377) offered, related to assessment work.

Chronology

Describe what was observed chronologically, over time, to tell the story from beginning to end.

Key Events

Present data by critical incidents or major events, not necessarily in order of occurrence but in order of importance.

Various Settings

Describe various places, sites, settings, or locations (doing case studies of each) before doing cross-setting pattern analysis.

People

Compose case studies of individuals or groups, if people are the primary unit of analysis.

Processes

Describe important processes, such as control, recruitment, decision making, socialization or communication patterns.

Issues

Illuminate key issues, such as how participation or percep-tions changed.

Similar to case study approaches, these methods need not to be mutually exclusive or exhaustive. They are simply an initial framework for organizing and managing data.

Observational data also can be shown as summary themes, organized in tables. Similar to interview results, context is important, so we recommend an introduction that describes the setting(s) as well as some explanatory text about the themes. Observation data can include quotations, though an effective way to convey examples of themes (both confirmatory and outlier) is also to describe specific situations through narrative.

Review Data Analysis

Love (2003) noted, "although categorizing and coding data are important, document analysis goes beyond these processes and seeks to understand the relationships and structural interconnec-tions among various categories" (p. 95). Many of the strategies for working with review data are similar to observation field notes. Organizing by chronology, key events, or processes, for example, is an effective way to make sense of data. Miles and Huberman (1994) provided numerous useful diagrams and figures that can help you visualize patterns to create clear and efficient data displays. Creating figures as part of the analysis phase also can help you tie (that is, make meaning of) various data sources together by revealing interconnections. For example, Biddix, Somers, and Polman (2009) created an event history display to bring interview and archival data together as a means of understanding the actions of students, administrators, and faculty during a campus protest.

Review data also can be communicated efficiently by displaying themes from analysis in a table. Generally, the quantity of reviewed data (number of documents, images, and so on) is commonly provided. Examples from text should be given to evidence themes, although presenting images or excerpts of the documents can be a powerful way to show results (for example, Certis, 2014).

Your Qualitative Skillset

Qualitative measures provide an important holistic component to assessment work, lending voice and perspective to individuals and groups and allowing us to evaluate the experiences and environments that affect learning. They can be tremendously impactful if done well, but a waste of resources if done poorly. It can be tempting to assume qualitative measures are less difficult than quantitative measures because they do not involve calculations, data modeling, or basic knowledge of statistical testing; however, a good qualitative skillset is equally complex to develop and maintain. Interviewing is a challenging skill even for experienced researchers, particularly since every interview is a unique experience. This is especially true for focus groups, which involve the additional ability to guide conversation. Similarly, learning what to look for and record, what to follow-up on and ignore, and how to deal with noise are observation skills that take a great deal of practice. Reviewing documents can be equally difficult, as this form of data collection requires a keen intuition as to what to look for in text as well as how to consider the context within which the text was created. Finally, learning how to reduce qualitative findings for summary reports in a genuine and meaningful way can be especially challenging.

Taking (or retaking) a qualitative methodology or digital tools class is a one way to improve your skills. Courses or seminars in counseling can help you build relatable proficiencies in interviewing, observing, and listening. Another way to enhance your listening, note-taking, and observation skills is to take notes at meetings and then review the notes with colleagues for accuracy. In addition, establishing a network of colleagues and faculty who regularly engage in qualitative assessment and research can be immensely beneficial, especially when planning projects, resolving issues that come up, and considering data analysis. Following is set of basic qualitative skills we believe assessment practitioners should work to develop and maintain.

- Fundamental understanding of the qualitative (that is, constructivist) perspective
- Awareness of how identities, experiences, and biases can inform and influence data collection, analysis, and interpretation
- Ability to negotiate access to sites and to build authentic rapport with participants
- Basic skills, building toward intermediate proficiencies, in interviewing, note-taking, and observation
- Ability to code data and to identify emergent themes across multiple data sources

Returning to College Town University

This chapter began with a case study describing the assessment project Brian wants to design to evaluate space use for a new residence hall at College Town University (CTU). There are several issues to consider. On the surface, it seems a utilization study could be efficiently completed with a simple but well-designed survey of building residents. This information could reveal student perceptions of the space, self-reported data on use, and satisfaction measures; however, Brian believes this will not be an accurate

(Continued)

representation of how students use the spaces at different times, how they interact, and what changes (if any) might be accommodated. These goals suggest a qualitative design might be more suitable.

Brian has a number of decisions to make prior to data collection. He would like to complete unobtrusive observations as well as conduct informal interviews in the spaces. In addition, he wants to conduct focus groups with students both within the same pods and with mixed groups. As he begins to plan, he knows he will need help. He asks the hall director as well as two student workers to serve on a project committee with him. The hall director also suggests that resident assistants on each floor can aid with data collection. Assuming Brian is given permission to conduct the project, we ask that you provide the answers to the following questions:

1. How should he conduct the observations and informal interviews?

2. Should the interviews consist of standard questions, or will they be open-ended?

3. Should he develop structured instruments, such as tally sheets for observations, or should he take free-form notes?

4. At what times and how often should he collect data?

5. After data collection is complete, how will he analyze and report the data?

6. How can Brian ensure that, if a team of observers is employed in data collection, their observations are consistent?

Discussion Questions

1. In what situations is it appropriate to collect qualitative assessment data?

2. What are some of the challenges to collecting qualitative data? Describe ways you might address those challenges.

3. What are some ways you can develop and demonstrate credibility when analyzing qualitative assessment data?

4. How can you present results from qualitative data analysis?

References

Biddix, J. P., Somers, P. A., & Polman, J. L. (2009). Protest reconsidered: Activism's role as civic engagement educator. *Innovative Higher Education, 34*(3), 133–147.

Certis, H. (2014). The emergence of Esther Lloyd-Jones. *Journal of Student Affairs Research and Practice, 51*(3), 259–269.

Chickering, A. (1969). *Education and identity.* San Francisco, CA: Jossey-Bass.

Cooper, R. M. (2009). Planning for and implementing data collection. In J. H. Schuh & Associates (Eds.), *Assessment methods for student affairs* (pp. 51–76). San Francisco, CA: Jossey-Bass.

Creswell, J. W. (2014). *Educational research: Planning, conducting, and evaluating quantitative research* (5th ed.). Boston, MA: Sage.

Denzin, N. K., & Lincoln, Y. S. (2011). *The Sage handbook of qualitative research* (4th ed.). Thousand Oaks, CA: Sage.

Emerson, R. M., Fretz, R. I., & Shaw, L. L. (2011). *Writing ethnographic fieldnotes.* Chicago, IL: University of Chicago Press.

Gasparatos, A., El-Haram, M., & Horner, M. (2008). A critical review of reductionist approaches for assessing the progress towards sustainability. *Environmental Impact Assessment Review, 28*(4–5), 286–311.

Gasparatos, A., El-Haram, M., & Horner, M. (2009). The argument against a reductionist approach for measuring sustainable development performance and the need for methodological pluralism. *Accounting Forum, 33*(3), 245–256.

Glaser, B., & Strauss, A. (1967) *The discovery of grounded theory.* Hawthorne, NY: Aldine.

Green, A. S., Jones, E., & Aloi, S. (2008). An exploration of high-quality student affairs learning outcomes assessment practices. *NASPA Journal, 45*(1), 133–157.

Johnson, R. B., & Christensen, L. B. (2014). *Educational research: Quantitative, qualitative, and mixed approaches* (5th ed.). Thousand Oaks, CA: Sage.

Love, P. (2003). Document analysis. In F. K. Stage & K. Manning (Eds.), *Research in the college context: Approaches and methods* (pp. 83–97). New York, NY: Brunner-Routledge.

Manning, K. (1992). A rationale for using qualitative research in student affairs. *Journal of College Student Development, 33*(2), 132–136.

Marsh, J. A., Pane, J. F., & Hamilton, L. S. (2006). *Making sense of data-driven decision making in education.* Santa Monica, CA: RAND Education.

Retrieved from http://www.rand.org/content/dam/rand/pubs
/occasional_papers/2006/RAND_OP170.pdf

Marshall, C., & Rossman, G. B. (1995). *Designing qualitative research.*
Thousand Oaks, CA: Sage.

Merriam, S. B. (1998). *Qualitative research and case study applications in education.* San Francisco, CA: Jossey-Bass.

Merriam, S. B. (2002). *Introduction to qualitative research.* In S. B. Merriam
& Associates (Eds.), *Qualitative research in practice* (pp. 3–17). San
Francisco, CA: Jossey-Bass.

Merriam, S. B. (2009). *Qualitative research: A guide to design and implementation.* San Francisco, CA: Jossey-Bass.

Miles, M. B., & Huberman, A. M. (1994). *Qualitative data analysis: An
expanded sourcebook* (2nd ed.). Thousand Oaks, CA: Sage.

Patton, M. Q. (1990). *Qualitative evaluation and research methods* (2nd ed.).
Thousand Oaks, CA: Sage.

Patton, M. Q. (2015). *Qualitative research & evaluation methods: Integrating
theory and practice.* Thousand Oaks, CA: Sage.

Rubin, H. J., & Rubin, I. S. (2012). *Qualitative interviewing: The art of hearing
data.* Thousand Oaks, CA: Sage.

Saldana, J. (2012). *The coding manual for qualitative researchers.* London, UK:
Sage.

Schuh, J. H., & Associates. (2009). *Assessment methods for student affairs.* San
Francisco, CA: Jossey-Bass.

Seidman, I. (2006). *Interviewing as qualitative research: A guide for researchers
in education and the social sciences* (3rd ed.). New York, NY: Teachers
College Press.

Stage, F. K., & Manning, K. (2003). *Research in college context: Approaches and
methods.* New York, NY: Brunner-Routledge.

Strauss, A., & Corbin, J. M. (1998). *Basics of qualitative research: Techniques
and procedures for developing grounded theory* (2nd ed.). Thousand
Oaks, CA: Sage.

Suskie, L. A. (2009). *Assessing student learning: A common sense guide*
(2nd ed.). San Francisco, CA: Jossey-Bass.

Thomas, D. R. (2006). A general inductive approach for analyzing qualitative
evaluation data. *American Journal of Evaluation, 27*(2), 237–246.

Upcraft, M. L., & Schuh, J. H. (1996) *Assessment in student affairs: A guide for
practitioners.* San Francisco, CA: Jossey-Bass.

Wagner, E., & Ice, P. (2012). *Data changes everything: Delivering on the
promise of learning analytics in higher education.* Washington, DC:
EDUCAUSE.

Webb, E. J., Campbell, D. T., Schwartz, R. D., & Sechrest, L. (2000). *Unobtrusive measures.* Thousand Oaks, CA: Sage.

Wolcott, H. F. (1987). On ethnographic intent. In G. Spindler & L. Spindler
(Eds.), *Interpretive ethnography of education* (pp. 37–57). Hillsdale, NJ:
Erlbaum.

8

USING QUANTITATIVE TECHNIQUES IN CONDUCTING ASSESSMENTS

The use of quantitative techniques for assessment dates back to the early years of the student affairs profession, when Northwestern President Walter Dill Scott and his colleagues L. B. Hopkins and future *Student Personnel Point of View* coauthor Esther Lloyd Jones administered tests and measures to evaluate the academic and extracurricular well-being of students (Biddix & Schwartz, 2012). With a few exceptions, contemporary student affairs assessment is not nearly as holistic as those early efforts, which necessiated a dedicated personnel office to coordinate (Certis, 2014). Much of today's quantitative-based assessment work takes the form of aggregated student behavior, attitudes, utilization, and learning outcomes associated with individual facilities and programs.

A proliferation of research and assessment tools have been made available to student affairs practitioners in the past decade, including student response systems, external benchmarking studies, corporate vendors, and effortlessly configured electronic surveys. Each has contributed to a renewed interest and expanded use of quantitative-based evidence by simplifying data collection, analysis, and reporting. While some practitioners philosophically may reject a reductionist approach to demonstrating the value of their services, concisely reported statistics get the attention of interested stakeholders and are used for the accountability function of assessment as Chapter 1 describes. This is particularly true within the contemporary national context favoring summarized numerical data as indicators of postsecondary value and accountability. Added to this was the high-profile publication of *Academically Adrift* (Arum & Roska, 2011), a book-length study that gained national attention when results from the research suggested students failed to improve in critical thinking, complex reasoning, and writing during the first two years of college.

The increasing emphasis on summarized academic outcomes such as retention and graduate rates, as primary indicators of college impact, have left practitioners with little room to demonstrate the importance of their services. In the past, large-scale, national, longitudinal survey programs such as the National Survey of Student Engagement (NSSE) have helped practitioners evidence how cocurricular involvement and programming can influence broad student outcomes; yet, even these have come under recent criticism (Pike, 2013). Further, despite a historic trend valuing assessment proficiencies (Sandeen & Barr, 2006), researchers continue to demonstrate a mismatch between practitioners desired competencies and reported abilities. Herdlein, Riefler, and Mrowka (2013), in a recent meta-analysis, found assessment, evaluation and research skills as among the most important and highly desired competencies for practitioners; however, in a large-scale validation study, Sriram (2014) showed research values, skills, and behaviors were among the lowest self-rated competencies in student affairs. This context leads to the importance of developing and strengthening quantitative skills for assessment practice.

Definition and Use of Quantitative Techniques

Quantitative, or numerical, data are generally used to describe trends or to explore relationships between variables, helping to answer "what" and to some extent "why" questions (Creswell, 2014). Quantitative data are used widely in student affairs to assess needs, satisfaction, learning outcomes, the environment, cost effectiveness, postgraduate experiences, and student involvement (Astin & antonio, 2012; Banta & Palomba, 2014;

Bresciani, Moore Gardner, & Hickmott, 2009; Schuh & Upcraft, 2001; Suskie, 2009). A major benefit of using quantitative data is that it can be collected efficiently, helping offset the lack of time and resources that practitioners cite as barriers to assessment practice (Bresciani, 2010).

Quantitative assessment data are most often gathered by administering a survey or extracting variables from an existing database. Assessment surveys generally involve developing a set of questions, tailored to specific goals, to collect data at a single point. Surveys allow assessment coordinators to collect a variety, and potentially a volume, of data efficiently. Existing datasets also can be used in quantitative analyses. Chapter 6 offers further discussion of using datasets.

A major focus of this chapter is on promoting interpretation and use of quantitative techniques in student affairs assessment. We begin by presenting a case study for undertaking a quantitative-focused assessment project and conclude the chapter by demonstrating how the study might be completed. We introduce a keyword approach for aligning assessment project goals with question selection and data analysis. Common techniques for analyzing quantitative assessment data are also included, along with tips for effectively presenting results.

Campus Recreation at Big-Time Football University

Anthony is assistant director of campus recreation at Big-Time Football University (BTFU). He has responsibility for the leadership, planning, content, training, organization, supervision, and evaluation of programs offered through Campus Recreation Services. Assessment has a high priority in his responsibilities. Anthony is directly tasked with collecting, maintaining, and reporting data

(Continued)

on users and participants, evaluating the department's impact on departmental, divisional, and institutional missions and values, and assessing learning outcomes associated with participation in programs and services. He advises the director and staff regarding findings and records decisions and changes influenced by these findings.

Anthony is an active member of his professional organization. At the last annual meeting, he learned about a recreation and wellness national benchmarking survey. The project involves an online assessment administered to a sample of users and nonusers of on-campus recreational facilities and programs. The survey provides utilization data on facilities, activities, and programs; outcomes related to utilizing campus recreation including social, academic, emotional, and wellness; satisfaction data with facilities and programs; and user needs and expectations.

Participation in the survey affords two major benefits. First, responses can provide data to aid Anthony in performing his internal assessment responsibilities. Second, the benchmarking component will allow him to compare BTFU's findings to peer institutions, which can help him recommend ways to tailor services. The price for participating in the study is considerable at $2,000 per administration, but his supervisor, as well as the associate vice chancellor for student affairs, agrees it will offer a good return on investment.

Selecting Quantitative Techniques: A Keywords Approach

An important early decision in the design and planning phases of an assessment project is whether using a quantitative approach is appropriate (see Chapter 2 for more details about selecting an assessment method). Primarily, this choice should be evaluated based on the purpose(s) of the study. To aid with this considera-tion, we introduce four keywords that can be used to tie project goals with quantitative techniques: *describe, differ, relate,* and *predict*. Integrating the keywords can help practitioners to ensure intended outcomes are met. The primary value of this approach is that each keyword also links with specific quantitative analysis techniques. An overview of the four keywords follows as well as examples of how project goals might be reworded as keyword-related questions. Statistical measures associated with the keywords are referenced in the following and discussed in further detail later in the chapter.

Describe

Describe refers to explanatory data. There are three main categories of statistics that are used to describe data. The most basic category is frequencies, which includes summary counts, percentages, and rates. A second category has to do with measures of central tendency, which includes means, medians, and modes. The third category is variability, which includes range and standard deviation. Describe data used for assessment purposes are commonly employed to assess trends, opinions/perceptions, needs, utilization of services, and attitudes and beliefs of people or groups. This category of data seldom appears as the only analyses in journal articles; however, most published research studies (quantitative, qualitative, or mixed) include descriptive data as a precursor to the primary analysis. Statistics used to summarize data depend on the data form, or the level of measurement. For assessment purposes, we identify three types (nominal, ordinal, and scale), which will be defined later in the chapter.

Differ

Differ refers to comparison data. Studies evaluating differences between or among groups are commonly published in student affairs journals, yet are used less often in assessment. This is unfortunate, since they can provide a statistical distinction between two or more groups and when appropriately designed, can reveal larger trends in the population. Often, differ designs involve one or more "grouping" characteristics (that is, independent variables), such as male/female or resident/nonresident and one or more outcomes (that is, dependent variables), such as satisfaction with dining services or total number of hours a student group contributes to a service project.

Like describe statistics, differ calculations often appear as precursors to additional analysis in published journal articles. The idea of "difference" comes from confirming whether what is observed based on a randomly drawn sample is statistically distinct enough to say it might be true of a population. For example, let's say a random sample of residents and nonresidents from the total population of undergraduate students is asked about satisfaction with campus dining services. If the sample is truly random and large enough, the appropriate statistical test can be used to generalize findings from the sample to all students in the population. The distinction in differ studies lies in the statistical test used, which is based on the type of variables being tested (for example, nominal, ordinal, or scale). The more common include chi-square (difference between groups of categorical measures), t-tests (difference between two groups on continuous measures), and analysis of variance (ANOVA) (difference between two or more groups on continuous measures).

Relate

Relate refers to association data. Relate statistics are commonly used because they can be the simplest to interpret. In most cases, two or more variables are considered related (or correlated) when a change in one relates to a change in the other in some way, such as the positive link between high school GPA and ACT score (for example, the higher the GPA, the higher the ACT). Often, relate studies involve two variables, but some statistics allow for examining relationships between more than two. Relationships can be positive (the higher the GPA, the higher the ACT) or negative (the lower the level of fitness, the higher the level of stress), as well as strong (the closer to home, the lower the level of first-semester homesickness) or weak (the more computers in the library, the more hours students report studying). The concept of positive or negative can be misleading. Positive in this statistical sense means the variables are related in the same direction (that is, both go up or down), while negative means they are related in opposite directions (for example, when one goes down, the other goes up). Strong or weak indicates how closely the variables are statistically associated.

We have observed that in practice, quantitative assessment tends to use less relate statistics even though many of the purposes and questions lend themselves to the relate keyword. One explanation for this is that calculating a correlation statistic such as Pearson's r is not as straightforward in a database program or within an existing tool suite offered by a corporate vendor. Further on in this chapter, we will identify a few ways that relate statistics may be calculated and used effectively to examine and showcase assessment results. Among the advantages of using relate data include the possibility of understanding how programs or services might be addressing similar outcomes, or having the capability of showing figures and statistics that are interpretable to a wide audience.

Predict

Predict refers to causal data. This family of statistics permits estimating or projecting outcomes. Terms commonly associated with predict are *affect, effect, impact,* and *influence*. A benefit of this approach is that it can help demonstrate how one or more variables produce change in an outcome. Also, despite the ability to display a variety of statistics from a predict analysis, the results can be simplified and revealed in an easily interpreted format. Two primary weaknesses limit its common use in assessment. First, the statistical knowledge required to design and to conduct predict studies is beyond the training most professionals received in master's level graduate programs. Second, analyses require meeting conditions that even some of the most rigorous large-scale survey projects in higher education have a difficult time reaching.

Predict studies in student affairs often are used to determine which factors (such as group involvement or leadership status) affect an outcome (for example, civic engagement score). Common outcomes include measures of retention, graduation, academic engagement, social integration, and identity development. Data analysis employed in predict studies frequently falls into the broad category of regression studies. While predict studies do not receive as much attention in student affairs assessment as we think they should, an effectively designed and reported study could provide powerful evidence, such as programmatic impact. Advantages of using predict data include the ability to understand how one or more influences (such as joining a student organization or adding 50 more service hours) potentially could increase a measurable program, divisional, or institutional outcome. For example, a first-year studies coordinator might learn that participating in required tutoring sessions as part of an FYS course increases the likelihood of retention by three times.

Using the Keywords Approach

Often, we talk with practitioners who have developed a survey that seems to ask all the right questions, but cannot generate intended results due to inadequate wording or misalignment with analysis techniques. Specifically, a questionnaire with an assortment of responses types (for example, agree/disagree, ordered, multiple response, ranking) may have been created or selected without consideration for how to score the instrument or analyze data for interpretation and presentation. We propose directly incorporating keywords into the initial assessment questions to promote alignment between the planning, analysis, and reporting phases of the study.

For example, perhaps you are hoping to *describe* the basic functions of a service or to determine perceptions of its usefulness.

Or, you may be interested in finding out how student perceptions *differ* based on demographic (for example, race/ethnicity) or group (for example, commuter/noncommuter) characteristics. Or, you may want to know how perceived learning outcomes from participating in two leadership programs *relate*. Finally, you may want to know if a particular combination of influences (for example, student characteristics, involvement, self-rating of leadership ability) might be used to *predict* an engagement outcome.

While the preceding examples represent distinct studies, a quantitative assessment project may have more than one focus, necessitating several different keyword-based questions. Further, it is not problematic to use the same keyword multiple times to address several overall questions in a single project. Later in this chapter, we discuss common analysis techniques tied to each of the keywords. Subsequent chapters (such as Chapter 13) demonstrate ways to report and display results effectively.

Analyzing Quantitative Data

Statistics is a largely formulaic system of data analysis. Many practitioners we meet who are daunted by statistics view quantitative analysis as a massive, vague, and as a result, highly intimidating field. However, when the type of data (level of measurement) is matched with the type of question or desired outcome (keyword), the statistical technique frequently can be determined quite easily. This section begins with a review of commonly used terminology employed in statistical analysis. Then, an overview levels of measurement is presented, followed by specific recommendations on how to use keywords to select specific analysis techniques.

The statistical analyses presented in this section were selected because they represent common techniques used in student affairs assessment, are widely acceptable and recognizable in other fields, are relatively approachable as introductory but robust measures, and are foundational in nature in that basic concepts can lead to related analytical measures. The texts cited were selected because they are among the more approachable statistical references and can help to clarify concepts or be used to identify additional measures not covered in this overview.

Terminology

Population: All members of a group of interest (for example, all sophomore student leaders)

Sample: A set of members selected from a population (for example, a sample of 50 sophomore student leaders)

Descriptive statistic: A measure used to summarize, organize, or simplify data (for example, mean)

Inferential statistic: A measure used with samples to make generalizations about populations (for example, *t*-test)

Independent variable: A characteristic (for example, gender of sophomore student leaders), cause, or influence affecting or related to an outcome; often used as an input or environment

Dependent variable: An outcome or effect (for example, academic engagement scores) resulting from or related to a characteristic, cause, or influence

Group: A classification of individuals (for example, gender, student group membership)

Level: A subclassification of individuals within a group (for example, gender is a group with two levels, male and female)

Choosing a Level of Measurement

Statisticians classify variables using levels of measurement. Descriptions of nominal, ordinal, and scale measures follow. Interval measures were not included as this type of data is used infrequently in student affairs assessment and often treated as ratio data for analysis. Identifying the level of measurement is a fundamental proficiency that leads to selecting the correct statistic.

Data limited to categories usually based on characteristics or attributes are referred to as *nominal* data. Most often, these are demographic descriptors, such as gender, political party, or religious preference but they can also be agree/disagree questions. Other names used for this level of measurement are categorical, discrete, or string variables. When you see nominal, think *names* or *groups*.

Data limited to fixed categories usually representing choices are referred to as *ordinal* data. Most often, these are ordered or preference responses such as Likert scales. Another name used for this level of measurement is ranked data. When you see ordinal, think *ratings*.

Data that provide the opportunity to choose a numerical answer are referred to as *scale* data. Most often, these are truly variable responses such as age or number of hours worked. Another name used for this level of measurement is continuous data. When you see scale, think *numbers*.

It is important to note there are differing opinions on what types of data are most appropriate for certain statistics. Specifically, there is some disagreement in the research community on whether response data (such as Likert scale) should be treated as categorical, ordinal, or ratio. Our suggestion for assessment purposes is to treat response categories with five or more responses as ratio, though seven or more is preferable, as the added possible responses allow the data to vary.

Selecting the Correct Assessment Statistic

A quantitative assessment design is built on keywords, variables, and levels of measurement, which combine to suggest the appropriate statistical test. The basic approach looks like this:

Keyword + Variable/Level of Measurement = Statistic

Table 8.1:   Selecting the Correct Assessment Statistic

You Want to Know	You Have These Types of Variables	Use This
(Keyword)	(Level of Measurement)	(Statistic)
Describe	Names or Groups Ratings or Numbers Combinations of Names, Groups, or Ratings	Data display, percent, mode, range mean, standard deviation cross tabulations
Differ	Names or Groups **by** Names, Groups, or Ratings 1 Name or Group **by** 1 Rating/Number 2+ Name or Group **by** 1 Rating/Number	Chi-square *t*-test ANOVA
Relate	Names or Groups **to** Names or Groups Names or Groups **to** Ratings or Numbers Ratings or Numbers **to** Ratings or Numbers	Correlation
Predict	Any Variable(s) **on** 1 Name or Group Any Variable(s) **on** 1 Rating or Number	Logistic Regression Multiple Regression

Table 8.1 illustrates how this system works. The first column (Keyword) relates directly to the keyword selected in the early steps of the project. The second column (Level of Measurement) shows the types of variables associated with the keywords. Note that the differ, relate, and predict rows have bolded words to indicate how variables are combined for analysis. The final column (Statistic) shows the statistic associated with each Keyword and Level of Measurement combination. The next section provides an overview for how to calculate, interpret, and report each statistic listed in the table.

Describe Statistics

Describe data are the most commonly utilized quantitative assessment statistics for ease of use, straightforward interpretation, and concise presentation. Statistics used for describe data are generally summary values that fall into three categories, frequency (data display, percentage, cross tabulation), central tendency (mean, median, mode), and variability (range, standard deviation).

A frequency is a summarized count of raw data, often summarized as a data display in a table or graph. Examples of frequency displays are pie charts or bar graphs, which show all responses to a particular question efficiently. Percentage is among the most-often-used descriptive statistics, largely for its versatility. Nearly any level of measurement can be expressed as a percentage, which is calculated by grouping all like values, counting the number of occurrences in each group, then dividing each total by the total number of groups and multiplying by 100. A crosstabulation is a statistic used to summarize categorical data to show within-variable frequency distributions. Put another way, a cross tabulation is a table that combines the results of two variables to show how they relate with each other. The measure is widely used to show "breakdowns" of responses by a demographic category, such as how men and women individually replied on each level of a satisfaction with campus health services question. Cross tabulations can be calculated with a spreadsheet program, statistical software, or through tools offered by a corporate vendor service and are reported effectively in a table (such as a matrix) or bulleted format.

Central tendency is term used to describe the most common or average value. The most often used measure of central tendency is a mean, or arithmetic average, which is most appropriate for scale data, but also can be used with ordinal data. As previously noted, there is some disagreement about whether mean should be used with Likert scale or ranking data, which has to do with the lack of possible variance with a limited (1–5 or less) scale. Following field convention, we acknowledge a five-point scale is marginally acceptable for calculating mean and standard deviation, though we recommend a scale of seven points or more. In the case of nominal or response questions with four or fewer possible answers, the mode, or most commonly occurring response, is preferred. The median is the 50th percentile, with half the scores being above the median and half falling below the 50th percentile.

Variability (sometimes referred to as dispersion) is the spread of variables and is among the most useful, but least often reported, statistics in assessment. Range, appropriate for all levels of measurement, is the maximum value minus the minimum value. Standard deviation is best suited for scale data, but also can be used with ordinal data if mean is reported. The basic formula for calculating standard deviation is relatively easy to perform by hand; however, using a handheld or online calculator, spreadsheet program, or statistical software simplifies it further. Standard deviation can be used to determine how far apart most values or scores are in a distribution, simply by subtracting one standard deviation from the mean, and then adding one standard deviation to the mean (mean +/−1 standard deviation).

For example, let's say students are asked to rate their satisfaction with dining services on campus on a 1–7 scale, with 1 being lowest and 7 being highest. After a random sample of 150 students answers the question, you calculate a mean of 4.5 and standard deviation of 0.7. Subtracting and adding one standard deviation score to the mean (4.5 − 0.7 = 3.8) (4.5 + 0.7 = 5.2) tells us that the majority of scores (68 percent) fall between 3.8 and 5.2. Extending this to two standard deviations below and above the mean (4.5 − 0.7 − 0.7 = 3.1) (4.5 + 0.7 + 0.7 = 5.9) tells using nearly all scores (95 percent) fall between 3.1 and 5.9. Finally, extended this to three standard deviations below and above the mean $(4.5 - 0.7 - 0.7 - 0.7 = 2.4)$ $(4.5 + 0.7 + 0.7 + 0.7 = 6.6)$ tells us nearly all scores (99.7 percent) fall between 2.4 and 6.6.

Variability measures, and in particular standard deviation, reveal two valuable trends in data. First, they show whether responses (or other numerical data) are relatively close or located far apart. A small standard deviation, for example, suggests most responses are about the same, which makes the mean worthwhile to interpret. A larger standard deviation suggests responses diverge substantially from each other, which renders the mean as being less valuable since few responses are actually close to "average." Second, when comparing scores for two or more groups, standard deviations can reveal differences even when the means are nearly identical. Knowing which groups are similar on some measure or preference compared with those that are very diverse can help a decision maker tailor programming more precisely to address specific needs.

Describe data are often shown in data displays. The more common displays include frequency distributions, graphs, frequency histograms, bar graphs, and pie charts. Advantages to using describe data is that they are easy to calculate and can yield brief, easily interpreted reports.

Differ Statistics

Difference data can serve two functions. The first is to test for differences between two or more groups when all data for the groups are available. This is a descriptive function. The second also tests for group differences but is used when only sample data (sufficiently large and randomly drawn) for the groups are available. This is an inferential function. In other words, the descriptive function lets you see if a statistical difference exists between groups, while the inferential function allows you to estimate whether the difference tested also exists in the population. Both are calculated using the same statistics;

the distinction has to do with the sample (it must be random for inferential) and the goals of the analysis.

For example, let's say you are assessing the functionality of a web-based form for submitting parking ticket appeals. Using the descriptive function, if you have all the data for the time frame you are interested in, you could test to determine if men and women appeal tickets differently. If you have access to only some of the data, you could use the inferential function by randomly selecting a sample of men and women, and then inferring that the results of the test apply to all men and women parking ticket appellants.

Statistics for difference data are chosen using both the level of measurement along with the number of groups, as shown in table 8.1. More precisely, statisticians place these distinctions into two analysis categories, parametric and nonparametric statistics, which has to do with whether a variable is normally distributed (that is looks like a bell curve when plotted with a few values at the low and high ends and a majority grouping in the middle). Levin and Fox (2010) provided an excellent overview of this distinction, which is a core concept for understanding advanced statistics. An overview of three difference statistics useful for most assessment efforts follows.

Chi-square (χ^2) can be used with data in nearly any form (names, groups, or rating), is viable when groups are different sizes, and can be interpreted as difference or relate (depending on how you word the results). Chi-square is simply an extension of a cross tabulation, where variables are crossed for comparison. The difference between the crossed groups is tested and the results are interpreted as descriptive or extended as inferential. Chi-square can be calculated using an online calculator or statistical software and is reported effectively by including the χ^2 value and significance (for example, $p < .05$), generally shown at the bottom of a cross-tabulation table of results.

T-test and ANOVA (F test) evaluate the statistical difference between a group and a mean calculated from a rating or numerical value. The two statistics are identical in terms of design and reporting with the exception that *t*-test can handle only two groups (such as sorority member/nonmember) or two levels within a single group (for example, sorority/membership status: member/leader). Conversely, ANOVA can handle two or more groups (for example, sorority member/fraternity member/nonmember) or two or more levels within a single group (such as sorority membership status: member/appointed leader/elected leader). Advanced forms of ANOVA allow you to control for the influence of certain variables (ANCOVA) or test multiple outcomes at the same time (MANOVA). Field (2013) provided an approachable introduction to these and other concepts using SPSS. In any case, the outcome variable must be scale (a number) or treated as scale (for example, 1 to 5 or more rating). *T*-test and ANOVA can be computed with a spreadsheet program or online calculator, though we recommend using statistical software, since the process for organizing the data can be unclear for beginning users.

Differ data are reported effectively in a table showing mean, standard deviation, the *t* or *F* value, and significance (for example, $p < .05$). A useful tip when viewing seemingly complicated tables or in-text statistics is to look for the *p* value and interpret the sign. A < sign generally indicates groups are statistically different.

Relate Statistics

Correlation, the primary relate statistic for the purposes of assessment, tests the relationship between two or more characteristics. Researchers use correlation when building prediction models (highly correlated values are often predictive), to assess the validity or reliability of a measure (instrument testing), and to verify theory. Before reviewing the basic tenets of correlation statistics, two caveats are important to note: (1) correlation does not imply causation (that requires a predict statistic) and (2) extreme low or high scores (outliers) greatly affect correlation.

The most widely used relate test is the Pearson correlation, or Pearson's r, which is a bivariate (that is, between two) test using scale, rating (1–5 or more), or a combination of the two types of data. When comparing nominal data to other forms, researchers sometimes use point biserial (rpb), although that procedure is mathematically equivalent to Pearson's r and SPSS calculates it by default. Spearman's rank-order (ρ) is used with two ordinal, or ranked, variables (if you are not treating ranks as scale).

Correlations have three main properties that are important to understand: direction, form, and degree or strength. Direction indicates whether the relationship is positive (as one value goes up or down, the other goes up or down) or negative (values go in opposite directions). Form is the shape of the relationship and can be either linear (a straight line up or down) or curvilinear (values start high or low, then peak or dip, then return to high or low). Degree or strength indicates how closely related the variables are, specifically, when plotted on a line. This is expressed as a correlation coefficient and can fall between -1.00 and $+1.00$. The farther from 0, the more closely the variables are related. As a general guide: 0.00 = no correlation, $+/- .10$ = weak correlation, $+/- .30$ = moderate correlation, $+/- .60$ = strong correlation, and $+/- 1.00$ = perfect correlation.

Relate data are often shown in tables called matrices and include p or significance values, which are interpreted in the same way as differ values. In this case, a $<$ sign generally means the similarity is valid. Showing variables with up or down arrows to indicate the direction of their relationship can be an efficient and effective way to present results.

Predict Statistics

Predict statistics are used less frequently in assessment studies, likely because they require the most expertise and effort. The most common predict statistic used in student affairs research is regression. Regression datasets can be challenging to create, given the number of statistical assumptions that variables and models must meet for robust analysis. Further, reporting results effectively and accessibly for a wide audience requires a sufficient understanding of how to interpret and explain several different statistics. Nonetheless, incorporating predict statistics into assessment can evidence new insights and enhance long-term strategic plans. Predict statistics allow a researcher to use a set of independent, or "predictor" variables to determine how they can individually or in combination affect a dependent, or "outcome" variable. Astin (1973) notably applied this concept to student affairs research with his Input-Environment-Output (IEO) model, using student background and characteristics (I) to understand the impact of college effects such as joining student groups or participating in service (E) on measures such as academic achievement and psychosocial development (O).

Two types of regression are used in student affairs assessment contexts: logistic and multiple. The main difference is in the types of variables that can be used for predictors and outcomes. Logistic regression is the most flexible as it allows different levels of measurement to be used as predictors; however, its basic form allows prediction for only two possible outcomes. Logistic regression is widely used in institutional research because many outcomes of interest are discrete (for example, retain/not retain, graduate/not graduate). Multiple regression is more restrictive, as it cannot accommodate nominal variables without special coding; furthermore, its basic form restricts the outcome variable to continuous data, or numbers. Multiple regression is used less often in institutional contexts, but is widely used with national datasets such as the NSSE.

Conducting predict assessment studies is beyond the scope of this text; however, its prominent use on campus and in national conversations surrounding student outcomes warrants your attention. As noted, institutional research officers use predict studies to understand persistence and retention outcomes. Further, institutions that partner with national studies to understand and evaluate student engagement likely also are using prediction equations or have the ability to do so with the data collected. Minimally, we suggest practitioners learn the basics of how to read regression tables and identify how data need to be collected and formatted for inclusion in predict studies. We recommend Mertler and Vanetta (2013) and Field (2013) as two different approachable, step-by-step guides to setting up, completing, and reporting predict studies. Advocating for the inclusion of cocurricular experiences in a measurable and meaningful way in predict modeling has the potential to include student affairs more prominently in strategic and budgeting decisions.

Predict data are often shown in tables including variable coefficients (such as beta weights), p or significance values, and an indicator of overall model fit. In this case, a $<$ sign generally means the predictor variable produces a change in the outcome. When used for assessment, predict results should be displayed in a simplified and interpretable format.

Your Quantitative Skillset

Quantitative assessment measures are relatable to a broad audience, and inform most research-based practices in the field. Understanding and using quantitative techniques for assessment can be a valuable (and marketable) skillset. Taking (or retaking) a statistics course is one way to build expertise, though professional associations regularly offer workshops at annual or regional meetings. Following is a set of basic quantitative skills we believe assessment practitioners should work to develop and maintain.

- Ability to create and manage a dataset, preferably in a spreadsheet program

- Ability to conceptualize and create effective statistical graphs, figures, and tables
- Relationship with the institutional research office and/or other potential assessment partners
- Beginning knowledge (interpretation) of predict statistics
- Intermediate knowledge (interpretation and basic calculation) of differ and relate statistics
- Advanced knowledge (interpretation and advanced calculation) of describe statistics

Returning to Big-Time Football University

This chapter began with a case study describing the benchmarking assessment project Anthony planned to implement at Big-Time Football University (BTFU). The instrument he will use already exists, which saves him considerable implementation time. Anthony also chose to partner with a corporate vendor to collect the data, which will allow him to track response rates, easily request basic statistics, and generate an exportable file for sophisticated analyses. Assuming he wants to know more about the results than the basic percentages and cross tabulations, we ask that you provide the answers to the following questions.

1. What keywords should Anthony use to address the purpose and goals of his project?

2. Using the keyword approach, which statistics should Anthony use when analyzing data?

3. What sample should he target and how many participants does he need?

4. When should he administer the survey?

5. How should Anthony present results to the various stakeholders on campus?

Discussion Questions

1. In what situations is it appropriate to collect quantitative assessment data?

2. What are some of the challenges in collecting quantitative data? Describe ways you might address those challenges.

3. What are some ways you can develop and demonstrate credibility when analyzing quantitative assessment data?

4. How can you present results from quantitative data analysis?

References

Arum, R., & Roksa, J. (2011). *Academically adrift: Limited learning on college campuses*. Chicago, IL: University of Chicago Press.

Astin, A. W. (1973). Measurement of determinants of the outputs of higher education. In L. Solomon & P. Taubman (Eds.), *Does college matter? Some impacts of higher education*. New York, NY: Academic Press.

Astin, A. W., & antonio, a. l. (2012). *Assessment for excellence: The philosophy and practice of assessment and evaluation in higher education*. Lanham, MD: Rowman & Littlefield.

Banta, T. W., & Palomba, C. A. (2015). *Assessment essentials: Planning, implementing and improving assessment in higher education* (2nd ed.). San Francisco, CA: Jossey-Bass.

Biddix, J. P., & Schwartz, R. (2012). Walter Dill Scott and the student personnel movement. *Journal of Student Affairs Research and Practice, 49*(3), 285–298.

Bresciani, M. J. (2010). Understanding barriers to student affairs professionals' engagement in outcomes-based assessment of student learning and development. *Journal of Student Affairs, 14,* 81–89.

Bresciani, M. J., Moore Gardner, M., & Hickmott, J. (2009). *Demonstrating student success: A practical guide to outcomes-based assessment of learning and development in student affairs*. Sterling, VA: Stylus.

Certis, H. (2014). The emergence of Esther Lloyd-Jones. *Journal of Student Affairs Research and Practice, 51*(3), 259–269. doi:10.1515/jsarp-2014–0027

Creswell, J. W. (2014). *Research design: Qualitative, quantitative, and mixed methods approaches* (3rd ed.). Thousand Oaks, CA: Sage.

Field, A. (2013). *Discovering statistics using IBM SPSS Statistics* (4th ed.). London, UK: Sage.

Herdlein, R., Riefler, L., & Mrowka, K. (2013). An integrative literature review of student affairs competencies: A meta-analysis.
Journal of Student Affairs Research and Practice, 50(3), 250–269.
doi:10.1515/jsarp-2013–0019

Levin, J., & Fox, J. A. (2010). *Elementary statistics in social research: Essentials*
(3rd ed.). New York, NY: Pearson.

Mertler, C. A., & Vanetta, R. A. (2013). *Advanced and multivariate statistics
statistical methods: Practical application and interpretation* (5th ed.).
Glendale, AZ: Pyrczak.

Pike, G. R. (2012). NSSE benchmarks and institutional outcomes: A note
on the importance of considering the intended uses of a measure of
validity studies. *Research in Higher Education, 2013*(54), 149–170.
doi:10.1007/s11162–012–9279-y

Sandeen, A., & Barr, M. J. (2006). *Critical issues for student affairs: Challenges
and opportunities.* San Francisco, CA: Jossey-Bass.

Schuh, J. H., & Upcraft, M. L. (2001). Conducting focus groups. In J. H.
Schuh & M. L. Upcraft (Eds.), *Assessment practice in student affairs:
An application manual* (pp. 42–56). San Francisco, CA: Jossey-Bass.

Sriram, R. (2014). The development, validity, and reliability of a psychometric instrument measuring competencies in student affairs. *Journal of
Student Affairs Research and Practice, 51*(4), 349–363.

Suskie, L. A. (2009). *Assessing student learning: A common sense guide*
(2nd ed.). San Francisco, CA: Jossey-Bass.

9

DEVELOPING AND SELECTING
INSTRUMENTS

This chapter provides recommendations for developing and selecting instruments and includes information related to assessing instrument quality. Most often, instruments are created, rather than chosen, for assessment efforts to ensure alignment between program, unit, or divisional goals. Unless a decision-maker predetermines the methodology, the assessment coordinator is responsible for choosing the instrument that best fits the study. In this chapter, we describe and evaluate eight types of assessment instruments: four qualitative questionnaire formats, an observation form, a document review guide, and two types of quantitative surveys. After considering instrument types, we turn to wording and sequencing questions, before closing with a discussion of quality.

Definition and Use of Instrumentation

Instrumentation is the process of selecting a tool, or instrument, to gather data for an assessment project. Developing an instrument refers to the process of creating a survey, questionnaire, observation form, or document review guide. Selecting an instrument refers to choosing and receiving permission to use an existing instrument. Instrumentation also should involve assessing the quality of the instrument and the validity of the data collected. A case study follows to illustrate these concepts.

Learning Outcomes for Tour Guides at Small Private College

Jana is an admissions representative at Small Private College (SPC). Her primary responsibilities include traveling throughout the region in the late fall and early spring to recruit prospective SPC students from area high schools and participating in various college fairs. SPC is a religiously affiliated institution located in a rural area with a total enrollment of 2,500 students. Jana has a smaller territory than her four colleagues who hold similar positions because she also is responsible for coordinating the campus tour guide program. She selects, trains, supervises, and coordinates the schedules of 12 undergraduate work-study funded students who lead campus tours. Most of the tour guides are juniors and seniors and have served for multiple years.

Following a recent accreditation visit, student affairs staff members were challenged by the reviewers to document student learning outcomes from various programs on campus. After talking with several colleagues at other institutions, Jana wants to evaluate outcomes from the tour guide program, with the hope of demonstrating what current students learn and using the results to enhance the experience for future students. Because of the small number of tour guides, she feels qualitative methods may be best to use for now, but eventually wants to transition to a pre/post survey design she can use long term. She begins by reviewing student learning outcomes from various documents to compose outcomes for her office. Then, she uses the new outcomes to develop a structured questionnaire to interview tour guides individually at the beginning, middle, and end of the upcoming academic year. Based on the results, she will develop a pre/post survey to administer to tour guides in subsequent years.

Developing Instruments

When you know what you want to assess, developing a tool for gathering that information may seem a simple task. However, developing an instrument can be deceptively challenging. It is not uncommon for even experienced assessment professionals to complete data collection, only to find that poorly worded or confusing questions, measures mismatched to intended outcomes, or data that require additional analytical expertise have severely limited the potency of the project. This section provides an overview of assessment instruments recommended for student affairs projects. For the purpose of clarity, we refer to qualitative instruments as questionnaires and quantitative instruments as surveys.

Questionnaires

Berg (2004) differentiated three formats of qualitative questionnaires: standardized, semi-standardized, and unstandardized, all of which can be used as guides for interviewing individuals. The major difference between the three formats is the degree of rigidity, which Berg (2004) illustrated as a continuum ranging from formal (that is, structured) to informal (that is, nondirective). Each format also might be used for either scheduled or casual (that is, "walk-up") interviews, and can involve individuals or groups. Group questionnaires can take on any of these characteristics, but some adjustment is needed when conducting group interviews. Additional considerations are included as a fourth questionnaire format in this section.

A *standardized questionnaire* includes a list of predetermined questions, arranged and asked in a set order, with limited provision for follow-up, explanation, or clarification. A major benefit for using this format is that it is highly focused and can yield the most consistent results, ensuring you will address the topics you expect to cover in the allotted time. As a result, a standardized interview can be the most efficient in terms of time. Another major benefit is that this format is the easiest to train someone to use, further maximizing efficiency. Finally, this format requires little researcher intuition, or sense of when to change or alter the interview based on the flow of the session.

Often, researchers are reluctant to use standardized question-naires because of their inherent inflexibility. As such, this format may be less well regarded in the larger qualitative community because it is the least conceptually qualitative (that is, construc-tivist) in terms of allowing participants to freely share and elab-orate on points. The trade-off for this rigidity is consistency and credibility to an external audience (Patton, 1990). Even when the answers vary considerably, a reader can be sure that all topics were covered in the same way with each participant. In a related view concerning the reliability of surveys, Fowler (2009) supported this perspective, noting, "The researcher would like to be able to make the assumption that differences in answers stem from differences among respondents in what they have to say rather than differ-ences in the stimuli to which respondents were exposed" (p. 88).

An *unstandardized questionnaire* generally does not include a set list of questions, set order, or set wording. Berg (2004) char-acterized this format as "completely unstructured," but this does not imply the interview is without direction or order. An unstan-dardized questionnaire might look like a topical outline or listing of ideas with a few essential questions. These questions may or may not be ordered, based on the primary goals for the study.

A major benefit to this approach is that it allows for ques-tions to arise during the interview. This gives the researcher the flexibility to cover, or "probe" an important point without con-cern for covering other topics. In addition, the format is more natural and conversational, which can help the interviewer estab-lish and maintain rapport and trust with the participant. A major drawback is that this approach can yield inconsistent results. This potential is particularly challenging when you have an exact idea about the things you want to uncover during the interview. The format also can be the least efficient in terms of time, and should not be used if more than a few specific points need to be cov-ered. Using an unstandardized interview requires a great deal of researcher intuition and experience, since the format is highly dependent on a sense of when to probe, redirect, or simply to listen. As a result, this approach may not be best suited for new or novice researchers.

A *semi-standardized questionnaire* often includes a brief list of predetermined questions and might also include a listing of topics that could be explored depending on the conversation. A benefit of this approach is that it offers some standardization between interviews while also providing the interviewer with the flexibility to explore topics further. A common approach is to develop three questions, ask each individually, and then to follow up on responses with additional questions sparked by the answers. Three sample questions appear in the following:

1. What's it like to be a student here?
2. What do you like best about your college experience?
3. What could we change to improve your experience?

A *group interview questionnaire*, or focus group protocol, can follow any of the previous three formats. The main difference is that in a group setting, individuals have the opportunity to explain, elaborate, or even amend their comments based on the discussion. The nature of the data collection process shifts from interviewer/participant to participant/participant dialog. A major benefit and attractive feature of this approach for busy professionals is efficiency, especially when compared to conducting several individual interviews. The trade-off for this approach can be an inability to gain in-depth, individualized perspectives from the participants.

Focus group interview questionnaires often include far fewer questions than individual interview protocols, since the general goal of a group interview is to facilitate discussion rather than to address multiple or varied topics. Hence, a semi-standardized approach is generally preferable to structured or unstructured group questionnaires. This allows the interviewer to cover the most important topics and to make comparisons across focus group sessions. Using a semi-standardized questionnaire also allows for the flexibility to facilitate discussion or probe further. Kelly (2003) emphasized opportunities for interviewees to rationalize their responses to the group. She noted, "when participants publically defend their responses in the presence of others and within the context of challenges expressed by fellow group members, the researcher witnesses the strength of the conviction held" (p. 51).

Observation Forms

An *observation form* guides note taking and provides consistency and continuity when collecting observational data. Consistency also can be referred to as interrater reliability, defined by Vogt (2005) as "Agreement or consistency among raters; the extent to which raters judge phenomena in the same way" (p. 157). While researchers can go into an observation with simply a pencil and a notepad, we do not recommend this approach. The novice researcher or even someone more experienced but out of practice may find it helpful to develop a listing of phenomena to observe prior to collecting data. An observation form is generally researcher-developed and customized to the particular inquiry. The form can be either structured and include set items to be checked off as observed, or semi-structured with some items listed for focus but in general left open for narrative entries.

Common to all observation forms should be a space for contextual details including the time, date, and location as well as information about the physical setting. Also, an observation form should note the focus for the data collection session. Observers often record what social interactions or activities took place, including movement or change within the setting Saunders and Cooper (2009) suggested observers might attend to what people are doing or not doing as well as the layout of the activity (that is, how individuals negotiate the space). They also recommended developing a list of questions to help guide the observation (for example, how are students interacting with each other in the space?). A final, but important aspect of data collection is the observer's feelings, reactions, and reflections about meaning or significance, which can reveal missing information and suggest additional questions, as well as facilitate interpretation and analyses.

Pragmatically for assessment purposes, we follow Emerson, Fretz, and Shaw's (2011) recommendation to complete an initial observation (or several) to generate ideas of what might be observed more formally later. Notes from these first sessions might be turned into checklists if specific behaviors or actions are notable (consistent or inconsistent), but an observer should be ready to record events beyond the list as outliers might become frequent enough to be considered normal practices. A potential problem with developing and using a checklist for observation is that this approach can devolve into an emphasis on frequency counts of activities, which may cause you to miss other aspects in favor of ensuring accurate counts. If counts are necessary, we suggest developing the list, then either training others to record activities while you focus on the broader setting or completing several observations varying between using the checklist and open note-taking.

Using an observation form also can help minimize bias, preconceived notions, early judgments, or generalizations that can cause the observer to look for confirmatory practices as opposed to maintaining openness to data collection (Emerson, Fretz, & Shaw, 2011). However, Patton (1990) noted that observers are not simply recording machines; biases should be recorded, but marked separately with brackets, parentheses, or asterisks to delineate interpretations. After collecting data, Emerson, Fretz, and Shaw (2011) suggested first writing initial impressions, then describing key events or incidents, followed by information about aspects or individuals in the setting perceived as significant or important. If it is possible to talk with participants after an observation, follow-up interviews can provide additional information or clarification on actions, interactions, and events.

Document Review Guides

A *document review guide* is a standardized form used for recording notes collected from documents and records. Notes are inclusive of context, facts, and researcher observations. Documents and records refer to text and images. Examples include e-mails, meeting agendas and minutes, newspaper articles, and photographs. Similar to interview and observational tools, developing a standardized way of examining text and images helps to establish consistency and continuity (Saunders & Cooper, 2009). A document review guide is often researcher-developed and can be highly structured or semi-structured with some standardized elements, checklist-type prompts, and room for open comments. This standardization establishes commonality across notes, even when using different sources, and facilitates data analysis in the case of multiple assessment team members, helping to assure interrater reliability.

Document review guides should include contextual details such as the date the document was acquired, the origin of the document and purpose, the author(s), intended audience, a brief summary of contents, influences and/or conditions under which it was produced, and any other context in which it was written (for example, temporal, political, historical, or economic) (Merriam, 1998; Yin, 1994). Neither the influence nor context(s) may be easy to determine without some background knowledge or access to other sources. Data typically do not exist without the influence of outside factors. For example, perhaps you are assessing perceptions of campus policy for posting fliers and during your initial review of the student handbook you find very restrictive guidelines. You may have been on campus long enough to know those were developed after an offensive party flier was posted. Or, you may be new to campus and when asking others, you discover strong opinions about the policy. This example illustrates that document data generally has a contextual backstory. It is important to understand and bracket (that is, make your own observations about) those influences as you collect and analyze data.

Yin (1994) noted, "no document is a literal recording of an event" (p. 87). Depending on the goals of the assessment project, a document review guide also might include questions related to assessing authenticity. These considerations are more important when the document is an e-mail or personal record. Examples questions include:

- Has the document been tampered with or edited?

- What biases might have influenced the creation of the document?

- What other documents or evidence might exist to verify the information?

Surveys

Surveys used in quantitative studies are common data collection tools for student affairs assessment, due both to an emphasis on demonstrating value using numerical data and to the efficiency of data collection. Among the major benefits of surveys are that they can be cost-effectively delivered, scaled to fit large or small samples, and analyzed efficiently if structured properly. Further, depending on the goals of the assessment, it is possible to collect survey data using a small sample and generalize results to the larger population of interest. Finally, using standardized measures can permit comparison of results to internal or external benchmarks. Researcher-developed and existing surveys are reviewed in the following.

A *researcher-developed survey* is deceptively difficult to create. Superficially, it may seem easy to write questions aligned with your project. Unfortunately, many novice as well as seasoned survey developers have constructed and administered surveys without considering how to analyze data or whether the responses to the survey will contribute relevant information to the study. Fowler (2009) captured this sentiment, noting, "good questions maximize the relationships between the answers recorded and what the researcher is trying to measure" (p. 87).

Nonetheless, the ability to create and/or tailor questions is a major benefit of developing a survey. Although it can take a considerable amount of time to write questions, a well-developed survey can directly align with project goals, outcomes, and analytical techniques. This provides the researcher with control often not achievable with an existing instrument. Developing a survey also may be more efficient than purchasing a commercially available instrument, depending on how long it takes to gain permission or to fund the cost of using an established instrument. Finally, it is important to note that a researcher-developed instrument should be piloted tested, meaning " ... the entire study with all its instruments and procedures is conducted in miniature" (Vogt, 2005, p. 237) before the study is conducted.

An *existing survey* offers several advantages. Most notable is that questions are already developed and ideally validated, saving a considerable amount of time and potentially lending credibility to data collection. Ensuring that the instrument is a fit for the study context and sample is essential; therefore, we still advocate pilot testing existing surveys. A significant disadvantage can be locating and accessing a survey that matches the needs of the assessment. This includes meeting any conditions that using the instrument may require, such as cost of obtaining copyright from the author or organization if the survey is not designated for free or fair use.

We are often asked if a researcher can use or adapt questions from an existing instrument when creating a new one. For example, let's say you are developing your own survey. You write some questions, but find an instrument online that has three that match your assessment goals or intended outcomes. Some survey authors or agencies encourage users to include individual questions to permit comparison to existing data or benchmarks (Hyman, Lamb, & Bulmer, 2006). Often, large-scale national survey providers do not object to researchers using a few questions as long as the proper credit is given. However, our experience has been that unless the survey is licensed for fair or free use, it is essential to secure permission from the instrument's copyright holder before using questions from another instrument.

Guidelines for Developing Instruments

As an initial step before developing an instrument, we suggest reviewing previous reports and files as well as reaching out to former employees to identify any previously used instruments. Having an example that can serve as a basis for developing an instrument can help identify what worked (or did not work) in the past. Reviewing literature on the topic also can help shape the study and ground it in current research. Further, we recommend involving others. Even if you are conducting the assessment alone, asking others to be involved in developing an instrument can help to ensure alignment in the project as well as to promote external legitimacy.

Although we have distinguished between various instrument formats, each also shares common characteristics. Some general guidelines follow for how to write and sequence questions in addition to further considerations for developing instruments. Although much of the information is more appropriate for survey research, keep in mind that a core characteristic of qualitative data collection is asking questions. You may find referencing the subsequent information while developing an instrument (or considering using an existing instrument) will help you to consider additional ways to enhance data collection from observation or document review.

Using Open-Ended Questions

Open-ended questions allow respondents to answer, using their own words, yields responses that may be more reflective of individual views, and produce unanticipated findings (Fowler, 2009). This format generally is associated with interview research, which has a central goal of getting people to elaborate. Many times when we review qualitative questionnaires or transcripts, we see strings of questions so narrow that respondents needed only single words to answer. Further, sometimes interviewers believe that simply removing choices from a question makes it open-ended; however, in most cases this practice creates a boundary of possible responses. Patton (1990) warned that asking series of such questions could feel more like an interrogation than an opportunity to share experiences. The truly open-ended question, conversely, allows respondents to draw from their own broad possibilities, permits the interviewee to dictate the direction of the interview, and allows them to select the words and ordering of the words they want to use.

Using Closed-Ended Questions

Closed-ended questions limit participitants to predetermined responses (Vogt, 2005). A significant advantage to using closed-ended questions for assessment purposes is that the predefined categories or labels can be directly aligned to the project. Noting the consistency afforded by this approach, Fowler (2009) stated, "the simplest way to give respondents the same perceptions of what constitutes an adequate answer is to provide them with a set of acceptable answers" (p. 97). Closed-ended questions favor a quantity of responses over the potential depth allowed by open-ended options. Generally, they are best reserved for surveys or provided as a separate form to interviewees if more than a few demographic questions are necessary. Example categories of questions used for close-ended surveys follow.

- *Agree-Disagree items* ask respondents to decide if their opinions are similar (agree) or dissimilar (disagree) to a given statement. These types of questions can limit data analysis by putting respondents into only two categories, regardless of the number of choices. Fowler (2009) used the example of the statement "my health is fair" to which a person could agree or disagree because their health is good or poor. This can lead to confusion, as saying that your health is good is disagreeing that it is poor. Although this approach seems to be a common way to form questions, we agree with Fowler's (2009) advice to avoid agree-disagree questions when possible to promote clearer and more reliable responses.

- *Ordered questions* provide prearranged categories of responses to participants. Most often, these are feeling or opinion questions that have been assigned a continuum of acceptable responses. Common formats are Likert Scale (for example, strongly disagree to strongly agree), intensity (for example, not at all to extremely), or rating (for example, poor to excellent). Respondents are asked to consider the potential responses and put themselves into a category. A limitation is that respondents can differ in how they interpret categories. Ordered scales are most meaningfully and effectively used to classify people into groups, not to suggest something is good or better than something else. Using ordered questions to make comparative statements between groups or within comparable samples over time is an effective way to analyze and report data.

- *Multiple response questions* provide a listing of categories and allow more than one answer to be selected. This type of question can be advantageous to use when trying to keep a survey questionnaire brief. A way to develop multiple response items is following analysis of an open-ended question. For example, an open-ended satisfaction question might ask parents to list additional comments about parent orientation programming. Analysis of these responses may reveal multiple, but distinct, items that could be used in a subsequent multiple response question. Overusing these types of questions is not advisable as analysis can be limited to percentages or cross-tabulations between responses and other questions. Also, inexperienced researchers can find it challenging to set up a dataset properly for analysis.

- *Ranking questions* allow respondents to assign positions to some or all responses to a question. Ranking questions are a blend of ordered and multiple response questions. Analysis of ranking questions, beyond percentages, is limited to ordinal statistics, which can be challenging for novice researchers to select and interpret the correct measures.

The choice of whether to use open- or close-ended questions often is dependent on pragmatic considerations such as available support resources. The decision should not be decided simply on methodological preference. Ideally, the choice will be based on alignment with the goal and intended outcomes of the project. Two questions might be used to aid in this decision:

- Do the questions give respondents opportunities to answer in a way that addresses the project goals?
- Will the response types allow you to present data in meaningful way?

Specific Types of Questions

Following is a list of specific types of question that can be incorporated into an assessment instrument. The questions can be either open- or close ended, depending on whether choices are provided to respondents. A survey or questionnaire often incorporates multiple types.

- *Background/demographic questions* concern characteristics, traits, or attributes. Responses help the interviewer describe participants individually and in relation to others. These types of questions also can reveal aspects of a person's life that may shape his or her views, such as political affiliation or socioeconomic status.

- *Experience/behavior questions* concern descriptions of experiences and behaviors as well as related actions and activities. Responses can help the interviewer understand how aspects of an individual's background can influence his or her choices and/or actions.

- *Opinion/values questions* concern perceptions and interpretations. Responses reveal what a person thinks about a topic or issue and can give insight to intentions and values.

- *Feeling questions* concern emotional responses and thoughts about experiences. Patton (1990) noted that when asking feeling questions, the interviewer is looking for adjective responses such as the extent to which a person is happy, sad, confident, or uncertain. Feeling questions are distinct from opinion/values questions because of the intent to stimulate an emotional, rather than an analytical or interpretive response.

- *Knowledge questions* concern factual information or knowledge. These are things a person knows—not opinions or feelings. Responses can supply factual information to the researcher about the study, but also can reveal what a person believes to be factual.

- *Sensory questions* concern sensations. Responses give insight to how people physically experience things. Sensory questions are distinct from opinion or feeling questions because of the intent to enlighten how environmental stimuli might affect an experience. They also might be used to reveal an additional level of knowledge about a situation.

Sequencing Questions

An easily overlooked feature of an instrument that can be critical to its usability is how it is organized. Even an unstructured interview, which by definition would not have a fixed sequence, generally should exhibit a logical flow. Patton (1990) advocated beginning an instrument with easily answered, noncontroversial questions about present situations to encourage participants to talk descriptively. Asking participants for opinions or feelings should follow to help establish context. Questions about the future can be more difficult for respondents because they require speculation, which may be less reliable than questions about present or past experiences, opinions, feelings, or knowledge.

Many authors recommend saving demographic questions for the end of an instrument; however, some types of analyses are dependent on participant characteristics, so the choice of where to add them can vary. Generally, questions nonessential to the immediate study should be reserved for the end of an instrument.

Asking Clear Questions

Questions that are confusing or unclear to participants return responses unrelated to the intent of the question. With regard to survey questions specifically, Fowler (2009) cautioned "questions should all mean the same thing to all respondents. If two respondents understand the same question to mean different things, their answers may be different for that reason alone" (p. 92). Unclear questions can also affect rapport with an interviewee adversely, which can influence an entire session. Asking one question at a time can remedy many of the problems researchers encounter with clarity.

Another consideration is the audience. It is not necessary to use casual or slang terms to ask questions, but it can be important to learn if there is a preferred or specific term that participants use related to the topic. Patton (1990) noted that this means

> ... taking special care to find out what language the interviewee uses to describe the program, the staff, program activities, or whatever else the evaluator is interested in talking about, and then using that language provided by the interviewee in the rest of the interview. (p. 312)

Avoiding Leading Questions

Often, unclear questions are related to leading questions. Validity threats can arise when an interviewer looks for a specific response by suggesting it in the question. In many cases, interviewers do not recognize they are influencing responses. For example, an interviewer may have strong opinions that can be revealed when questions, either verbally or indirectly with an intonation or visual cue, encouraging the respondent to answer in ways aligned with the interviewer's beliefs. Frustration, which can arise when the interviewer is limited by time, also can lead to more direct and suggestive questioning. To help minimize problems with leading questions, Patton (1990) recommended being attentive to rapport and neutrality. Rapport is related to the interviewee; neutrality is related to the content of what a person says. Pragmatically, this means showing care about the content and the sharing (that is, building rapport) but not showing judgment about the content of the response (that is, maintaining neutrality).

Using Follow-Ups and Probes

At times, interviewers may want additional detail about a particular topic to provide richness to the data. Follow-up questions normally are not written prior to an interview, but some prompts might be listed on an instrument in case the interviewer wants to find out more detail. Researchers sometimes use the terms follow-up and probe synonymously, though a follow-up is generally a question, while a probe can be a question or a visual cue. Patton (1990) classified various forms of follow-ups such as *detail-oriented* questions (that is, basic questions to add detail to responses such as when, who, how, and so on), *elaborative* probes (that is, a gentle nod of the head, other visual cue, or simple request for more detail aimed at keeping the participant on the topic), *clarification* probes (for example, gently asking for additional explanation or restatement), and *contrast* probes (for example, asking how something compares to something else). Asking follow-up questions and probes requires skill beyond simply asking questions. Knowing when to probe or request additional detail comes from learning to listen very carefully to responses, being sensitive to the content an interviewee reveals, and knowing when to explore further, use the appropriate probe, or move on to the next question.

Assuring Quality

This chapter has stressed the importance of using researcher-developed or selected instruments to promote consistency, credibility, and standardization in assessment work. The value of the data collected is directly related to the quality of the instrument as well as the role and choices of the researcher. A number of methods and measures exist to judge the quality of data. We advocate piloting (prior to data collection) and pausing (during data collection) as two strategies of ensuring data are consistently collected and contribute to the focus of the project. For larger scale and external quantitative research projects, measures assessing external validity, content validity, test/re-test reliability, and internal consistency should be included as part of the pilot testing phase. For most student affairs assessment purposes, genuine attentiveness to pilot testing and pausing can address many of the major concerns related to quality.

Piloting

While there is no single process of determining validity and reliability of an instrument, administering a pilot prior to data collection often can address many of the more significant potential concerns for quality. For questionnaire research, we recommend that two to four individual interview sessions or two small focus groups be conducted to allow for adjustment between interviews. Ideally, the pilot sessions should allow the opportunity to test the type, sequence, wording, and clarity of questions as well as the need for additional probes or follow-ups that might be listed as prompts on the instrument. For survey research, we recommend pilot testing with at least two groups with 10–20 participants in each group (ideally, 30 in total) to meet minimal stability for statistical measures. Also, while it is ideal to administer the pilot survey under the same conditions as the full survey, administering an online survey in person can allow for clarification questions, give a general sense of how long the survey will take, and provide for immediate results to be analyzed and considered.

A major goal of piloting an instrument is to promote usability, or the ease with which an instrument can be administered, interpreted by the respondent, and scored by the researcher. Researchers who pilot surveys with individuals similar to those they will sample can address usability concerns efficiently. Fowler (2009) noted, "reducing measurement error through better questioning is one of the least costly ways to improve survey estimates" (p. 112). In a pilot test, the survey or questionnaire should be administered under the same conditions it will be given (addressing potential administration problems), pilot testers or interviewees should be asked to make notes about problematic questions (addressing potential interpretation issues), and afterward the responses should be scored or coded to see if the questions are individually and collectively interpretable and aligned with the goals of the project (addressing potential analysis problems).

Pausing

Pausing is a means of continually assessing quality during data collection. Qualitative researchers, partially in response to criticisms regarding validity and reliability, have developed a number of criteria for judging the viability of qualitative data. We advocate for pausing, or stopping at periodic points during data collection, and applying the following checks adapted from Lincoln and Guba's (1985) criteria for judging qualitative research, to ensure the quality of data regardless of type or form.

Assessment data collected from individuals or groups often are based on perceptions or perspectives, making participants the ultimate judge of *credibility*, or authenticity of the data from the viewpoint of the participant. Using member checking, the investigator asks participants, "Do these results seem accurate, based on your perspective?" Extending this technique to observation, event attendees or space users might be asked if the description seems accurate, just as a document creator or frequent user might be asked to review notes about the record for accurateness.

Our view is that all data are biased. Even a standardized survey instrument has to be chosen by an individual, as do the context and setting in which it is administered. Recognizing and accounting for the preconceptions and predispositions of the person who designed/selected the instrument and collected the data is known as *confirmability*, or the likelihood that the results could be similarly established or corroborated by others. Techniques to promote confirmability include maintaining a detailed record when examining data throughout the study, pursuing and documenting instances and outliers contradicting or opposing themes or results, and seeking bias or distortion during data collection and analysis.

Assessment data nearly always exist in a specific context and contexts frequently shift. How well data hold up in the face of change or differ by circumstance refers to *dependability*. In a way, the concept is related to statistical reliability, or the likelihood of obtaining comparable results under similar study conditions. Enhancing dependability means being attuned to changes in the setting describing how these changes affect the research.

Administering the Instrument

After determining and evaluating instrument, the next consideration is deciding who will collect data. Will you be working alone, or will data collection be a team effort or aided by assistants? Schuh and Upcraft (2000) emphasized the importance of recognizing biases among those collecting data. When using instruments that are researcher-driven, such as semi- or unstandardized interviews or unstructured observation forms, it is especially important to consider what personal stake those collecting the data may have in the study or its outcome. Similarly, we suggest caution when using assistants with no familiarity with the project, particularly when collecting qualitative data, as a lack of contextual understanding or nuances may limit their ability to recognize or to distinguish significant issues that may arise or be referenced. Interrater reliability must be ensured to minimize researcher bias.

Survey fatigue, which encompasses both survey and questionnaire-based research, is another issue that can affect data collection. With increasing pressure to publish among faculty and graduate students, an emphasis on undergraduate research at many college and universities, expanded use of external surveys on campus, and existing campus efforts such as course and program evaluations as well as regular institutional research studies, survey fatigue is likely to endure as well as to intensify. Gansemer-Topf and Wohlgemuth (2009) suggest some ways of overcoming survey fatigue, such as varying sampling techniques and delivery methods and sharing results with participants, which can help them feel as though their contribution is valued and meaningful.

Both of these considerations suggest the need for a student affairs divisional assessment coordinator who works with decision-makers to prioritize and maintain a master schedule of projects. Each calendar entry should include data collection dates as well as the target population to avoid oversurveying a particular group. Having a macro view of who is participating in various efforts also can help individual project coordinators identify potential partners for assistance with various aspects of an assessment study. For a further discussion of the role of a student affairs division assessment coordinator, see Livingston and Zerulik (2013).

Additional Considerations for Interviewing

Interviewing is a personal approach to data collection and as a result, some additional considerations should be kept in mind.

- The location of the interview can be important, even with casual questions. Participants may feel most comfortable in their setting; however, it may be distracting. Conversely, having participants meet in an office can be intimidating. When possible and when the content of the interview permits, we advise using neutral, public, but not overcrowded locations.

- If the investigator intends to record the interview, equipment should be checked in advance of the interview. Too often, we have recorded an interview only to find out that the microphone was placed in the wrong spot and did not pick up the audio very well.

- The instrument should be pilot tested for clarity with a similar audience, especially for new or inexperienced interviewers. It is disappointing to realize during a session that the questions, as worded, are not eliciting the responses that were intended.

- Recognize interview biases—these can come through in questions, during the session, and afterward when analyzing data. Qualitative researchers acknowledge that research is a subjective process, but being mindful of bias can help establish rapport and ensure neutrality.

- Watch and listen actively during the interview. An interviewee may not answer the question you asked or you may detect a visual or verbal cue that the interviewee has more to say.

- Realize that while it is desirable that interviewees feel comfortable enough during the interview to speak candidly, the interviewer is ultimately in control. Patton (1990) noted that maintaining control is knowing (1) what one wants to find out prior to the session, (2) asking the right questions, and (3) giving appropriate verbal and visual feedback. While some interviewees may have little to say or it is difficult to get long responses to questions, others will provide long-winded or irrelevant responses to questions. To maximize the time allotted for the session, a skilled interviewer needs to know when to carefully intervene to bring the interview back into focus. This might be done by saying, "I appreciate what you have told me, but I want to be sure to get your thoughts on . . . ."

As a final thought, we recall Merriam's (1998) advice that "the key to getting good data from interviews is asking questions; asking good questions takes practice" (p. 75). And an effective way of concluding an interview is to ask this question—Is there anything else you would like to let me know before we finish this conversation?

Additional Considerations for Surveys

Among the most often overlooked aspects of survey data collection are how to score and present results. When surveys ask respondents to rate something on a five-point scale of "strongly disagree" to "strongly agree", then later asks them to rate another item from "least applicable to me" to "most applicable to me" on a four-point scale, confusion may result. Still later, the survey might ask the respondents to circle a number ranging from 1 to 3. To allow for the most flexibility in data analysis, we advise consistency in response choices. When the initial version of a survey has been drafted, you might ask yourself, can most of these questions be asked using the same response type? If this is not possible given the nature of the questions, perhaps items can be grouped into sections as opposed to being mixed among each other.

We recommend analyzing results from the pilot test of the instrument prior to beginning the actual assessment. This process can reveal problems well before it is too late to make adjustments to the instrument.

Returning to Small Private College

This chapter began with a case study describing the assessment project Jana wanted to design to evaluate learning outcomes from participating in the admissions tour guide program at Private Small College (PSC). Jana ultimately wants to develop a pre/post survey, but feels she needs to create the instrument based on preliminary interview data. Assuming Jana is given permission to conduct the project, we ask that you provide the answers to the following questions about assessment, assuming that you are consulting with Jana in designing her instruments:

1. What type of questionnaire format and which types of questions should Jana ask?

2. What are the main reasons for choosing the format and question types?

3. What if she decided to conduct focus groups instead of interviews? How would the instrument change?

4. Assuming she completes the qualitative component of her assessment and is designing the survey, what other sources might she consider to help refine the questions?

5. Overall, how will she assess the quality of her instruments?

Discussion Questions

1. In what situations is it necessary to collect demographic data? What are some situations when it may not be necessary?

2. The chapter lists several advantages to piloting an instrument. Choose one of the instruments listed in the chapter. What are some ways you might pilot it?

3. Create a short list of questions that could be used across the division of student affairs in all data collection efforts. What are some reasons it would be beneficial to add a few standard questions to additional assessments?

4. Obtain and evaluate an existing instrument using the criteria provided in this chapter. What are some ways the instrument might be improved?

References

Berg, B. L. (2004). *Qualitative research methods*. Boston, MA: Allyn & Bacon.

Emerson, R. M., Fretz, R. I., & Shaw, L. L. (2011). *Writing ethnographic fieldnotes*. Chicago, IL: University of Chicago Press.

Fowler, F. J. (2009). *Survey research methods*. Thousand Oaks, CA: Sage.

Gansemer-Topf, A. M., & Wohlgemuth, D. R. (2009). Selecting, sampling, and soliciting subjects. In J. H. Schuh & Associates (Eds.), *Assessment methods for student affairs* (pp. 77–106). San Francisco, CA: Jossey-Bass.

Hyman, L., Lamb, J., & Bulmer, M. (2006). The use of pre-existing survey questions: Implications for data quality. *European Conference on Quality in Survey Statistics* (pp. 1–8). Retrieved from http://tinyurl.com/p32e4n7

Kelly, B. T. (2003). Focus group interviews. In F. K. Stage & K. Manning (Eds.), *Research in the college context: Approaches and methods* (pp. 49–62). New York, NY: Brunner-Routledge.

Lincoln, Y. S., & Guba, E. G. (1985). *Naturalistic inquiry.* Newbury Park, CA: Sage.

Livingston, C. H., & Zerulik, J. D. (2013). The role of the assessment coordinator in a division of student affairs. In J. H. Schuh (Ed.), *Selected contemporary assessment issues* (pp. 15–24). New Directions for Student Services no. 142. San Francisco, CA: Jossey-Bass.

Merriam, S. B. (1998). *Qualitative research and case study applications in education.* San Francisco, CA: Jossey-Bass.

Patton, M. Q. (1990). *Qualitative evaluation and research methods* (2nd ed.). Thousand Oaks, CA: Sage.

Saunders, K., & Cooper, R. M. (2009). Instrumentation. In J. H. Schuh & Associates (Eds.), *Assessment methods for student affairs* (pp. 107–140). San Francisco, CA: Jossey-Bass.

Schuh, J. H., & Upcraft, M. L. (2001). Conducting focus groups. In J. H. Schuh & M. L. Upcraft (Eds.), *Assessment practice in student affairs: An applications manual* (pp. 42–56). San Francisco, CA: Jossey-Bass.

Vogt, W. P. (2005). *Dictionary of statistics & methodology* (3rd ed.). Thousand Oaks, CA: Sage.

Yin, R. (1994). *Case study research: Design and methods* (2nd ed.). Thousand Oaks, CA: Sage.

10

ASSESSING STUDENT CAMPUS ENVIRONMENTS

Colleges and universities are expected to create high-quality environments supportive of student learning and success. Features of the campus environment include just about everything one envisions when thinking about college: residence halls, parking lots, stately buildings and lawns, arches, arboretum, carillons, stadiums, computers, classrooms, libraries, laboratories, bicycles, faculty, students, staff, groundskeepers, Greek letter houses, buses, and so on. How all this works together produces a distinct campus culture. The environment in which college students live and learn is vast and encompasses a wide range of dimensions including the physical, structural, organizational, psychological, social, pedagogical, cultural, and virtual. Understanding the significant effect that the campus environment has on the quality of students' experience, and the potential to design and shape it to be beneficial for student learning and success, makes it an important topic for assessment.

Arising from the common definition of environment that we use to frame this chapter, which comprises the circumstances, objects, and conditions that surround and act on individuals, college and university environments are distinct and have a significant influence on students, the quality of their experience in college, and a host of desirable outcomes. Astin (1968) defines the campus environment broadly as "including any characteristic of the college that constitutes a potential stimulus for the students" (p. 3), and asserted the powerful influence of the environment on student development. Pascarella (1985) further theorizes that institutional characteristics, including size, location, type and mission, and the campus environment influence student develop-ment and that together these elements produce a unique college climate.

College student behavior is also influenced by the envi-ronment, including physical space, norms of student cultures, and the perceptions of students (Kuh, Kinzie, Schuh, Whitt, & Associates, 2010; Kuh, Schuh, Whitt, & Associates, 1991). The influence of campus climate has been further examined employing an ecological framework, which conceptualizes the relationship between students and the college environment as both reciprocal and dynamic (Milem, Chang, & antonio, 2005). The campus and its environs, what some have called "place," is also a powerful resource for making positive change on campus (Kenney, Dumont, & Kenney, 2005). Given the significant role of the campus environment in students' college experiences—their development, learning, and success—and that the environment can be manipulated, it is critical to understand the campus and know how to assess it.

Scenarios Related to Student Environments

To contextualize the important work of assessing campus environ-ments consider the following scenarios:

- An urban campus is interested in creating a greater sense of intellectual vibrancy and increased interaction among students and faculty. Although the current student pattern is to leave campus as soon as classes end, attendance at university events is unpredictable—sometimes standing room only, and other times practically deserted—and faculty report that most contact with students is via the learning management system.

- The new division of student success is striving to achieve enhanced collaboration and connection to provide more holistic student support across its offices of learning support, advising, counseling, and financial aid. Cross-training has increased professional staff members' understanding of the relationship between their responsibilities, but staff wonder if the distance between these offices and services, and the historical "bad reputation" of one of the offices, is inhibiting effectiveness.

- Prospective students and visitors to a metropolitan university are frequently found wandering around the admissions office building, searching for the right entrance. Fortunately, attentive groundskeepers, public safety officers and faculty are around to guide guests to the second-floor welcome office. Once there, visitors find a friendly admissions staff and informative tour guides.

- Scores on the Supportive Environment measure of the National Survey of Student Engagement (NSSE), specifically students' perception of institutional emphasis on support to succeed academically, and quality of interactions with peers, have risen significantly over the past five years since the campus implemented enhancements to the study spaces in the residential living units, expanded access to group study rooms in the library and student center, and improved coffee and other snack services adjacent to group study space.

- A campus committed to fostering a caring community and for creating opportunities for constructive participation in a multicultural world, learned from its Campus Climate for Diversity Study that Latino students had higher rates of attrition than other groups, perceived the campus environment as hostile, and had numerous problems in their adjustment to campus life.

These scenarios illustrate different images of the campus environment and the ways it can be affirming, helpful, inclusive, and clear, or discouraging, alienating, and confusing. The scenarios also suggest important questions about what is known about the campus environment and how assessment results can be useful to a campus. What might the urban campus do to learn more about student patterns, students' motivations for participating in events, and habits for interacting with faculty? How far apart are the support offices in the new division of student success, and what information is available about the reputation of the offices? How are visitors directed to the admissions office and what do prospective students and families think about the quality of tours? How is the campus using its NSSE scores to affirm the investment in improving campus space and what else does it need to document? How should the campus respond to the concerning campus climate results?

This chapter introduces the concept of the campus environment as an important consideration for assessment. First, a conceptual overview of the theory of campus environments is presented. Then, several approaches to assessing campus environments are introduced. Examples of environmental assessments are also highlighted.

Conceptualizing and Theorizing Campus Environments

In the broadest definition, the term *campus environment* refers to the entirety of the college and university surroundings and conditions in which people live and function. It includes all the conditions and influences, such as physical, biological, organizational, and social stimuli, that affect the growth and development of living things (Strange, 2003). The concept implies a multiplicity of individuals, forces, and systems interacting, and usually suggests a physical space, or a virtual equivalent, and a dynamic network of factors and conditions. Every institution has its own culture, language, behavior, artifacts, rules, and symbols that make it unique (Kuh, Schuh, Whitt, & Associates, 1991).

Bess and Dee (2008) add that the general environment consists of broad forces that affect all organizations, while the proximate environment includes specific external factors that affect a particular organization. Examples of the former could be political, social, or economic trends, while examples of the latter could include customers, competitors, or special interest groups (see Bess & Dee, 2008, for further details about organizational environments).

Most relevant for assessment and the goal to use information to evaluate and improve educational quality and the student experience, campus environments are important to understand because they exert an influence on students. Likewise, students bring their own life experience to the collegiate experience, which then crosses with the campus environment. At this intersection, the campus environment has a significant effect on the quality of students' experience, influencing how students feel and what they do by presenting complex choices and opportunities, with consequences that may or may not be productive for learning and success.

Models and theories have been advanced on the dynamics of campus environments in higher education. Several resources provide a thorough introduction to the concept of campus environment including the work of Strange and Banning (2001, 2015), Strange (2003), Kuh (2009), and Cuyjet (2011), just to name a few. These resources provide the necessary background and extensive theoretical foundations for employing the concept of campus environment in assessment. A brief review of several central concepts provides a rudimentary introduction to the topic.

One of the theorists identified in student affairs literature as contributing to understanding human behavior and the influence of the environment is Kurt Lewin. Lewin (1936) explored the relationship between the person and the environment and proposed the straightforward formula $B = f(P \times E)$ to explain that behavior (B) is a function (f) of the interaction between person (P) and the environment (E). The application of this theory to the college setting led to the understanding that students shape the environment and are in turn shaped by it (Cuyjet, 2011; Kuh, 2009). Huebner and Lawson (1990) employed Lewin's line of thinking in their assessments of college environments and found that the theory helps explain and guide environmental assessment activities. However, they point out that there are far more environmental variables that affect students and the complexity of the interactions are difficult to comprehend and control, while Cuyjet (2011) asserts that the formula may overemphasize the cultural majority of students on campus and ignore the differences that may exist among people who do not reflect the dominant culture.

Strange and Banning (2001, 2015) offer a four-dimensional model for understanding campus environments. The *physical dimension*, which addresses features of the campus natural and synthetic physical plant; the *human aggregate dimension*, which includes the transmission and reflection of the collective characteristics of the campus human population; the *organizational dimension*, which emphasizes the structures that serve specific goals that enhance or inhibit certain environmental characteristics or outcomes; and the *constructed or perceptual dimension* which emphasizes the collective perceptions and meanings that campus members put on these interactions. This comprehensive four-dimensional framework is useful for the development of a scheme for educational design and for framing environmental assessment studies.

Kuh (2009) conceptualizes a broad overview of the more important contextual conditions that foster student development and learning, outlines a process for assessing these conditions, and highlights how student affairs professionals can positively shape campus environments. Several identifiable dimensions of college and university environments have an impact on students, including classroom experiences, pedagogies, coursework, institutional environments, and cultures. Moreover, institutional properties such as location, physical, social and psychological environments, and faculty and student cultures influence student behavior. For example, the size and shape of built structures, location of faculty offices in relation to classrooms, and students' perceptions of what the institution emphasizes in terms of the nature of student-faculty interaction, all contribute to how often students interact with faculty outside the classroom and the extent to which this interaction is meaningful and helpful or infrequent and unsupportive.

Three sets of institutional properties substantially influence student success, including an institution's mission and philosophy, student engagement in educationally purposeful practice, and campus cultures (Kuh, 2009). An example of the way a salient institutional mission clarifies expectations for behavior, includes the emphasis of internationalism and multiculturalism that one finds at Macalester College; this mission orients student, faculty, and staff to the importance of affirming difference and international understanding. The properties of student engagement, best exemplified in the assessment activities associated with the National Survey of Student Engagement (NSSE) and the Community College Survey of Student Engagement (CCSSE), accentuate the characteristics of engagement, and the importance of creating and maintaining supportive campus environments, including supports for students to succeed academically and socially, and fostering high-quality relationships among students, faculty, and the institutions' administrative personnel. At Fayetteville State University, for example, there is a strong ethos of support for students to be successful and to help students rise to meet high expectations. The third element for campus environments is campus culture. This perspective is demonstrated at campuses interested in fostering student-centered cultures to enhance undergraduate learning (Kinzie & Kuh, 2007). Student cultures also exert an influence on student learning because they determine the kinds of people with whom students spend time, and the values that are reinforced, including, for example, how much to study and when.

Finally, ecological perspectives on campus environment, such as Bronfenbrenner's (1979) ecological framework, add another level of complexity to campus environment models. Ecological theory reinforces that individual development is influenced by interactions with others and their immediate surroundings. This framework is perhaps the broadest model for understanding campus environments and is particularly salient for considering the multiple influences of family, communities/ neighborhoods, culture, and the connections between all these elements, in today's students' complex lives. For example, a new community college student may be simultaneously engaging closely with his or her family, off-campus employer, and other students, and also with the policies and demands of the college.

These fundamental conceptualizations illustrate the dynamics of understanding campus environments. Implicit in the perspective of the campus as an environment is the assumption that colleges and universities bear responsibility for the design and creation of environments, and arranging them so that they serve their educational mission and support students' educational pursuits. Educational settings designed with an understanding of the influence of the environment and the dynamics of human interaction are more likely to achieve these ends. Although campus environments are indeed a mix of the deliberate and the accidental—a combination of planned and unanticipated events—educators and practitioners of assessment can benefit from understanding how environment affects students and the approaches to studying the environment, and then modifying conditions in ways that support students and their learning and success.

The Purpose of Assessing Campus Environments

Given the influence of the campus environment on all aspects of the college experience, and the unique conditions that exist at every institution, there is considerable interest in understanding how the various elements and dimensions of the college or university environment affect student development, learning, and success. For example, understanding the extent to which a growing urban campus is as welcoming to a new cadre of traditional-aged students as it has been to its predominately adult professional, part-time students, is critical as the institution makes decisions about investing in traditional student interests, including student activities and residence halls, or if the design of more lower-division learning communities will serve students' needs. Simply put, "environmental assessment determines and evaluates how various elements and conditions of the college campus milieu affect student learning and growth" (Upcraft & Schuh, 1996, p. 167). Every campus has unique concerns and questions about the campus environment that deserve exploration.

The purpose of environmental assessment is to develop a deeper understanding of the conditions of the environment, and most importantly, for educators and all those responsible for the campus environment to use this information to optimize the circumstances for students to learn and grow. The idea that campuses can learn from environmental assessments and use this information to improve is illustrated in the growing emphasis on the value of campus climate studies to make the institution more inclusive of lesbian, gay, bisexual, and transgendered (LGBT) students. For example, an LGBT campus climate study completed at a large state university, which employed data from a statistically valid and reliable national survey, complemented with 50 individual interviews and a dozen focus groups with students and faculty, suggested that LGBT students, staff, and faculty found the environment in which they study and work to be personally challenging and perceived a lack of support from many of those around them; they were also twice as likely as heterosexuals to say they had been targets of derogatory remarks and singled out as the "resident authority" on LGBT issues, and shared many personal examples of harassment. This extensive climate study resulted in a series of actions to make the campus more inclusive including allowing students the ability to have a preferred name on their ID cards, integrating LGBT issues in curricular and cocurricular education, and increased training for bias incident and hate-crime reporting systems, among others. Like all assessment activities, an important phase of the assessment project is making use of results for improvement purposes.

The assessment of campus environments is complicated because of the multidimensional facets of environments, including the physical, human, and perceptual, plus the interaction of all three. To develop the most complete understanding of campus environment, it is important to acknowledge and study as many of the elements as possible. Further complicating the assessment of campus environments is the fact that every person on campus is affected differently; thus it is possible to have multiple unique, and competing, perspectives of the environment. Despite these complications, the assessment of campus environment is an important approach to develop rich, institutionally nuanced perspectives of the campus.

Assessing Campus Environments

To understand the various elements and conditions of the college campus that affect student learning and growth and then to consider what this means for the design of effective educational environments that support student learning and success, it is necessary to thoughtfully approach the assessment of campus environment. Assessment results about the campus environment, including perceptions of students, faculty, and staff, considered in relation to environmental frameworks, and combined with research about educational practices that support learning and success, can provide campus leaders with immediately useful information to inform efforts to improve educational quality.

There are many approaches to assessing college environments including surveys, observation, focus groups, interviews, cultural audits, and ethnography. Surveys to assess student and faculty

experiences with the elements of the institutional culture and climate for inclusion, and instruments that ask students about their
behaviors and perceptions of support and institutional emphasis,
coupled with observations of student behaviors in campus settings and offices, and in-depth studies of particular student groups
or cultures, are long-standing approaches to collecting information about campus environments. This section introduces several
approaches and examples for assessing campus environment.

Approaches and Frames for Assessing Campus Environments

Leonard Baird (1988) articulated a simple frame of the essential
elements in any assessment of the campus environment. Baird
identified four approaches: (1) demographic, which includes the
use of data such as student characteristics, enrollment patterns,
and major distribution; (2) perceptual, which relies on responses
to surveys and interviews to access perceptions and impressions of
the campus environment; (3) behavioral, which assesses observ-
able actions of students, faculty, staff, and others on campus; and
(4) multimethod, which employs a combination of demographic,
perceptual, and behavioral assessments. These four organizing
concepts may be employed to structure a comprehensive study of
campus environments.

Strange and Banning's (2001, 2015) four facets of an
environmental assessment model—*physical, human aggregate,
organizational, and constructed*—provide a more explicit framework through which Baird's (1988) approaches to studying
environments can be emphasized. The four dimensions are
briefly defined next, and connected to assessment examples.

The *physical* environment is one of the easiest dimensions to
observe and understand. Physical properties are obvious in nature
and comprise such things as landscaping, architecture, climate,
lighting, and the placement of sidewalks and buildings. It can also
include layout and space, accessibility, and cleanliness. Physical

features can convey nonverbal messages sometimes more strongly than can verbal messages by either welcoming or discouraging, or valuing or disrespecting. For example, a lack of seating near classrooms discourages students from arriving early or meeting with classmates and faculty for informal discussions after class, in the same way a large wall in the student union adorned with photos of campus leaders, but featuring few images of students of color, can reduce underrepresented minority students' sense of belonging overall, and alienate them from positions of campus leadership (Kinzie & Mulholland, 2008). Marshall (2012) assessed aspects of the physical space in an academic advising office, noting the connection between lighting and psychological arousal and overheated spaces to hostility (Graetz & Goliber, 2003), and how the layout of the advisor's desk can present a formal or friendly impression. The assessment of physical properties of the campus can inform the creation of welcoming space and an environment conducive to learning and success.

An assessment of the physical environment would be a useful way to explore the opening scenario involving the lost visitors at a metropolitan university. The assessment could involve a mix of observations about the actions of visitors when they arrive at campus, a review of signs and maps leading to the admission office, and interviews with public safety and other staff who typically interact with lost visitors, as well as a survey to assess the impressions of recent visitors about getting to the office, as well as their perceptions of services. Information from a quick environmental assessment could help identify aspects of the physical environment that could help guide visitors to the office and bolster their positive interaction with staff.

The *human aggregate* dimension is founded on the concept that environments are transmitted through people and reflect the collective characteristics of the people who are influenced by them. This component refers to how the environment reflects the dominant characteristics of the people in it, and is akin to identifying the campus's "personality" or student culture.

People in the environment are pleased or dissatisfied with their environment based on their interactions (Strange & Banning, 2001, 2015). The characteristics of the human aggregate dimension are comprised of demographics (such as gender, age, or race-ethnicity) and psychological traits (personality types, interests, and styles). One emphasis in the human aggregate theory is person-environment interaction. Specifically, the degree of congruence between persons and their environment is important to understanding how someone will function within the environment and whether they will adapt to it, leave it, or try to change it.

The aggregate dimension is important to the assessment of campus climate for underrepresented populations. For example, according to Rankin (2003), assessments of campus climate can illustrate that while institutional missions suggest that higher education values multicultural awareness and understanding and the creation of welcoming and inclusive climates, the college environment is a focused aggregate dominated by heterosexism, with dynamics that are incongruent with LGBT student interests and needs. This frame is also illustrated in the components of the opening scenario regarding the campus climate for diversity, in that the study featured demographic information about Latino student retention, and surveys about students' perceptions of the environment and interactions with others and interview data to understand students' adjustments experiences, disaggregated by race-ethnicity.

The *organizational* facet includes the organized structures in the environment that serve specific goals, including decision-making, rules, and rewards. Established policies and procedures, the distribution of resources, protocols, and how goals are achieved construct the organizational dimensions of any environment. This dimension reflects how colleges and universities are organized, including the division of labor, distribution of power, execution of policies and procedures, and decisions about how things are done.

The policies and procedures in place at many colleges and universities exist to assist students to be academically successful. For example, practices and policies that encourage students to take advantage of academic support services, writing centers, tutoring, leadership opportunities, and other educational programs, are organizational structures that create and sustain a culture that promotes student success. Information about organizational productivity and the extent to which the environment supports student success, as monitored by measures such as NSSE, or revealed in studies of the frequency of use of the writing center and observing students' interactions with tutors in the writing center, can point to areas of campus life that are problematic, or underperforming in general or for particular groups of students. The organizational frame could similarly be employed to assess the concerns in the opening scenario about barriers to integrating the offices of learning support, advising, counseling, and financial aid.

The *constructed* environment assumes that the collective perceptions of how participants subjectively characterize the context and culture of the setting creates the reality for the environment they inhabit (Museus, 2008; Strange & Banning, 2001, 2015). This environment is entirely dependent on each inhabitant of the environment. Therefore, the main source of information about the constructed environment is the perception of each student. This aspect of the model is amenable to traditional forms of assessment including self-reports of participants' activities and perceptions of institutional emphasis or by interviewing students and students in groups about their perspectives. The opening scenario reporting results from the campus climate study could be expanded by conducting a more intensive study of Latino students' experiences on campus including more in-depth interviews and observations to understand Latino students' expectations for adjusting to the campus and what they find supportive and inhospitable.

Assessing Environments Using Surveys

Surveys are a popular approach for assessing the campus environment. Surveys designed for institutions to understand the aggregate experience of students on campus include the NSSE, and the companion two-year instrument, the CCSSE. The instruments are multidimensional, evidence-based, and have been tested for validity and reliability. These assessment tools have provided more than 2,000 campuses with information about students' engagement in educationally effective practices and importantly, their perceptions of the environment for learning. Student engagement results, combined with results from the Faculty Survey of Student Engagement (FSSE) about faculty practices and perceptions of student engagement, can provide institutions a portrait of the student experience, the opportunity to disaggregate and explore by subpopulations and, for example, identify aspects of the learning environment misaligned with the institutional mission. Additional information about the technical aspects of conducting surveys is included in Chapters 6 and 9.

The opening scenario involving the institution with improved NSSE scores illustrates how survey results can first be used to pinpoint aspects of the physical and aggregate environment that are below institutional expectations or to benchmarked institutions. The low Supportive Environment scores helped that campus launch a more extensive examination, involving focus groups with students in particular campus locations to learn more about where they study, interact with peers, and study in groups, and so on. The campus took action to improve, and then examined follow-up NSSE survey results to determine if anything improved and to gauge if the changes made a difference in students behaviors and perceptions.

Focused instruments to measure campus climate, for example, or to study the experience of underrepresented student populations, and to explore specific environments, including residence halls and the student union, or to query specific student subcultures, such as athletes and students in Greek life, are available. For example, the Higher Education Research Institute's Diverse Learning Environment (DLE) survey, which assesses the impact of the diverse environments that help shape student learning, captures student perceptions regarding the institutional climate; campus practices as experienced with faculty, staff, and peers; and student learning outcomes (see http://heri.ucla.edu /dleoverview.php). Diverse student populations are at the crux of the survey, and the instrument is based on studies of diverse students and the complexity of issues that range from student mobility to intergroup relations (Hurtado, Arellano, Cuellar, & Guillermo-Wann, 2011; Hurtado, Griffin, Arellano, & Cuellar, 2008).

Assessing the campus climate by employing the Diverse Learning Environments (DLE) survey provides campuses information about students' perceptions regarding the institutional climate and campus practices. One campus learned, for example that with respect to the factor score for Sense of Belonging, their under-represented minority students (URMs) scored significantly lower than comparison groupings. Results related to the measure of Institutional Commitment to Diversity were particularly concerning given the significant difference between URMs and other respondents. On the other hand, measures of Curriculum of Inclusion and Co-Curricular Diversity Activities were positive for URMs. Though no one single measure can capture the complex interactions, behaviors, peer effects, attitudes, perceptions, and so on, associated with campus climate, the DLE results provided valuable data regarding the different perceptions, attitudes, and experiences of the institutions' diverse undergraduate population.

Surveys that are designed to assess the dimensions of quality and experiences of students in particular environments are useful for focused assessments of particular offices and units. For example, a suite of questionnaires available through Educational Benchmarking Inc. (EBI), is available to assess housing quality and the influence of different environmental conditions. By electing to use more focused surveys, assessment professionals can secure the information they need to evaluate effectiveness, examine performance in relation to professional or national standards, and inform continuous improvement initiatives.

Although approaches using quantitative measures can provide helpful information to pinpoint strengths and shortcomings in the college environment, they do not fully capture all the elements of college environments, nor are they sufficient for collecting information about environmental aspects that can be readily observed, such as how students interact in the campus union, or how well a new learning commons is facilitating study groups.

Assessment professionals who can actively explore the environment with an eye toward inventorying what transpires in campus spaces, and to determine if students are using spaces as intended, provides salient information about the campus environment. For example, concern about low NSSE Support Environment scores caught the attention of the campus in the opening scenario. However, the institution needed to supplement survey results with additional demographic information about student grade point averages by residence hall, observational studies of how students were using study space in residence halls, the union, and the library, as well as swipe-card analysis from the coffee shop and snap surveys to assess perceptions of space and who was using group study spaces. These assessments were compiled and provided to administrators who used the results to design improvements to campus space. Follow-up results on NSSE provide some evidence that the enhancements made a difference.

Assessing Campus Culture

Culture is a powerful element in all organizations. It is what connects and gives meaning to activities and events, and it deeply affects everything that happens on college and university

238 ASSESSMENT IN STUDENT AFFAIRS

campuses (Kuh, 2009). Kuh and Whitt (1988) define culture as the "collective, mutually shaping patterns of norms, values, practices, beliefs, and assumptions that guide the behavior of individuals and groups in higher education and provide a frame of reference within which to interpret the meaning of events and actions" (pp. 12–13). Culture gives meaning to members by emphasizing the institution's unique characteristics. Culture is difficult to identify and assess because it represents the taken-for-granted beliefs and assumptions that form the basis for how people interact and make sense of the environment. Culture is difficult to explain, and the complexity of layers of culture, and influence of subcultures, make it challenging to grasp and describe. Despite these challenges, the assessment of campus culture can provide an in-depth analysis of the cultural properties of the institution, reveal how members interpret and make meaning of properties and events, and expose the formation and behavior of groups within the institution.

Several resources are available to assist in conducting assessments of campus culture. Kuh (2009) summarizes the key issues in assessing environmental influences and conducting an audit of an institutions culture and its policies and practices. Cultural assessments and audits can be conducted campus wide or focus on a particular context, such as examining the impact of recently constructed suite-style residence halls on community building and belonging. Assessment practitioners seeking a step-by-step approach to conducting a cultural assessment could begin with the *Inventory for Student Engagement and Success* (Kuh, Kinzie, Schuh, & Whitt, 2005), which provides structured prompts and templates for guiding explorations of the influence of campus culture.

The adoption of a cultural lens to study campus environment has been increasingly employed in efforts to understand campus diversity and cross-cultural engagement, and to create inclusive campus environments (Museus, 2007, 2008; Rankin & Reason, 2008). Museus (2008) outlined the qualitative and quantitative approaches, including surveys, interviews, and observations, and the review of institutional documents, that can be employed to assess the impact of cultural factors on the experience and behavior of college students and to understand the elements of campus culture, and articulated a dozen practical guidelines for designing and conducting a campus culture assessment. Some of these recommendations include: focusing on student attitudes, feelings, thoughts, and experiences as the primary sources of data to understand cross-cultural engagement; diversifying data sources by exploring subcultures; being prepared to hear things that challenge existing conceptions of institutional culture; investing resources to study culture since such studies can be costly in terms of time and money; expecting culture studies to be messy; and considering the value of involving external assessors and evaluators to gain objective or new perspectives, among others.

Ethnography is a methodological tradition that has long served as a guide in pursuing the examination of culture. Ethnographic work aims to uncover and explicate the ways in which people come to understand, account for, take action, and otherwise manage their day-to-day situation (Magolda 1999; Schuh & Whitt, 1988). Iloh and Tierney (2014) introduce the ways that ethnography is useful for understanding recent shifts in higher education, including online education, for-profit colleges, and adult students, and offer methodological recommendations and directions for greater use of ethnographic approaches in higher education. An ethnographic study of a campus can contribute a deeper understanding of the culture, and for example, how the institution is helping students achieve their educational goals. A mission statement may express an institution's dedication to student success, but what are students' constructions and understandings of this mission? Interviews with students may pose broad questions, such as How do you define student success? and What does the institution do to support student success? Combined with other more extensive ethnographic approaches, including participant observation in offices on campus dedicated to student success, could be useful. Ethnographic approaches to studying campus culture could be helpful to the urban campus in the opening scenario, in trying to understand intellectual vibrancy and students' participation in campus life. Observations and interviews with students at events and immediately after class could bring into focus campus culture and student life.

Assessing Campus Climate

Although *campus culture* and *climate* are terms that are sometimes used interchangeably, Bauer (1998) asserts that the terms are distinct. Campus climate refers to the current perceptions, attitudes, and expectations that define the institution and its members. It is different from culture, which is holistic and focused on deep patterns of beliefs and organizational values. Climate can reference specific sections of parts of an environment, and is distinctly about the atmosphere or style. The major features of climate include participant attitudes, perceptions, or observations, and patterns of beliefs that can be compared among groups or over time. In addition, climate is considered to be more susceptible to change than culture.

Greater awareness of the extent to which members of the campus community experience the environment differently based on their group membership and group status on campus (Museus & Harris, 2010; Rankin & Reason, 2005), and concerns about creating more inclusive campus environments have increased assessments of campus climate. Campus climate is conceptualized as "the current attitudes, behaviors, and standards of faculty, staff, administrators, and students concerning the level of respect for individual needs, abilities, and potential" (Rankin & Reason, 2008, p. 264). This includes the experience of individuals and groups, and the quality and extent of the interaction between those groups and individuals.

Assessments of the campus climate for diversity have been undertaken on many college campuses. Hurtado, Milem, Clayton-Pederson, and Allen (1998, 1999) conceptualized a climate for diversity framework with four dimensions: (1) compositional diversity, (2) historical legacy of inclusion or exclusion, (3) psychological climate, and (4) behavioral climate. These elements can all be assessed for a full understanding of campus climate for diversity. For example, compositional diversity is simply the proportional representation of various student populations, whereas historical legacy of inclusion or exclusion accounts for the history that a university has with the target population, and psychological climate refers to group members' sense of inclusion and support. These dimensions are useful ways to frame a campus climate study of diversity. Institutions have conducted surveys to assess a range of diversity dimensions, for example, many of the University of Wisconsin system institutions have employed the Campus Climate Survey to measure the climate of diversity and inclusiveness on campus with regard to race, ethnicity, gender identity, and sexual orientation, religious affiliation, veteran status, and so forth. Some campuses have also conducted qualitative assessments to capture students' perspectives on the campus climate for diversity using a combination of survey data, existing documentation about campus diversity efforts, focus groups with students, and interviews with faculty and administrators to foster efforts to improve campus climate.

The purpose of conducting climate assessments often is to influence a foundation for institutional change by evaluating the environment's relations to issues of diversity and the climate for racial diversity (Harper & Hurtado, 2007; Hurtado et al., 1998; Museus, 2008; Rankin, 2006; Smith, 2009). Assessments of the climate for LGBT students and for gender identity on campus have been the more recent focus of climate surveys (Rankin, 2006). Rankin (2003) was the first to conduct a national study of campus climate for LGBT students. This study demonstrated that a third of LGBT undergraduates had experienced harassment within the year, and found that derogatory remarks were the most prominent form of harassment. These national assessments of campus climate and local surveys have provided institutions insights and directions to create more inclusive and affirming practices and policies.

Closing Thoughts about Assessing Campus Environments

The campus environment is vast, encompassing a wide range of dimensions including the physical, structural, organizational, psychological, social, pedagogical, cultural, and virtual, and exerts a significant influence on students and their experiences in college, shaping students perceptions and behavior. The campus environment can be welcoming or inhospitable, clear or confusing, or engaging or dull, and unique conditions exist at every college campus.

The features and properties of campus environments affect the extent to which students feel they belong and are supported in their learning. Given the role that campus environment plays in supporting or inhibiting student learning and success, and that environment can be manipulated and improved, it is critical for colleges and universities to understand the campus environment and know how to assess it. Assessments of campus environments can provide colleges and universities vital information about the dimensions of students' experience and insights into what needs to improve. To more fully understand how students function in their environment and how campus environments can be optimally designed to ensure all students succeed and thrive, it is important to conduct a range of assessments of the campus environment.

Discussion Questions

1. Consider again the five opening scenarios and the questions raised about them:

   a. What might the urban campus do to learn more about student patterns, students' motivation for participating in events, and habits for interacting with faculty?

   b. How far apart are the support offices in the new division of student success, and what information is available about the reputation of the offices?

   c. How are visitors directed to the admissions office and what do prospective students and families think about the quality of tours?

   d. How is the campus using its NSSE scores to affirm the investment in improving campus space and what else does it need to document?

   e. How should the campus respond to the concerning campus climate results?

   f. What environmental assessments could be conducted to further explore these contexts? Which scenarios would benefit from a climate assessment or an assessment of the campus culture?

2. Select one of Strange and Banning's (2015) four dimensions of the campus environment. Then identify an example of this dimension on your campus and interpret what if anything this expresses about student success.

3. What are the benefits and limitations of conducting assessments of the campus environment?

4. What campus climate studies might be important to conduct to understand today's college students and institutions?

References

Astin, A. (1968). *The college environment*. Washington, DC: American Council on Education.

Baird, L. (1988). The college environment revisited: A review of research and theory. In J. Smart (Ed.), *Higher education: Handbook of theory and research* (Vol. 4, pp. 1–52). New York, NY: Agathon.

Bauer, K. W. (1998). Editor's notes. In K. W. Bauer (Ed.), *Campus climate: Understanding the critical components of today's colleges and universities* (pp. 1–5). New Directions for Institutional Research no. 98. San Francisco, CA: Jossey-Bass.

Bess, J. L., & Dee, J. R. (2008). *Understanding college and university organization*. Sterling, VA: Stylus.

Bronfenbrenner, U. (1979). *The ecology of human development: Experiments by nature and design*. Cambridge, MA: Harvard University Press.

Cuyjet, M. J. (2011). Environmental influences on college culture. In M. Cuyjet, M. Howard-Hamilton, & D. Cooper (Eds.), *Multiculturalism on campus: Theory, models, and practices for understanding diversity and creating inclusion* (pp. 37–63). Sterling, VA: Stylus.

Graetz, K. A., & Goliber, M. J. (2003). Designing collaborative learning places: Psychological foundations and new frontiers. In N. Van Note Chism & D. J. Bickford (Eds.), *The importance of physical space in creating supportive learning environments* (pp. 13–22). New Directions for Teaching and Learning no. 92. San Francisco, CA: Jossey-Bass.

Harper, S., & Hurtado, S. (2007). Nine themes in campus racial climates and implications for institutional transformation. In S. R. Harper & L. D. Patton (Eds.), *Responding to the realities of race on campus* (pp. 7–24). New Directions for Student Services no. 120. San Francisco, CA: Jossey-Bass.

Huebner, L., & Lawson, J. (1990). Understanding and assessing college environments. In D. G. Creamer (Ed.), *College student development: Theory and practice* (pp. 127–151). ACPA Media Publication #49. Alexandria, VA: American College Personnel Association Publications.

Hurtado, S., Arellano, L., Cuellar, M., & Guillermo-Wann, C. (2011). *Diverse Learning Environments Survey Instrument: Introduction and select factors*. Retrieved from http://www.heri.ucla.edu/dleoverview.php

Hurtado, S., Griffin, K. A., Arellano, L., & Cuellar, M. (2008). Assessing the value of climate assessment: Progress and future directions. *Journal of Diversity in Higher Education, 1*(4), 204–221.

Hurtado, S., Milem, J., Clayton-Pedersen, A., & Allen, W. (1998). Enacting campus climates for racial/ethnic diversity through educational policy and practice. *The Review of Higher Education, 21*(3), 278–297.

Hurtado, S., Milem, J., Clayton-Pedersen, A., & Allen, W. (1999). *Enacting diverse learning environments: Improving the climate for racial/ethnic diversity in higher education*. Washington, DC: The George Washington University.

Iloh, C., & Tierney, W. (2014). Using ethnography to understand twenty-first century college life. *Human Affairs, 24*, 20–39.

Kenney, D. R., Dumont, R., & Kenney, G. (2005). *Mission and place: Strengthening learning and community through campus design*. Westport, CT: Praeger.

Kinzie, J., & Kuh, G. D. (2007). Creating a student-centered culture. In G. Kramer (Ed.), *Fostering student success in the campus community* (pp. 17–43). San Francisco, CA: Jossey Bass.

Kinzie, J., & Mulholland, S. (2008). Transforming physical spaces into inclusive multicultural learning environments. In S. Harper (Ed.), *Creating inclusive campus environments for cross-cultural learning and student engagement* (pp. 103–120). Washington, DC: NASPA.

Kuh, G. D. (2003). What we're learning about student engagement from NSSE. *Change, 35*(2), 24–32.

Kuh, G. D. (2009). Understanding campus environments. In G. S. McClellan & J. Stringer (Eds.), *The handbook of student affairs administration* (3rd ed., pp. 59–80). San Francisco, CA: Jossey-Bass.

Kuh, G. D., Kinzie, J., Schuh, J. H., & Whitt, E. J. (2005). *Assessing conditions for student success: An inventory to enhance educational effectiveness*. San Francisco, CA: Jossey-Bass.

Kuh, G. D., Kinzie, J., Schuh, J. H., Whitt, E. J., & Associates (2005/2010). *Student success in college: Creating conditions that matter*. San Francisco, CA: Jossey-Bass.

Kuh, G. D., Schuh, J. S., Whitt, E. J., & Associates. (1991). *Involving colleges: Successful approaches to fostering student learning and personal development outside the classroom*. San Francisco, CA: Jossey-Bass.

Kuh, G., & Whitt, E. J. (1988). *The invisible tapestry: Culture in American colleges and universities*. ASHE-ERIC Higher Education Report, no. 1. Washington, DC: Association for the Study of Higher Education.

Lewin, K. (1936). *Principles of topological psychology*. New York: McGraw-Hill.

Magolda, P. M. (1999). Using ethnographic fieldwork and case studies to guide student affairs practice. *Journal of College Student Development, 40*(1), 10–21.

Marshall, M. (2012). Environmental conditions and their influence on academic advising offices. *The Mentor: An Academic Advising Journal*. Retrieved from http://dus.psu.edu/mentor/2012/09/environmental-influence-on-advising/

Milem, J., Chang, M., & antonio, a. (2005). *Making diversity work on campus: A research-based perspective*. Washington, DC: Association of American Colleges and Universities.

Museus, S. D. (2007). Using qualitative methods to assess diverse campus cultures. In S. R. Harper & S. D. Museus (Eds.), *Using qualitative methods in institutional assessment* (pp. 29–40). New Directions for Institutional Research no. 136. San Francisco, CA: Jossey-Bass.

Museus, S. D. (2008). Focusing on institutional fabric: Using campus culture assessments to enhance cross-cultural engagement. In S. R. Harper (Ed.), *Creating inclusive environments for cross-cultural learning and engagement in higher education* (pp. 205–234). Washington, DC: National Association of Student Personnel Administrators.

Museus, S. D., & Harris, F., III. (2010). Success among college students of color: How institutional culture matters. In T. E. Dancy II (Ed.), *Managing diversity: (Re)visioning equity on college campuses* (pp. 25–43). New York, NY: Peter Lang.

Pascarella, E. T. (1985). Students' affective development within the college environment. *Journal of Higher Education, 56*(6), 641–663.

Rankin, S. R. (2003). *Campus climate for gay, lesbian, bisexual, and transgender people: A national perspective.* New York, NY: The National Gay and Lesbian Task Force Policy Institute. Retrieved from http://www.thetaskforce.org/static_html/downloads/reports/reports/CampusClimate.pdf

Rankin, S. (2006). Campus climates for sexual minorities. In R. Sanlo (Ed.), *Gender identity and sexual orientation* (pp. 17–23). New Directions for Student Services no. 111. San Francisco, CA: Jossey-Bass.

Rankin, S., & Reason, R. (2005). Differing perceptions: How students of color and white students perceive campus climate for underrepresented groups. *Journal of Student College Development, 46*(1), 43–61.

Rankin, S. R., & Reason, R. D. (2008). Transformational tapestry model: A comprehensive approach to transforming campus climate. *Journal of Diversity in Higher Education, 1*(4), 262–274.

Smith, D. (2009). *Diversity's promise for higher education: Making it work.* Baltimore, MD: Johns Hopkins Press.

Strange, C. C. (2003). Dynamics of campus environments. In S. R. Komives, D. B. Woodard Jr., & Associates (Eds.), *Student services: A handbook for the profession* (4th ed., p. 312). San Francisco, CA: Jossey-Bass.

Strange, C. C., & Banning, J. H. (2001). *Educating by design: Creating campus learning environments that work.* San Francisco, CA: Jossey-Bass.

Strange, C. C., & Banning, J. H. (2015). *Designing for learning: Creating campus environments for student success* (2nd ed.). San Francisco, CA: Jossey-Bass.

Upcraft, M. L., & Schuh, J. H. (1996). *Assessment in student affairs.* San Francisco, CA: Jossey-Bass.

11

ASSESSING QUALITY THROUGH COMPARISONS

While institutions have distinct missions and internal ways of measuring their achievement, assessing quality can also involve using external data, standards, and frameworks against which to compare local practices and outcomes. Making comparisons creates context. It is one thing to know that you are achieving your goals; it is another thing to know how those achievements and goals compare to peer and aspirant institutions, to national data, or to professional criteria and standards. This chapter begins with a case study that illustrates the need for and uses of such comparisons. It then looks at various ways of measuring how institutions are performing along a variety of dimensions. It explores the role of benchmarking, accreditation, professional standards of practice, governmental or national data, and commercial products and services as avenues to assess effectiveness and quality.

Assessment Planning at North State University

North State University, a mid-size regional public institution, is five years away from the next reaffirmation of its regional accreditation. The current strategic plan calls for increasing the institution's profile and focuses on high-quality programs and services, a student-centered learning environment, retention, and financial stability. A new Director of Institutional Effectiveness has been charged with conducting an audit of assessment practices

(Continued)

across the institution to determine what is in place and what could enhance their assessment plan. Upon review, the Director identifies the following:

- The previous reaffirmation was successful. In addition to four areas of commendation, there were six recommendations, and all but two have been addressed successfully.
  - One is related to documentation of student support services and learning outcomes for the degrees offered through the online distance education program.
    - The online programs have evolved slowly over the past 15 years. Initially only a few courses were offered, but as demand and enrollment grew, others were added until a limited number of majors are now available completely online.
  - The other is related to the need to establish a regular cycle for systematic program reviews across the institution.
    - The on-campus academic programs have been reviewed on a five-year cycle for nearly 20 years. The institution's approach is consistent and well established; it involves a structured self-study, student and alumni input, and the use of external reviewers.
    - There is no comparable system in place for student support services, student affairs units, or the distance program.
- The institution participates in the Cooperative Institutional Research Program (CIRP) Freshman Survey (CIRP; Higher Education Research Institute, 2015) and the National Survey of Student Engagement (NSSE; Center for Postsecondary Research, 2015b) on alternating years, but the Director can find no documentation of how those results have been used.
- The Department of Housing and Residential Life contracts with Skyfactor (formerly EBI-MAP-Works) to conduct assessment

with residents. Considering all of this, the Director develops a summary of what is in place, with the most recent reports appended, and a plan for addressing the gaps.

A review of articles, websites, commercial ads, or conference programs related to higher education quickly reveals that the concept of "quality" is ubiquitous. We want high-quality programs, services, experiences, and outcomes, and we seek ways to "assure" that quality will be the result of our various efforts. What is less often defined, however, is what we mean by the term "quality." As Arminio and Creamer (2004) described it,

> Defining quality is the first hurdle to establish a convincing link between standards (input) and quality (output). The task is made more difficult by the fact that an accepted definition may vary from institution to institution, from program to program, and from person to person. Within those variations, certain themes emerge regarding quality. Quality is achieving one's goals; quality is meeting or exceeding the expectations of stakeholders; quality is creating an outcome consistent with institutional goals (such as student development); quality is adding value; and quality is the result of maintaining educational programs and services that adhere to minimum standards and guidelines as proscribed by practitioners in the field. (p. 19)

Assessing quality begins in defining what quality is and what quality looks like.

Assessment Is Grounded in Comparison

One way of thinking about assessment is that, at its core, it is grounded in comparison. Assessment of student learning is based on learning objectives or intended outcomes; the mark of quality is the extent to which the student experience results in students who meet those objectives. High-quality experiences, then, are those that yield the desired outcomes. From a programmatic perspective, the objectives are framed at the aggregate or administrative level. High-quality programs are those that yield the desired effect on a group of students, or that achieve a desired level in areas like participation, revenue, or efficiency. In this way, assessment of quality can be contextualized at the local level. What do we want our students to learn? What are our goals for this program? One could argue that the local level is, after all, the most important, since it is framed by distinct institutional mission, student demographics, academic curricula, goals for student learning, student affairs services and initiatives, available resources, and the like (see Chapter 1). However, a different—and arguably useful—perspective comes from comparisons beyond the local level. While this can lead to a variety of challenges, such as ratings based on dubious metrics, it can also lead to understanding informed by and situated in a broader context.

Assessing quality in this way begins with defining quality through identifying the object of comparison. Is the best point of reference another program or student group at the institution, or should the point of reference be another institution, whether peer or aspirant? Is quality reflected by a set of outcomes or standards, such as those published by accreditation agencies or professional organizations? What are the questions driving the process? Where are the points of evaluation, and who determines the level of achievement? The choice of the basis and means for comparison creates the lens through which the results are viewed and serves as the touchstone for the determination of quality.

If the definition of "quality" is reflected in the objectives, outcomes, exemplars, or standards chosen as the basis for comparison, the idea of "quality assurance" incorporates a sense of process. A strict interpretation of *assurance*, however, connotes simply giving confidence, for example, to assure someone that the outcome will be positive (Assurance, 2015); perhaps it is more accurate to talk about *ensuring* quality, where the focus is on making sure it is accomplished. Quality assurance, from this perspective, may be little more than platitudes and claims with no evidence, but to ensure quality is to create and implement a process that is certain to yield positive results. The measure of quality, then, must be in both the basis for comparison and the process used to compare. Ensuring quality involves using a sound process to compare local efforts to a carefully chosen set of criteria.

This approach represents a departure from the identification and adoption of "best practices" as a means of improvement. While practices that have been successful at other institutions may provide good ideas, they do not automatically translate to success in a new context. There is no singular "best practice," but through assessment, practice can be evaluated and improved (Shutt, Garrett, Lynch, & Dean, 2012).

Approaches to Assessing Quality

A variety of comparisons can be used as a basis for assessing quality in programs and services. In the broadest sense, all comparisons involve a form of benchmarking, since the identification of the comparison is, in effect, the identification of the benchmark. Given that, benchmarking is described first in the following section, followed by a discussion of accreditation and use of professional standards of practice, governmental and other large databases, and commercial instruments. The chapter concludes with consideration of the role of the assessment industry in supporting assessment practice.

Benchmarking

To evaluate local practice by comparing it in a larger context, rather than simply implementing what works elsewhere, it is important first to select carefully the basis for comparison. In a broad sense, as previously asserted, all such comparisons are a form of benchmarking (Yousey-Elsener, 2013). Suskie (2009, p. 234) identified several forms of benchmarking:

External peer benchmarking	How do our students compare to peers at other institutions?
Best practices benchmarking	How do our students compare to the best of their peers? OR How does our program compare to other high-quality programs?
Value-added benchmark	Are our students improving over time?
Historical trends benchmarking	Is our program improving over time?
Strengths-and-weaknesses perspective	What are our students'/programs' relative strengths and weaknesses?
Capability benchmark	Are our students/programs doing as well as they can?
Productivity benchmark	Are we getting the most from our investment? How do programs/services compare relative to cost?

As this chart illustrates, the first step is to clarify the questions to be answered. For example, is the goal to compare one group of students with another (such as first-year students with seniors), or to the same group over time (this year's living-learning residents to last year's)? Is it helpful to know how one institution's outcomes compare to those of another, similar institution? Or is the question whether a particular functional area unit is working in ways that are consistent with national standards? Is the question whether local practice meets accreditation criteria? In other words, what is the unit of comparison?

Once the unit of comparison is determined (for example, living-learning program, or LLP), and the objects of comparison, or benchmarks, are identified (for example, GPA, retention, designated learning outcomes, process for establishing new LLPs), then the data sources and metric must also be decided. Identifying data sources involves determining those sources that are judged to offer a relevant basis for comparison; this process should include consideration of both the political and pragmatic elements of the decision. Although, as previously indicated, benchmarking can be used internally, to compare students with each other or over time, the more typical connotation of benchmarking involves looking outside the institution for the basis of comparison. Many institutions have identified their peer and aspirant counterparts, and there may be an expectation (or at least advantage) that those are included in any benchmarking effort. Beyond those already designated by the institution, others are often identified through the professional networks and knowledge of the staff. It is important at this stage to clarify the goal of the benchmarking. Is the intent to see how local practice compares to a range of others, or to gather information about programs or services that are judged to be strong and so can offer insight into ways to improve local practice? The goal will determine whether it is more useful to identify the sources to be used through comparable characteristics like institution type, size, and location, or to identify the best examples of the unit of comparison through identifying those that have won awards, published about their successes, or otherwise been recognized as exemplars. Taking the time to consider and carefully identify relevant data sources will increase the likelihood that the results are useful and helpful.

The metric to be examined can range from the simple and discrete (for example, retention rate, participation as a percentage of target group) to the complex (for example, the admission process for online degree programs from first contact through application to matriculation). With the elements clearly defined and delineated, a process can be created to gather the relevant data, examine the practice in question in light of it, and draw conclusions from the comparison. If the questions are narrow, the basis for comparison clear, and the questions specific, this process is not difficult; a simple comparison of relevant local or national data sets or a brief e-mail or telephone call to professional counterparts at other institutions can yield the needed information. However, if the questions are broader and the process to be examined more complex, the development of the framework itself can be challenging and subject to local biases and blind spots.

The scale of the benchmarking project also must be considered in light of the scale of the program. The term *program* is used to refer to structured interventions of various sizes; the residence life program, for example, includes all of the elements created to support residents and student staff, while a hall program may be a one-time workshop coordinated by a resident assistant. Regardless of scale, however, the program must be designed intentionally to achieve its goals (Liddell, Hubbard, & Werner, 2000), and benchmarking is a useful process through which to inform design. The larger the scale of the program, the more complex the set of questions that benchmarking must answer.

This kind of benchmarking, developed and conducted locally, is essentially a way of defining a standard of practice through gathering data to establish a baseline against which current practice can be compared. For some purposes, this is the most appropriate and useful source of such a baseline. It provides criteria for assessment; however, it may not offer the context needed for evaluation, as Chapter 1 defines. Further, it is most useful for program development and improvement, but may not communicate the strength or needs of the program situated in a larger framework.

Accreditation

One of the most commonly used forms of benchmarking, or ways to ensure quality, is found in the process of accreditation. According to the Council for Higher Education Accreditation (CHEA, 2002), accreditation is "a process of external quality review used by higher education to scrutinize colleges, universities, and educational programs for quality assurance and quality improvement" (p. 1). At its core, accreditation uses comparison against external standards as a mechanism for ensuring quality. In the United States, nongovernmental agencies carry out accreditation, while in many other countries accreditation is a governmental function. The question of quality assurance has grown in importance globally: The International Network for Quality Assurance Agencies in Higher Education (INQAAHE) comprises over 200 organizations and offers the means for sharing and generating discussions related to quality assurance strategies and initiatives (INQAAHE, 2015). Internationally, the idea of quality assurance is the unifying concept that brings together organizations interested in enhancing excellence and accountability (Brusoni et al., 2014).

Although accreditation in the United States is technically a voluntary system, Title IV of the Higher Education Act of 1965 established a number of federal financial aid programs and tied student eligibility for them to attendance at an accredited institution (Eaton, 2015; Suskie, 2015). This legislation, in effect, made accreditation a necessity for virtually all postsecondary institutions. Regional accreditation at the institutional level may be the most familiar form of accreditation; administered by six regional private, nonprofit organizations, 98 percent of institutions holding regional accreditation are degree-granting and nonprofit (CHEA, 2002, p. 1). Other groups classified as national accrediting organizations also review colleges and universities at the institutional level; of these institutions, most are nondegree granting and for-profit, and many are single-purpose institutions with narrow program offerings (for example, educational technology, faith-based curriculum; CHEA, 2002). Finally, specialized accrediting organizations review mostly at the program (for example, business schools, nursing programs) and service level (for example, counseling centers). Regardless of the level and scope of accreditation, the basic process is that an institution or program conducts a self-study comparing itself to the organization's criteria for accreditation and providing evidence of compliance, including evidence of student learning (Suskie, 2015). A team of external reviewers from other institutions, trained by the accreditation agency, then evaluates the evidence and findings and makes a recommendation about whether the institution or program warrants accreditation (or renewal of accreditation, often called reaffirmation), as well as any changes needed to comply with the criteria. Decision-making bodies comprised primarily of institutional representatives make the final judgments. In this respect, accreditation can be considered a form of collegial peer review (Eaton, 2015; Suskie, 2015).

Of course, in accreditation, the criteria that are to be used are not a matter of choice. In the case of institutional regional accreditation, for example, the criteria are established by the agency and the broad outlines of the process are predetermined. Even in that case, though, there is latitude in terms of the smaller assessment projects that create the building blocks of the self-study, ideally aligned with the institution's mission, goals, strategic plan, and resources. Still, the priorities reflected in accreditation criteria have direct implications for campuses. Kuh, Jankowski, Ikenberry, and Kinzie (2014) reported that regional and program accreditation are the primary factors prompting assessment of student learning outcomes, with institutional improvement cited third.

Institutional accreditation is designed to ensure that the basic elements of institutional effectiveness and appropriate administration are in place. As such, it serves as a panoramic view of institutional functioning rather than as a snapshot of one division, a close-up of a particular program, or a microscopic look at one specific outcome. It is important that efforts at every level are aligned so that they combine to contribute to the bigger picture (Henning, 2013). While it is crucial that each unit is cognizant of how its assessment data may contribute to the larger picture, that alone is not sufficient to develop an understanding of how things are working and where improvements are needed. For that, a more targeted look is needed.

Professional Standards of Practice

The challenge of developing credible local criteria, and the lack of programmatic specificity in institutional level accreditation criteria, contributed to the development of standards of practice for a variety of areas within higher education. The Council for the Advancement of Standards in Higher Education (CAS) publishes the most comprehensive set of such standards for student affairs programs and services, broadly defined. Created in 1979, the original discussion that led to the development of CAS focused on the preparation of counselors and student affairs professionals (CAS, 2015). From that philosophical discussion of the best way to assure quality in professional preparation, two paths diverged: one yielded the Council for the Accreditation of Counseling and Related Educational Programs (CACREP), which accredits graduate counselor education programs, and the other led to the creation of CAS, a consortium of 42 professional associations that collaboratively develops and promulgates standards of practice for graduate student affairs preparation programs and for more than 40 areas across higher education. The founders of CAS believed in self-regulation, meaning that given the appropriate tools and processes, professionals themselves are in the best position to understand their local context, review their programs and services, and identify areas in need of improvement. The standards, designed primarily for program review, emphasize "the integrity of campus programs through comprehensive structural soundness and ethical excellence" (Komives & Arminio, 2011, p. 27). Each set of CAS standards is structured in the same 12 sections: mission; program; organization and leadership; human resources; ethics; law, policy, and governance; diversity, equity, and access; internal and external relations; financial resources; technology; facilities and equipment; and assessment (CAS, 2015). The use of a common structure across areas facilitates systematic review and provides a consistent framework for units engaged in self-study across a division. The various areas for which CAS publishes standards are referred to as *functional areas*, reflecting work that is done, whether or not an office or unit is dedicated to it. For example, there are standards for functional areas typically housed in a single office, such as career services or student conduct, but there are also standards for functions that on some campuses may be decentralized, such as academic advising or internship programs. Additionally, some units are assigned several different programmatic responsibilities. It may be necessary to draw from multiple sets of standards to compile the criteria for review of a multi-function office. Because the CAS standards are designed to be used for self-assessment, there is no one right way to use them, other than to respect the integrity of the statements and the process of using them to assess practice (Komives & Arminio, 2011).

Designed to reflect the essentials of good practice, the CAS documents include both *standards*, which are necessary and indispensable requirements, and *guidelines*, which describe enhanced practice beyond the basic level. The standards comprise two types of statements. The *general standards* appear verbatim in all functional area documents and represent essential practices across units (for example, "Programs and services must develop, disseminate, implement, and regularly review their missions"; CAS, 2015, p. 31). *Specialty standards* relate to a specific area (for example, "The primary mission of career services is to assist students and other designated clients in developing, evaluating,

and implementing career, education, and employment plans";
CAS, 2015, p. 131).

Comprehensive assessment must examine both administrative effectiveness and the outcomes of the work. CAS also has
developed a set of learning and development outcomes; these are
contained within the program section, and the standards require
that programs and services identify their intended outcomes,
assess them, and provide evidence of their accomplishment. Use
of the CAS standards for program review, then, will involve
assessment of both the administrative aspects of the program and
its effect on student learning.

It is important to note that the standards are intended to
provide a baseline, or threshold, of expectation for practice;
any program or service doing good work can reasonably be
expected to meet the standards. The standards are not inherently
aspirational, in the sense that they describe good practice rather
than define best practice. As such, they are not as prescrip-
tive as are standards written from the perspective of a single
functional area.

Such functional area standards exist for some units in higher
education. Developed and published by individual professional
associations, these standards can offer more specific guidance
to practitioners since the narrower focus permits more depth.
Standards in areas such as housing (ACUHO-I, 2014) or career
services (National Association of Colleges and Employers,
2013) may be particularly useful when there is reason to do a
particularly thorough examination of a unit, such as impending
change related to reorganization. Professionals should think critically about the standards on which they choose to base program
evaluation, since each set differs in its underlying assumptions,
values, and areas of emphasis. The areas identified through
review as in need of change will reflect those differences, and
so reviewing available frameworks carefully will help professionals choose those most suited for the project (Young, Dean,
Franklin, & Tschepikow, 2014).

Standards of practice are designed to guide the way that programs and services are delivered; they offer professionals a way to consider local practice in light of a broader context. Deciding to use them also involves deciding *how* to use them. While they can provide a basis for new employee orientation, staff training and development, design of new programs, or informal review of an area, the use of standards to structure a full program review creates a solid foundation for effective assessment and evaluation. As previously described, assessment based in comparison must involve both an appropriate basis for comparison, such as that provided by professional standards, and an appropriate process by which the comparison is made. Program reviews can be structured in various ways, but CAS (2015) recommends several principles that can contribute to an effective process. First, documentation, data, and evidence related to the standards should be compiled. Assessment is, at its core, an evidence-based process, so judgments without evidence to support them are just opinions—informed opinions, perhaps, but opinions without the support needed to demonstrate accountability or achievement. Second, a review team should be assembled, made up mostly of individuals outside the area to be reviewed. These may include others in the student affairs division, staff from related areas (for example, facilities, business services), faculty members, students, and in some cases, alumni, parents, or community partners. The composition of the team should reflect the mission, goals, and program of the area. The director or head of the unit under review might serve on the committee as an ex-officio member or as a resource to it but should not chair it, since an important role of the committee is to bring different perspectives to the review. The role of the committee, then, is to review compliance with the standards based on the evidence provided and to come to consensus about areas of particular strength and areas in need of improvement. This information can be used by the staff in the area reviewed to generate an action plan to address the needs identified. Some divisions or institutions also incorporate a step in which external reviewers are invited, often through a campus visit, to review the self-study and provide further perspective on the functioning of the unit. While a well-done standards-based program review can be time- and labor-intensive, it provides valuable information about how a program compares to professional standards, creating a level of credibility that can be hard to achieve without the larger context that standards provide.

Governmental and Other Datasets

In some cases, the needed points of comparison are the facts and figures that reflect the circumstances and profiles of other institutions. This need highlights the distinction between assessment and evaluation: An institution knows its own data and trends, but without a basis for comparison, it can be difficult to evaluate that information and make judgments about program renewal, modification, or perhaps dissolution. A major source of data for such comparisons is the Integrated Postsecondary Education Data System (IPEDS), a system of interrelated annual surveys resulting in a database managed by the National Center for Education Statistics, part of the U.S. Department of Education (NCES, n.d.). IPEDS gathers data from every postsecondary institution that participates in the federal student financial aid programs, totaling more than 7,500 institutions; all participating institutions are required to report specified data annually (NCES, n.d.).

> IPEDS collects data on postsecondary education in the United States in seven areas: institutional characteristics, institutional prices, enrollment, student financial aid, degrees and certificates conferred, student persistence and success, and institutional human and fiscal resources.... Institutional characteristics data are the foundation of the entire IPEDS system. These include basic institutional contact information, tuition and fees, room and board charges, control or affiliation, type of calendar system, levels of awards offered, types of programs, and admissions requirements. (NCES, n.d., paras. 7–8)

The IPEDS database is available to the public electronically; it offers the capacity to make a wide range of comparisons with other institutions. The data included are vast and easily accessible, and the longitudinal data that are available allow for examination of trends over time; however, because the categories are broad, they do not allow comparisons at the programmatic or unit level (Schuh, 2002).

In some cases, state databases are also available for within-state comparisons. Similarly, professional organizations or institutional consortia may gather data and make them available for their members. One of the best examples of this is NACUBO, the National Association of College and University Business Officers, which offers benchmarking data related to student financial services, tuition discounting, endowments, and a wide range of operational and strategic benchmarks (Mosier & Schwarzmueller, 2002; NACUBO, n.d.). Data gathered by institutional consortia may be particularly useful since member institutions share specific characteristics. AAUDE, the Association of American Universities Data Exchange, is "a public service organization whose purpose is to improve the quality and usability of information about higher education. [The] membership is comprised of AAU institutions that support this purpose and participate in the exchange of data/information to support decision-making at their institution" (AAUDE, 2012, para. 1). The Association of Public and Land-grant Universities (APLU, n.d.) and the Council of Independent Colleges (CIC, 1997–2015) are other examples of consortia that provide comparative data to their members. Such comparisons, however, are limited to the kind of factual data that such systems collect.

Commercial Instruments

Comparisons are in some ways a national pastime; we like to know how sports teams, restaurants, and movies fare in the eyes of experts, stack up against rating systems, and compare to each other on various metrics. Institutions of higher education are no different. *U.S. News & World Report* (2015) is well known for its annual college ratings edition, and other resources like Peterson's (http://www.petersons.com/) exist to help prospective students to compare institutions against one another and against the students' own criteria and preferences. Such sources of information have their place, and some would argue that they have helped prospective students and their families become decision-makers who are better informed. The other perspective, however, is that the metrics used may not be the most important ones, and that the systems lack appropriate controls, so they may not always reflect reliable and comparable measures. In fact, as Pascarella (2001) pointed out, "they are based on institutional resource and reputational dimensions, which, at best, have only minimal relevance to what we know about the impact of college on students … the factors that are important in shaping a college's impact on its students [indicate] that within-college experiences tend to count substantially more than between-college characteristics" (p. 20). These resources are designed to provide information as a basis for comparison and are not intended to be used for institutional assessment, but their popular use certainly involves value judgments based on the data.

One way that institutions gather data not only for their own use, but also to help describe themselves to others, is through the use of commercially available instruments. One well-known and widely used example is the National Survey of Student Engagement (and its counterparts designed for use with groups including faculty, beginning students, and community college students; Center for Postsecondary Research, 2015b). The NSSE was conceived in part in reaction to the popular ratings systems; it is theoretically grounded in the concept of student engagement.

> Student engagement represents two critical features of collegiate quality. The first is the amount of time and effort students put into their studies and other educationally purposeful activities. The second is how the institution deploys its resources and organizes

the curriculum and other learning opportunities to get students to participate in activities that decades of research studies show are linked to student learning. (Center for Postsecondary Research, 2015a, para. 1)

Administered to first-year and senior students, the survey collects information about how students spend their time and about the institutional activities in which they participate. It can provide a measure of progress, by comparing the two groups of students at one point in time (for example, are first-year students engaged differently than seniors?), or by comparing the same group of students over time (for example, is this cohort of students engaged differently as seniors than they were in their first year?). While there are methodological issues to be considered in these examples, the survey has been researched extensively and is a valid and reliable measure of the constructs (Center for Postsecondary Research, 2015c). By understanding their various metrics of student engagement, institutions can use the information as one piece of their assessment plan, used as an indirect measure of student learning for internal benchmarking and goal setting, and as a source of data about their areas of strength and distinctiveness. NSSE also offers institutions the opportunity to compare their scores to the overall annual results, based on administration at over 700 institutions, and to select groups of other institutions for comparisons of engagement indicators (for example, collaborative learning, student-faculty interaction), high-impact practices (for example, service-learning, study abroad), and individual survey items (Center for Postsecondary Research, 2015a). As with any standardized instrument, professionals must consider carefully whether the population in the comparison group is similar enough to their own to permit valid comparisons, but the NSSE and other instruments similar to it offer an avenue for understanding important patterns and factors at the local level and for considering them in a broader context.

Another widely used source of data is the CIRP Freshman Survey (Cooperative Institutional Research Program; Higher

Education Research Institute [HERI], 2015). Administered to entering students before they start classes, the survey "covers a wide range of student characteristics: parental income and education, ethnicity, and other demographic items; financial aid; secondary school achievement and activities; educational and career plans; and values, attitudes, beliefs, and self-concept" (HERI, 2015, para. 2). However, because it collects data prior to enrollment, the information is best used as a needs assessment to better understand incoming students. Similar to the NSSE, it also offers the option of requesting comparisons to selected other institutions as well as the opportunity to compare local results to national data and trends.

The ACHA-National College Health Assessment (NCHA), administered annually by the American College Health Association (2014), is an example of a more focused national survey that can be used by institutions to gather data about their student body as well as to consider national data as a basis for comparison. Designed to examine students' health habits, behaviors, and perceptions, NCHA data can inform campus interventions, health promotion activities, and planning for health services. Originally administered in 2000, the availability of longitudinal data permits consideration of trends and changes over time.

Commercial instruments such as those previously described offer broad information about national patterns that can be useful for constructing local assessment and programmatic efforts, but if institutions decide to participate in them, they can provide a wealth of information about the student body, as well as the means to consider that information in a larger context.

Assessment Industry

The practice of assessment in higher education has become increasingly complex. As expectations for the amount and sophistication of assessment have increased, administrators have been challenged to find the staff resources and expertise to manage expanding assessment-related activity and reporting. A number of assessment companies specializing in educational technology now offer services and products that campuses can contract or purchase to expand their assessment-related capacity. The specific nature and purpose of the various options varies from company to company, but all are intended to augment campus assessment efforts. As with the approaches previously described, many of them also offer a basis for comparison as an element of assessment.

One of the earliest of these companies, Skyfactor, was founded in 1994 as EBI (Educational Benchmarking Incorporated) and originally was created to provide assessment and benchmarking services for MBA programs (Skyfactor, 2015). Its scope has since expanded to provide benchmarking in multiple student affairs and academic program areas, as well as a hosted software system focused on student success and retention.

Campus Labs, founded in 2001 as StudentVoice, was initially "formed with a very simple goal: to collect information from students that could be used to impact programs and services" (Campus Labs, 2015, para. 1). The founder had the idea when, as a student leader, he was asked what students thought and realized that there was a need for a systematic way to find out. The company has expanded to include a wide array of assessment-related products and services, including data collection, reporting, management, and a platform that allows integration across academic affairs, student affairs, and institutional research. Campuses have the option to participate in benchmarking projects with other institutions as well.

These are just two examples of assessment industry companies; there are many others, with new ones created frequently. For institutions with the resources and support to engage external firms, partnering with commercial vendors can significantly expand capacity and can allow campuses to engage in assessment at a level otherwise not feasible for them. As is true for any instrument or approach used, it is important that professionals know their needs, the questions they want to answer, and the characteristics of their own institutions so that they can make informed and appropriate decisions about any avenue chosen, including assessment industry partners.

Final Considerations

There is a saying that "comparison is the thief of joy," and while that may be true in personal matters, it does not always hold in the practice of assessment. Comparison creates context, and context informs understanding. Used judiciously, comparisons can offer the means to evaluate how a given level of attainment measures up against a chosen metric or exemplar. The basis for comparison must be chosen carefully, since it will frame the results, and an ill-defined comparison is useless or, worse, harmful to clear understanding. However, comparisons can set baselines, inform reasonable goals, and describe good practice, and making purposeful use of them can be an important step in ensuring quality.

Back to North State University

Identifying the institution's assessment needs, questions, and context served as the initial step for the Director of Institutional Effectiveness at NSU. The next step is to consider the goals of the strategic plan and to identify progress toward those goals, with supporting evidence. In considering the plan's elements of high quality programs and services, a student-centered learning environment, retention, and financial stability, the Director recognized that comparison data will be useful in understanding where NSU stands. In consultation with administrators across campus, the Director created the following questions to be addressed and suggested potential sources of information:

- Which peer and aspirant institutions offer online degree programs?

(Continued)

       ✓ Data available through IPEDS, including enrollment numbers and demographic profile

  o What student support services do they offer? Through what mechanisms?

       ✓ Benchmarking—review of websites; follow-up questionnaire or phone calls as needed

  o What are the intended outcomes for those programs? Do they differ from their on-campus counterparts? How are the outcomes assessed?

       ✓ Benchmarking—review of websites; follow-up questionnaire or phone calls as needed

       ✓ Check accreditation criteria for specific requirements

- What mechanisms are available for program review of student support services, student affairs units, and distance programs?

       ✓ Review available professional standards; identify relevant CAS standards and self-assessment process; establish planning committee to develop program review cycle and plan

  o Should program review in these areas mirror the structure used for review of academic programs?

       ✓ Charge planning committee to benchmark with comparable institutions and make a recommendation

- How can we use the data we receive from CIRP, NSSE, and Skyfactor to improve our practice and inform progress on the strategic plan?

       ✓ Compile most recent results; highlight data related to the goals of the strategic plan. Look specifically at NSSE topical modules on Civic Engagement and Global Perspectives.

> ✓ Use national and designated group comparison data to evaluate current results
>
> ✓ Set goals based on assessment of available resources and in light of comparison data

Discussion Questions

1. In the example of North State University, what other questions could be answered through the use of comparative information? What questions should not be answered this way?

2. What considerations or cautions are there in the decision to use comparisons in assessment? How do these apply to the reporting of comparative results?

3. In what circumstances are national, overall data most useful? When do comparisons warrant use of targeted institutional or programmatic examples?

4. What are the factors or local priorities that would support the use of commercial instruments or assessment industry partners? How should those possibilities be evaluated?

5. What are the best examples you have seen of using comparisons to inform assessment? Have you seen instances where comparisons have been used poorly? If so, what changes would you recommend to improve the process?

References

ACUHO-I. (2014). *ACUHO-I standards & ethical principles for college & university housing professionals.* Columbus, OH: Author. Retrieved from http://www.acuho-i.org/Portals/0/2014_Feb_Standards_Ethical _Principles_1.pdf

American College Health Association. (2014). *About ACHA-NCHA.* Retrieved from http://www.acha-ncha.org/overview.html

Arminio, J., & Creamer, D. (2004). Promoting quality in higher education: The Council for the Advancement of Standards (CAS) celebrates 25 years. *NASPA Leadership Exchange, 2*(1), 18–21.

Association of American Universities Data Exchange. (2012). *Welcome.* Retrieved from http://aaude.org/home

Association of Public and Land-grant Universities. (n.d.). *Accountability and transparency.* Retrieved from http://www.aplu.org/projects-and-initiatives/accountability-and-transparency/

Assurance. (2015). *Oxford Dictionaries.* Retrieved from http://www.oxforddictionaries.com/us/definition/american_english/assurance

Brusoni, M., Damian, R., Sauri, J. G., Jackson, S., Kömürcügil, H., Malmedy, M., ... Zobel, L. (2014). *The concept of excellence in higher education.* European Association for Quality Assurance in Higher Education, Occasional Paper No. 20. Brussels, Belgium: European Association for Quality Assurance in Higher Education. Retrieved from http://www.enqa.eu/indirme/papers-and-reports/occasional-papers/ENQA%20Excellence%20WG%20Report_The%20Concept%20of%20Excellence%20in%20Higher%20Education.pdf

Campus Labs. (2015). *About us.* Retrieved from http://www.campuslabs.com/about-us/

Center for Postsecondary Research. (2015a). *About NSSE.* Bloomington, IN: Center for Postsecondary Research, Indiana University School of Education. Retrieved from http://nsse.iub.edu/html/survey_instruments.cfm

Center for Postsecondary Research. (2015b). *National Survey of Student Engagement: Survey instrument.* Bloomington, IN: Center for Postsecondary Research, Indiana University School of Education. Retrieved from http://nsse.iub.edu/html/survey_instruments.cfm

Center for Postsecondary Research. (2015c). *NSSE's commitment to data quality.* Bloomington, IN: Center for Postsecondary Research, Indiana University School of Education. Retrieved from http://nsse.iub.edu/html/psychometric_portfolio.cfm

Council for the Advancement of Standards in Higher Education. (2015). *CAS professional standards for higher education* (9th ed.). Washington, DC: Author.

Council for Higher Education Accreditation. (2002). *The fundamentals of accreditation: What do you need to know?* Washington, DC: Author. Retrieved from http://www.chea.org/pdf/fund_accred_20ques_02.pdf

Council for Independent Colleges. (1997–2015). *About the benchmarking services.* Retrieved from http://www.cic.edu/Research-and-Data/Benchmarking-Tools-and-Services/Pages/Benchmarking-Services.aspx

Eaton, J. (2015, January/February). Accreditation: What it does and what it should do. *Change*. Retrieved from http://www.chea.org/pdf/CHANGE%20article-Accreditation_Judith_Eaton.pdf

Henning, G. W. (2013). Documenting student learning and institutional effectiveness. In K. R. Allen, B. Elkins, G. W. Henning, L. A. Bayless, & T. W. Gordon (Eds.), *Accreditation and the role of the student affairs educator* (pp. 6–13). Washington, DC: ACPA.

Higher Education Research Institute. (2015). *CIRP freshman survey*. Los Angeles, CA: Higher Education Research Institute, UCLA. Retrieved from http://www.heri.ucla.edu/cirpoverview.php

International Network for Quality Assurance Agencies in Higher Education. (2015). *What can INQAAHE do for you?* Retrieved from http://www.inqaahe.org/main/about-inqaahe/what-can-inqaahe-do-for-you

Komives, S. K., & Arminio, J. (2011). Promoting integrity through standards of practice. In R. B. Young (Ed.), *Advancing the integrity of professional practice* (pp. 27–34). New Directions for Student Services no. 135. San Francisco, CA: Jossey-Bass.

Kuh, G. D., Jankowski, N., Ikenberry, S. O., & Kinzie, J. (2014). *Knowing what students know and can do: The current state of student learning outcomes assessment in U.S. colleges and universities*. Champaign, IL: National Institute for Learning Outcomes Assessment. Retrieved from http://www.learningoutcomesassessment.org/documents/2013%20Survey%20Report%20Final.pdf

Liddell, D. L., Hubbard, S., & Werner, R. (2000). Developing interventions that focus on learning. In D. L. Liddell & J. P. Lund (Eds.), *Powerful programming for student learning: Approaches that make a difference* (pp. 21–33). New Directions for Student Services no. 90. San Francisco, CA: Jossey-Bass.

Mosier, R. E., & Schwarzmueller, G. J. (2002). Benchmarking in student affairs. In B. E. Bender & J. H. Schuh (Eds.), *Using benchmarking to inform practice in higher education* (pp. 103–112). New Directions for Higher Education no. 118. San Francisco, CA: Jossey-Bass.

NACUBO. (n.d.). *Getting started on benchmarking*. Retrieved from http://www.nacubo.org/Research/Benchmarking_Resources.html

National Association of Colleges and Employers. (2013). *NACE professional standards for college and university career services*. Bethlehem, PA: Author. Retrieved from https://www.naceweb.org/knowledge/assessment.aspx

National Center for Education Statistics. (n.d.). *Integrated Postsecondary Education Data System*. Retrieved from http://nces.ed.gov/ipeds/

Pascarella, E. (2001). Identifying evidence in undergraduate education: Are we even close? *Change, 33*(3), 19–23.

Schuh, J. H. (2002). The Integrated Postsecondary Education Data System. In B. E. Bender & J. H. Schuh (Eds.), *Using benchmarking to inform practice in higher education* (pp. 29–38). New Directions for Higher Education no. 118. San Francisco, CA: Jossey-Bass.

Shutt, M. D., Garrett, J. M., Lynch, J. W., & Dean, L. A. (2012). An assessment model as best practice in student affairs. *Journal of Student Affairs Research and Practice*, 49(1), 1–16. doi:10.2202/1949-6605.6227

Skyfactor. (2015). *Company history*. Retrieved from http://www.skyfactor .com/about/history/

Suskie, L. (2009). *Assessing student learning: A common sense guide* (2nd ed.). San Francisco, CA: Jossey-Bass.

Suskie, L. A. (2015). *Five dimensions of quality: A common sense guide to accreditation and accountability*. San Francisco, CA: Jossey-Bass.

U.S. News & World Report. (2015). *Education: Rankings and advice*. Retrieved from http://www.usnews.com/education

Young, D. G., Dean, L. A., Franklin, D. S., & Tschepikow, W. K. (2014). Effects of assessment on collegiate recreation programs. *Recreational Sports Journal*, 38, 82–95.

Yousey-Elsener, K. (2013). Assessment fundamentals: The ABC's of assessment. In D. Timm, J. D. Barham, K. McKinney, & A. R. Knerr (Eds.), *Assessment in practice: A companion guide to the ASK standards* (pp. 9–18). Washington, DC: ACPA–College Student Educators International.

12

GETTING ASSESSMENT PROJECTS STARTED AND ENSURING SUSTAINABILITY

The end goal for an effective approach to assessment is to have a clear plan for initiating and sustaining activities and to build the work into routine systems and improvement cycles. Assessment is not a "once and done" activity. Yet, reaching the goal of sustainable assessment is no small feat. Assessment projects can fall off the assessment schedule in favor of dealing with pressing campus concerns of the moment, or disappear after reaccreditation is achieved or with budget cuts, while others may never get started because of resistance or weak assessment leadership. Assessment projects can fall prey to many factors, but perhaps the most challenging stage of assessment is simply getting the work underway.

Although assessment has had a persistent presence in higher education for more than three decades, we have not yet reached the point of having established systems and streamlined processes for doing the work on many campuses. Assessment activities at most institutions fluctuate with shifting priorities and new pressures, emerging technologies, and evolving interests and needs. For example, many campuses have regular cycles for assessing the institution's climate for diversity, yet a racial incident or a new enrollment strategy that involves the recruitment of greater numbers of international students might create the need for a whole new assessment initiative to assess campus climate. Other campuses may want to strengthen their assessment activities, or refocus on student learning outcomes (Bresciani, Zelna, & Anderson, 2004), prompting a new approach to assessment.

Every assessment project has a starting point, and getting activities in motion demands thoughtful planning and attention. This chapter explores the topic of how to get assessment projects started, opening with a case study about the challenging task of implementing a learning outcomes assessment project in student affairs. Then, we introduce practical steps for getting started, barriers to assessment and strategies for taking action, models for leadership and coordination, and close with a discussion of the need for balance between developing routine and responsive approaches to assessment. Among the questions this chapter addresses are the following: How should an assessment project get started? How does one overcome resistance to conduct assessment? What is the role of assessment coordinators in a division of student affairs? What are the barriers to undertaking assessment? This chapter relates closely to Chapters 4 and 5 in the development of learning outcomes for individuals and programs.

Initiating Learning Outcomes Assessment in Student Affairs at Midstate University

The new provost at Midstate University made it clear in her remarks to the student affairs division leadership that learning outcomes needed more emphasis in student affairs assessment. "I believe in the value of student affairs, but need to see greater articulation and assessment of student learning outcomes that reinforce what student life and cocurricular experiences contribute to the quality of undergraduate education." The vice president for student affairs and the newly minted, enthusiastic director of student affairs assessment exchanged expectant glances at the end of the meeting, aware that they needed to step up their plans to implement a more comprehensive system of student learning outcomes assessment. In addition to the keen interest of the provost was the reality that the institution's regional accreditation review was a little more than four years away, so plans had to ramp up fast.

The vice president for student affairs and director of assessment met the following Monday to inventory the division's progress on and results from a smattering of efforts to assess student learning outcomes. A review of each unit's assessment plan revealed that most of the investment in assessment was at the level of tracking student participation in, or use of, facilities and services, satisfaction surveys, and some benchmarking of services and outcomes to professional standards. The director of assessment noted that while these efforts were fairly well systematized, and that most units were making use of their assessment results to inform decision-making and guide improvements, only about half had made progress on assessing program outcomes, and few had made much movement toward developing a meaningful approach to assessing learning outcomes. The vice president was disappointed that so few programs could articulate outcomes in relation to either the institution learning outcomes or the student affairs domains for learning. It was clear more work needed to be done to respond to the provost's call for evidence on student learning outcomes.

Three years earlier, the division of student affairs at Midstate adopted six learning outcomes domains based on the outcomes framework advanced in *Learning Reconsidered* (NASPA & ACPA, 2004): Cognitive Complexity; Knowledge Acquisition and Integration; Social Responsibility and Civic Engagement; Inter- and Intra-personal Competence; Practical Competence; Persistence and Academic Achievement. The creation of the framework was achieved when the division sponsored a series of professional development workshops on assessment, including reading discussion groups for major texts and articles on learning outcomes assessment, and a retreat to determine the divisional learning domains. The division and each unit next set out to develop learning outcome statements and devise plans to assess and report results across the outcomes framework. However, the assessment work seemed to have stalled at this phase, during the transition from a part-time assessment coordinator to the new director of assessment, and when a project to contribute to the institution's new strategic plan captured the time and attention of student affairs leadership.

(*Continued*)

As the new assessment director met with leaders in each department regarding the status of their learning outcome assessment work, she discovered that some units, particularly those that had consulted professional benchmarks, including those identified by the Council for the Advancement of Standards (CAS), had advanced their work, and had defined skills, outcomes, and examples for all six divisional learning domains (see www.cas .edu). The student activities department, for example, had defined the Social Responsibility and Civic Engagement domain skills to include learning to work with others to address social inequities, sustainability and environmental justice, initiating or managing community programs, ethical decision making, interaction with diverse others, and self-reflection, and had identified activities and leadership experiences that provided opportunities for students to develop these outcomes. Experiences such as the Inter-Group dialogue programs, study abroad, alternative-break programs, service-learning and community-based learning programs, cultural festivals, and identity group programming (for example, Black Student Union, LGBTQ), were identified as providing students with opportunities related to this learning domain. However, like many other units, the staff needed help specifying what they wanted to learn from their outcomes assessment work, explicating the learning outcomes in these activities, and how they were going to assess student gains.

To strengthen the student affairs departments' capacity to write learning outcomes, and determine manageable approaches to collecting evidence, the director of assessment scheduled a series of formal presentations about writing learning outcomes statements and data collection methods, and invited units that had made some headway on these topics to share their work. She then conducted small group meetings with units that needed more support in their efforts. For example, the leaders of the Alternative Break programs, which are short-term service-learning trips, immerse students in direct service and education, resulting in the creation of active citizens who think and act critically around the root causes of social issues, wanted to know what students were gaining from the experience. She helped the staff develop some ways to assess gains by, for example, taking advantage of the critical reflection journals that the alternative-break project students keep throughout the experience, and developing specific prompts to trigger their thinking around the social responsibility and civic engagement student learning outcomes established by the department. They developed a rubric to review the journals and to document achieved student learning outcomes, and also employed interviews and focus groups with participants to deepen their understanding of learning gains.

The director then worked with the vice president to set a deadline for departments to submit their learning outcomes assessment plans. A simple reporting template required departments to identify learning outcomes, define measures, associate their outcomes with the six defined learning domains, and specify a timeline for gathering evidence. Once these were submitted, the division's assessment council, led by the director and populated by six student affairs professionals, a member of the institutional research and assessment office, a faculty member, and two students, reviewed all the learning outcomes plans and offered specific feedback about the outcomes, measures, and timeline to each unit.

Midstate's learning outcomes assessment activities definitely were spurred by the provost's interest, but the effort benefited from the thoughtful approach taken by the director, who spent time getting to know the needs of particular units, using group workshops and consultations, and planning documents to keep the work organized and moving forward.

Starting Assessment Projects

As the Midstate case study illustrates, assessment projects can get started when an administrative leader demands evidence. Student learning outcomes assessment had waned, and the new provost provided a reboot to the process of assessment. But even in this example, it's clear that some assessment activity, including the use of information about student participation in and satisfaction with services, and outcomes related to standards, had become routine and were considered helpful information to guide student affairs practice. The fact that this work was seemingly established in student affairs provided the new director of assessment a foundation upon which to build and focus on advancing needed work on outcomes assessment.

Of course, not all assessment projects will receive a kick-start from the provost, and most demand more thoughtful design and planning to get underway. More important, to make assessment meaningful—and not simply a response to a demand, an exercise in compliance, or a data-collection activity—it is critical to be thoughtful about the purpose of assessment and intentional about how to do the work. A solid first step for getting started is to adopt a framework for conducting assessment. Chapter 2 outlines a comprehensive assessment model. However, Banta and Palomba's (2015) three distinct phases of assessment—*planning, implementing,* and *improving and sustaining* the process—provides a useful framework for getting work underway.

The *planning* phase involves engaging stakeholders—those who have roles in the assessment project and who will ultimately make use of results—in charting the course for assessment. This group must identify the purpose of the assessment project and then help develop an approach to assessment that is rooted in the purpose. A key question at this phase is What do we want to learn from this assessment project? The creation of an assessment plan should be guided by the purpose of the project. For example, the student activities and service-learning educators at Midstate University wanted to learn how their students were developing outcomes related to social responsibility and to what extent students participating in the alternative-break project, as an illustration, were developing these outcomes. This goal helped the group design a plan that involved capturing student work products in service-learning courses, developing prompts for and a rubric to evaluate alternative-break journal writing, interviews with students, and a process for reviewing and interpreting results. Assembling a written plan and a timeline for assessment is also useful. Setting a timetable for assessment projects–for example, determining what is to be included in annual assessment reports and how often certain national assessments will be conducted—will also help set expectations for doing assessment.

After some careful planning, the next phase is *implementing* assessment. There is no greater impetus for implementing assessment than having leadership that expects and supports assessment work. The message that assessment evidence is valued will get work started and help ensure that assessment results will be used. The next step in the implementation phase is data collection. Assessment methods should be connected to goals of the project and to the activities that support the outcomes. For example, the student activities educators at Midstate could have elected to survey their students about their experiences in the domain of social responsibility and civic engagement. However, that method is an "add on" and is disconnected from the goals of the experience and what students are doing in their service-learning and alternative-break project. Instead, the staff decided to take advantage of the reflective journals and course products to assess learning gains. Methods that allow for the collection of both direct and indirect evidence, include performance measures, and are embedded in experiences can help make assessment more robust. The implementation of assessment also demands training and support, and resources to do the work.

Although this chapter is concerned with getting assessment projects started, the final phase of the Banta and Palomba (2015) model—*improving and sustaining assessment*—is an essential consideration at the onset of assessment projects. Often, so much attention has been placed on collecting data there is little time dedicated to taking action once data are available and determining what the data mean for educational practice. One way to help ensure that assessment projects get underway is to discuss how and with whom results will be shared right from the start of the project. Keep in mind that sharing results broadly is important to develop more widespread involvement in the identification of conclusions and recommendations, and to interest more stakeholders in making use of assessment findings. This last step of making use of assessment findings is an important commitment to establish at the start of an assessment project. Assessment results should be used to improve educational processes and outcomes. Communicating how results will be disseminated and stating expectations for using findings to improve will go a long way toward ensuring that assessment projects get underway and are sustained.

Thoughtful assessment planning offers a reasonable approach to getting assessment underway. It is also likely that various internal and external pressures and mandates can provide motivation for assessment. For example, the internal pressure to justify the existence of student affairs in a state of declining resources provides a strong push for assessing effectiveness and providing evidence of the value of student affairs services and programming to valued institutional outcomes. Another press for initiating assessment projects may arise from the drive for greater accountability in higher education (Schuh & Upcraft, 2001). Student affairs staff interested in getting assessment started are wise to take advantage of the external and internal pressures for accountability to push to make evidence available, demonstrating the value of student affairs programs and services.

One growing external pressure for assessment in student affairs emanates from the increasing numbers of student affairs educators who are being called upon to participate in the regional accreditation process (Allen, Elkins, Henning, Bayless & Gordon, 2013). Many accreditation standards, as mentioned in Chapter 11, demand evidence that resides in the domain of student affairs, including evidence of students' use of academic support services, data about the quality of enriching learning experiences including internships, service-learning, and leadership, and information about support for diversity. Yet, student affairs educators are often not equipped with the knowledge and skills to maximize the opportunity that accreditation presents to demonstrate effectiveness and make improvements. Most important, accreditation provides an opportunity for student affairs to collaborate with partners across campus in a significant institutional accountability effort and demonstrate the division's contributions to student success and educational effectiveness. When accreditation is approached as an opportunity to reflect on institutional performance and improve, student affairs educators are wise to seize the opportunity to be involved and use years leading up to a review as leverage to get meaningful assessment projects underway.

The truth is, the way to get an assessment project started is the same as getting any task started. To paraphrase Mark Twain, the secret is to break your complex overwhelming tasks into manageable tasks, and then start on the first one. Assessment projects are a series of small tasks. Identifying what the unit wants to learn about itself, its programs and outcomes, and then identifying how to collect this information can be done one task at a time. Getting a mandate from the provost or the senior student affairs officer to do assessment is one way to get assessment going, and leveraging the pressure of "proving our worth" or accreditation can provide even greater impetus. However, adopting an intentional framework for designing and planning assessment projects provides an important structure for getting assessment underway. Thoughtful attention to the phases of assessment will help ensure a sustainable approach to assessment practice. However, there is nothing more helpful than just getting started.

Common Barriers to Understanding Assessment and Strategies for Success

Even in the best of situations, in which assessment is supported by leaders and there is proper oversight and a plan for implementation, it can be difficult to get assessment underway. Some of the barriers to assessment include a perception that it is burdensome, or "extra work," that there is simply no time or resources to dedicate to the task, or that the work is difficult to do well, and produces useless information. Outcomes assessment in student affairs may be particularly difficult owing to the fact that student affairs often has been overlooked within institutions for its specific contributions to student learning and development, and staff may not have helpful grounding in assessment methods, or connections across the institution to develop effective collaborations (Bresciani, Moore Gardner, & Hickmott, 2009).

This section briefly introduces seven common barriers that anyone involved in assessment is likely to encounter. Anticipating some of these obstacles at the beginning of an assessment project, and planning responses for working through the issue, is critical to not getting tripped up in the hurdles.

1. *Lack of time and sense of being overwhelmed by reporting requirements.* Many leaders in student affairs units are likely to already be burdened with bureaucratic tasks and reporting requirements, and may be reluctant to take on assessment projects that add to their daily demands. Bresciani, Moore Gardner, and Hickmott (2009) identified lack of time and competing priorities and uncertainty about reallocating responsibility as common obstacles to assessment in student affairs.

2. *Limited value in assessment.* The burden of assessment is likely to be perceived as onerous if there is little belief in the value of the work or information to the unit. Absent a sense of value, student affairs staff are understandably reluctant to undertake assessment efforts that take valuable time but

appear to have little influence on their daily work. Doing assessment to fulfill someone else's agenda does not provide a strong incentive to undertake the assessment process. Furthermore, if there is no hope that evidence can be used to make needed changes or to influence the investment of resources into a practice or experience that has significant benefits to student outcomes, there is little reward for partaking in assessment.

3. *Insufficient knowledge of how to conduct assessment.* Limits in student affairs professionals' knowledge and skills in assessment is a recognized barrier to assessment. The need for professional development and importance of increasing capacity was well articulated in the "ASK Standards: Assessment Skills and Knowledge Content Standards for Student Affairs Practitioners and Scholars" (ACPA, 2007) and in the identification of assessment skills as a key professional competency area for student affairs practitioners (ACPA & NASPA, 2010; Hoffman & Bresciani, 2012).

4. *Lack of central coordination of assessment.* The scope of assessment questions and the need to coordinate activities to ensure implementation and follow-up makes it vital to have some central coordination and leadership. A lack of central support limits the sharing of resources and knowledge and can make assessment uneven, and subject to the interest and whims of each office or unit.

5. *Striving for the perfect assessment project.* Designing an assessment project that controls for student inputs and selection effects on outcomes, and relies on survey results with greater than a 50 percent response rate, is admirable. However, having such exacting standards for assessment can be an obstacle to getting projects underway. Too often, useful analyses based on reasonably good data are put aside in favor of collecting more evidence.

6. *Indeterminate assessment results.* Assessment results can be ambiguous and sometimes findings do not rise to the level of statistical significance or are insufficiently credible to draw definitive conclusions. Assessment is a practical undertaking and findings are not always straightforward. In addition, as Pascarella and Terenzini (2005) acknowledged, since most learning outcomes associated with student affairs programs are indirect and are likely to be the result of a host of inter-related and mutually supporting experiences that occur both in and out of the classroom, it can be difficult to confirm outcomes. Even when the outcomes of student affairs programs can be quantified, the statistical measures of significance and effect sizes are often small and raise questions about the practical implications of the findings.

7. *Skepticism about how evidence will be used.* One insidious barrier to assessment is fear that assessment results will be used to discredit a program or eliminate an office, position, or project. The absence of trust in who will see results and suspicion about how findings will be used will weaken assessment projects.

Strategies for Overcoming Common Obstacles

Instead of addressing the aforementioned barriers one by one, it is more helpful to consider a combination of interrelated approaches to address common obstacles to getting assessment underway.

One of the most important strategies to thwart common obstacles is to emphasize the practical value of assessment. Focusing on the assessment payoff, whether that is improved understanding of students' experience, insights into program quality, funding for additional advisors that assessment evidence helped make the case for, or evidence of how student affairs contributes to prized institutional outcomes, is important to keep front and center. While this does not, by itself, guarantee buy-in, it reminds everyone of the practical intent and benefits. Furthermore, showcasing one small example of learning from assessment, and celebrating modest achievements along the way, will also communicate value.

One of the chief obstacles to getting assessment underway is placing assessment projects onto an already crowded student affairs agenda. Breaking assessment up into small tasks, providing templates and timelines to keep units focused and on task can help, but busy professionals need to know that assessment projects have meaning for them and that there is an incentive for doing the work. By framing and promoting assessment as "mission-driven, meaningful, and manageable," St. Olaf College was able to increase the appeal of assessment to their faculty and staff and get multiple projects underway (Jankowski, 2012). The institution's assessment "mantra" and practical framing helped mitigate concerns about time, suspicion about the value of assessment, and mistrust about how results would be used. To emphasize the value and purpose of assessment and help prioritize the work, it is important to continually communicate the purpose for undertaking an assessment project, what it will help the campus understand, and how findings will be used to improve campus conditions.

Keeping the assessment task simple—by narrowing the outcomes assessed year to year, negotiating convenient sampling strategies, or limiting data collection activities—goes a long way to address concerns about time and lack of knowledge. Celebrating "small wins" (Weick, 1984), for example, shining a spotlight on a concrete, complete, implemented assessment project of moderate importance, can help attract allies and collaborators, demonstrate value, and lower resistance to subsequent assessment tasks.

Another approach to reinforcing the priority of assessment and reminding educators about the value of findings was employed by Richard Light, director of the Harvard Assessment seminars, which explored how students made the most of their undergraduate experience. Each time a new assessment project was considered, Light (2001) would ask, "How will this project help professors, advisers, staff members, or students to do their work better?" (p. 218). This simple question can help clarify priorities of assessment projects and also communicates for whom findings must be useful.

When qualms about employing a less-than-perfect research design threaten to stall an assessment project, it can be helpful to emphasize the difference between assessment and research. Both activities strive to develop sound studies and reliable conclusions. However, research has higher expectations for design and control, while assessment generally must work with the best design possible— given what is practical, feasible, and most likely to produce reasonable results. The goal to design a perfect study can seriously stall the start of assessment projects. Blaich and Wise (2011) viewed this as a tendency among academics trained to strive for methodological purity and to distrust data collected through a less-than-perfect research design. For the purposes of assessment, the most feasible design must answer a specific question of interest to campus leaders about educational quality or student learning (Doyle, 2004). In assessment, as Walvoord (2010) observed, "You are not trying to achieve the perfect research design; you are trying to gather enough data to provide a reasonable basis for action" (p. 5). Even more, "enough data" is not necessarily about quantity—although one way to strengthen the usability of assessment results is to line up multiple points of evidence. One threshold for determining if enough data are gathered is when they provide evidence that is reasonably sufficient—perhaps good enough—to answer a specific question.

Keeping in mind the difference between research and assessment is also a way to address concerns about indeterminate results. Understanding the challenge of isolating the effect of student affairs programs on student learning is an important caution, but it does not mean that attempts to tease out, for example, the role of intergroup dialogue programs or the influence of involvement in identity groups on the outcome of social responsibility, are not worth doing. It does mean that results should be appropriately qualified. Chapter 1 provides definitions of research, assessment, and evaluation.

Investing in professional development is an essential strategy to getting assessment started and for addressing common obstacles. Increasing staff expertise in assessment can also eventually make the work more efficient and meaningful. Celebrating engagement in the process of assessment and acknowledging accomplishments will encourage the assessment process.

Leadership for Assessment

Leadership is essential to high-quality assessment (Maki, 2004; Suskie, 2009) and is needed to get assessment projects underway. Correspondingly, leadership for student affairs assessment functions has expanded and become increasing more professionalized over the past 20 years, shifting from ad hoc assessment committee work or assigning a small percentage of professional staff time to assessment activities, to more and more full-time, director-level positions who participate in professional conferences and organizations to support their work. For example, in 2015, most of the elected board of directors of the Student Affairs Assessment Leadership, an organization for educators that coordinate assessment in divisions of student affairs to discuss issues to improve their work, have titles such as "Director for Student Affairs Research, Evaluation, and Planning" or at least, "Coordinator for Student Affairs Research, Evaluation, and Planning" (see www.studentaffairsassessment.org /leadership). And many of these assessment leaders have PhDs and advanced professional training in assessment. Most of the full-time director roles have understandably developed at larger institutions, specifically research universities, with complex student affairs divisions.

The more commonly identified assessment leadership role in student affairs is the coordinator of assessment. Livingston and Zerulik (2013) assert that assessment coordinators play a central role in student affairs to ensure that assessment is a divisional priority. Coordinators are responsible for maintaining a broad perspective on divisional and departmental or unit assessment needs; planning, stimulating, and coordinating assessment projects; and maintaining a body of evidence about programs and services. The coordinator role for leading assessment is found across a variety of institutional types and student affairs units, and the success of the role varies by campus.

Assessment coordinators generally have a range of roles in student affairs divisions. A coordinator may serve as director of an assessment department or as chair of an assessment committee, or have a percentage of their full-time duties designated for assessment. Further, assessment coordinators may report to the chief student affairs officer or to the director of a department, or have a dotted-line reporting relationship to institutional research and effectiveness (Livingston & Zerulik, 2013). Assessment coordinators are usually responsible for creating and managing an assessment team made up of representatives from each department, who serve as champions for assessment in their departments and divisions. A critical function of the coordinator is to shape and lead the team by successfully recruiting suitable team members who will carry out their unit assessment responsibilities and who can contribute to a collaborative assessment environment. In particular, like many functions at smaller institutions, assessment leadership may only be a portion of professional staff members' responsibilities. It is common to find the models of assessment coordination or leadership by committee enacted at smaller institutions to ensure that a range of professional staff are responsible for conducting assessment projects.

Although assessment coordinators provide needed oversight for assessment projects, leadership for assessment in student affairs ought to exist at several levels. Green, Jones, and Aloi (2008) identified four levels of professional commitment essential to effective student affairs learning outcomes assessment practice, including vice presidents, directors/coordinators of assessment, assessment committees, and unit-level professional staff. Ensuring that staff at these four levels are trained and have some experience with assessment is also more likely to help them initiate and oversee assessment projects effectively.

Given that student affairs divisions commonly are based on a management culture (see Manning, Kinzie, & Schuh, 2014), senior student affairs officers can simply require assessment. In this situation, departments are likely to comply. However, the surest way to ensure that assessment occurs in student affairs is to hire a person whose responsibility is to coordinate assessment. Another effective and important way to provide leadership for assessment is for student affairs to work collaboratively with another division of the university, such as academic affairs, to jointly sponsor an office dedicated to assessment or to identify someone in institutional research as a liaison and collaborator to the division. This collaborative model is how many student affairs divisions organize for assessment and it has the added benefit of reinforcing valuable connections between student affairs and other valued campus departments, and of increasing the potential for partnering on important student success and educational effectiveness issues.

Student affairs organizations are not alone in the assessment process, and they do not need to act independently of other institutional efforts to achieve assessment goals. This is particularly true regarding the important topic of the assessment of learning outcomes. Actively collaborating with academic affairs on learning outcomes assessment is an important aspect of assessment leadership in student affairs.

Starting and Sustaining Assessment Projects

The prescription for starting an assessment project specifies a reasonable dose of curiosity about what students are getting out of their college experience or a clear problem about educational quality that demands exploration, a limited amount of assessment knowledge, but sufficient interest in asking questions, modest support for undertaking the project, and a little pressure to hold one accountable for making it happen. Assessment projects can be inspired by internal structure or pressure or external demands for greater accountability.

Assessment can get started quickly when it is inspired by or in response to a problem, such as declining student retention rates or rising campus incivility, or to comply with internal demands for justifying a program. It can also start sluggishly from a position of compliance if the mandate comes down from upper administration or to address the expectations of accreditation. However, assessment can also get underway by designing a thoughtful framework for organizing the work. This structure can outline routine processes to advance, for example, the collection of information about institutional learning outcomes and the extent to which programs and activities contribute to student proficiencies, and can chart the course for regular program reviews that help departments achieve their goals and improve, and provide standard information to administrative leaders and other internal and external stakeholders concerned about the effectiveness of the institution and its success. It is important for student affairs educators to realize that it is not necessary to wait for a mandate from a senior administrator to conduct an assessment project. Assessment projects can be undertaken from any place in an organization—from senior leaders, midlevel managers, or program staff themselves. Assuming that one has professional curiosity and a commitment to providing increasingly effective programs and learning experiences, any person in the division of student affairs can initiate an assessment project related to her or his areas of responsibility.

As the Midstate University case study illustrates and the discussion of steps to get started suggests, there is need for both responsive and routine assessment in student affairs. Both approaches help assessment projects get underway and are associated with common obstacles. It is important to balance the need to develop assessment routines and reliable processes for doing the work and being responsive to the demands of a new provost, or the need for evidence during a period of financial constraint and budget reallocation. As a typically responsive organization, student affairs divisions probably have an edge for getting assessment projects started in response to a pressing need or mandate. However, it is the thoughtful structuring of assessment work that allows for the development of routine processes that is most worth additional attention, to get assessment work started and to ensure its sustainability.

Discussion Questions

1. In your opinion, do student affairs staff members, in general, have the skills necessary to conduct assessment projects? If not, where can they go to get the technical assistance they require?

2. Other than those identified in this chapter, have you observed or encountered other reasons why student affairs staff resist beginning assessment projects?

3. Are there other incentives that can be offered to encourage staff to undertake assessment projects in student affairs?

4. What risks do student affairs staff take in initiating student affairs assessment studies if the results indicate that the objectives of the project have not been met?

5.   This chapter recommends that student affairs divisions identify a person to coordinate assessment projects. If an institution does not have such a person on staff, and cannot afford
to hire one, what alternatives might be available to meet this
need?

References

Allen, K. R., Elkins, B., Henning, G. W., Bayless, L. A., & Gordon, T. W.
(2013). *Accreditation and the role of the student affairs professional.*
Washington, DC: ACPA–College Student Educators International.

American College Personnel Association. (2007). *ASK standards: Assessment
skills and knowledge content standards for student affairs practitioners and
scholars.* Washington, DC: Author.

American College Personnel Association & National Association of Student
Personnel Administrators. (2010). *Professional competency areas for
student affairs practitioners.* Washington, DC: Authors.

Banta, T. W., & Palomba, C. A. (2015). *Assessment essentials: Planning, implementing, and improving assessment in higher education* (2nd ed.). San
Francisco: Jossey-Bass.

Blaich, C. F. , & Wise, K. S. (2011). *From gathering to using assessment
results: Lessons from the Wabash National Study* (NILOA Occasional
Paper No. 8). Urbana, IL: University of Illinois and Bloomington;
Indiana University, National Institute for Learning Outcomes
Assessment.

Blimling, G. (2013). Challenges of assessment in student affairs. In J. Schuh
(Ed.), *Selected contemporary issues in assessment* (pp. 5–14). New
Directions in Student Services no. 142. San Francisco, CA:
Jossey-Bass.

Bresciani, M. J., Moore Gardner, M., & Hickmott, J. (2009). *Demonstrating
student success: A practical guide to outcomes-based assessment of learning and development in student affairs.* Sterling, VA: Stylus.

Bresciani, M. J., Zelna, C. L., & Anderson, J. A. (2004). *Assessing student
learning and development: A handbook for practitioners.* Washington,
DC: NASPA.

Doyle, J. (2004). Student affairs division's integration of student learning principles. *NASPA Journal, 41*(2), 375–394.

Green, A. S., Jones, E., & Aloi, S. (2008). An exploration of high-quality student affairs learning outcomes assessment practices. *NASPA Journal,
45*(1), 133–157.

Hoffman, J. L., & Bresciani, M. J. (2012). Identifying what student affairs
professionals value: A mixed methods analysis of professional

competencies listed in job descriptions. *Research & Practice in Assessment, 7*(Summer), 26–40. Retrieved from http://www .rpajournal.com/dev/wp-content/uploads/2012/07/A2.pdf

Huba, M. J., & Freed, J. E. (2000). *Learner-centered assessment on college campuses: Shifting the focus from teaching to learning.* Needham Heights, MA: Allyn & Bacon.

Jankowski, N. A. (2012). *St. Olaf: Utilization-focused assessment.* Urbana, IL: University of Illinois and Bloomington; Indiana University, National Institute for Learning Outcomes Assessment (NILOA).

Light, R. J. (2001). *Making the most of college: Students speak their minds.* Cambridge, MA: Harvard University Press.

Livingston, C. H., & Zerulik, J. D. (2013). The role of the assessment coordinator in a division of student affairs. In J. Schuh (Ed.), *Selected contemporary issues in assessment* (pp. 15–24). New Directions in Student Services no. 142. San Francisco, CA: Jossey-Bass.

Maki, P. L. (2004). *Assessing for learning: Building a sustainable commitment across the institution.* Sterling, VA: Stylus.

Manning, K., Kinzie, J., & Schuh, J. H. (2014). *One size does not fit all* (2nd ed.). New York, NY: Routledge.

National Association of Student Personnel Administrators & Association of College Student Personnel Association. (2004). *Learning reconsidered: A campus-wide focus on the student experience.* Washington, DC: Authors.

Pascarella, E. T., & Terenzini, P. T. (2005). *How college affects students* (Vol. 2). San Francisco, CA: Jossey-Bass.

Schuh, J. H., & Upcraft, M. L. (2001). Conducting focus groups. In J. H. Schuh & M. L. Upcraft (Eds.), *Assessment practice in student affairs: An applications manual* (pp. 42–56). San Francisco, CA: Jossey-Bass.

Suskie, L. A. (2009). *Assessing student learning: A common sense guide* (2nd ed). San Francisco, CA: Jossey-Bass.

Walvoord, B. E. (2010). *Assessment clear and simple* (2nd ed.). San Francisco, CA: Jossey-Bass.

Weick, K. (1984). Small wins. *American Psychologist, 39*(1), 40–49.

13

REPORTING ASSESSMENT RESULTS AND BRINGING ABOUT CHANGE

The purpose of assessment is not simply to systematically collect data and report evidence or to prove the value of an educational program. The ultimate goal of assessment is to use information to ensure quality and to guide improvement actions. Simply put: "Assessment's true aim is using results, *harnessing evidence* to inform educational improvements" (Kinzie, Hutchings, & Jankowski, 2015, p. 56). Presenting assessment as more than measuring, and even more about change and improvement, places a significant emphasis on sharing results and ensuring accountability for making change. Approaches to assessment must be designed to help educators and administrators improve educational effectiveness and quality and, in the end, student learning.

Although the end goals of assessment are to demonstrate accountability and make improvements (see Chapter 1), these aims seldom are reached. Too often, assessment activities get caught in the phase of gathering evidence. Some assessment projects move past this stage, and achieve the production of a sleek, bound report about the quality of a program, or perhaps a dashboard with some flashy interactive graphs that display program participation rates by race-ethnicity or changes in student satisfaction with services over time. However, bringing about change from the results is a whole new level. As Blaich and Wise (2011) learned, their assumption that once an institution had robust assessment results, the data would be put to use for improvement, turned out to be wrong. Rather, most campuses put too much of their energy into getting piles of "perfect" data, and not enough time getting people organized, interested, and engaged all the way through the process, and in sharing information to inspire action on results.

Making the shift from assessment results to taking action is challenging. However, when assessment projects are undertaken in the spirit of continuous improvement, and support for change is high, action can result. For example, a priority of the East Carolina University's Student Affairs Division strategic plan was a comprehensive assessment design that included external program reviews and a series of assessment projects exploring dimensions of student success, such as first-year students' time studying in campus living units and a campus wellness study, with the clear mandate for improvement. The division's report, *Closing the Loop on 2011–2012: Celebrating and Using Assessment Results for Improvement* (East Carolina University, 2012), highlighted improvements completed including organizational restructuring, leadership personnel hiring, new technology enhancements, facility upgrades, and new program development. Another example of assessment activity that resulted in change is illustrated in the collaborative assessment project between institutional research and student affairs to understand student persistence at Grinnell College (Schuh & Gansemer-Topf, 2010). Assessment results revealing that student attrition was greater between the second and third year of college than between the first and second year, followed by in-depth focus group findings that exposed unique factors influencing attrition in the second year, led to improved sophomore advising, particularly related to enhanced educational and career planning.

What increases the likelihood of moving from assessment results to taking action to improve? How should results be reported to inspire action? This chapter takes up the vexing challenge of how to ensure that assessment results are used to inform change. Once evidence is collected, what are the ways that results can be reported and shared that engage relevant campus audiences and help inform change? What are the best strategies for putting assessment results to use to bring about improvements?

The History and Challenges of Assessment for Improvement

Any student or practitioner of assessment should be aware of the history of assessment for the purposes of improvement. The idea that assessment is for improvement is actually a defining characteristic of the work. The origins of assessment are rooted in demands for educational reform and quality improvement in higher education. The National Institute of Education's 1984 report, *Involvement in Learning*, for example, influenced early aspects of the assessment movement by proposing systematic study of what it takes to improve educational quality, such as identifying that organizational strategies, policies, and processes to maximize student learning and development. The report challenged colleges and universities to maximize the use of evidence to inform institutional improvement. This report and other more recent calls for improved educational quality (Commission on the Future of Higher Education, 2006; Harward, 2012; Kuh et al., 2015) envision assessment as a key lever for promoting transformation goals in higher education.

Calls to improve undergraduate education have grown more insistent during the past decade, including demands for greater accountability and transparency, and statements doubting the quality of undergraduate education (Carey & Aldeman, 2008; Commission on the Future of Higher Education, 2006; Harward, 2012; Leveille, 2006; National Commission on Higher Education Attainment, 2013). Although the press for improvement has been a consistent emphasis, it is sometimes outweighed by the push for accountability, assessment's other goal. Ewell (2009) identified these two assessment goals as being in conflict because the requirement for the demonstration of accountability demands that the unit or program look as good as possible, regardless of underlying performance,

(Continued)

while improvement requires the faithful detection of shortcomings that must be reported and acted upon. Discovering deficiencies is one of the major objectives of assessment for improvement yet this is clearly in opposition with the accountability goal.

To distinguish the two paradigms of assessment, Ewell (2009) outlined their features along eight dimensions, including the strategic purpose of assessment, methods, and reporting and use of results, and so on (see Table 13.1). In the "Improvement Paradigm," for example, the communication of results is through multiple internal channels and media and results are put to use in numerous feedback loops; in contrast in the "Accountability Paradigm" results are for public consumption and simply used for reporting evidence. Although the differences may not be this stark in real assessment practice, understanding the contrast is useful for pinpointing tensions in assessment work.

Table 13.1: Two Paradigms of Assessment

	Assessment for Improvement Paradigm	Assessment for Accountability Paradigm
Strategic Dimensions		
Intent	Formative (improvement)	Summative (judgment)
Stance	Internal	External
Predominant Ethos	Engagement	Compliance
Application Choices		
Instrumentation	Multiple/triangulation	Standardized
Nature of Evidence	Quantitative and qualitative	Quantitative
Reference Points	Over time, comparative, established goal	Comparative or fixed standard
Communication of Results	Multiple internal channels and media	Public communication
Uses of Results	Multiple feedback loops	Reporting

Source: From Ewell (2009, p. 8).

First-Year Student Interest Groups
at Mid-North College

To illustrate the tension between assessment for improvement and accountability (Ewell, 2009) and how this can influence how assessment plays out in practice, consider, for example, an assessment project that starts out as an exploration of the influence of Freshman Interest Groups (FIGs) to first-year student retention and learning that is undertaken to assess and enhance the FIG program at Mid-North College (MNC).

MNC's FIG director wanted to make sure that the influence of the program was assessed systematically and planned to undertake a mixed-methods project, that included assessing the extent to which students who participated in the program were retained by the college for their sophomore year. The director also was interested in student learning, and planned to conduct a number of focus groups when the students returned for their sophomore year to explore such issues as how participating in the groups affected the participants' thinking about their college experience, what they had learned from their FIG experience, and how it affected their plans for their sophomore year. Preliminary analysis conducted in the early summer after the conclusion of the academic year indicated that participation in the FIGs had a positive influence on retention in that participants had registered for fall classes at a rate higher than those who had not participated in FIGs, but additional analysis needs to be undertaken to confirm actual persistence. And, the focus groups would not be conducted until the early fall. However, when the dean of undergraduate studies saw some early positive results, and started asking for more robust statistical tests, comparable groups, and a public communication plan—before the staff who run the FIGs had even had a chance to review or consider what the results suggest for improving the program or had conducted deeper levels of analysis—it was evident that the purpose of the assessment project had shifted from a formative study to a summative report on the value of FIGs.

This example offers a quick depiction of how the dual purposes of assessment can creep into assessment activities and shift the purpose and direction of a project.

To close our discussion of the practical considerations of the two tracks of assessment for improvement and accountability, it is important to point out the role that these dual purposes have had in terms of inspiring reform initiatives at most colleges and universities to improve student success and demonstrate educational effectiveness (Ewell, 2009; Harward, 2012; Kezar, 2009; Kezar & Eckel, 2002; National Commission on Higher Education Attainment, 2013). Yet, while most institutions have increased their assessment activities and are better at using formative and summative information to support campus change efforts and to monitor progress (Banta, 2009; Banta & Palomba, 2015; Kuh & Ikenberry, 2009; Kuh, Jankowski, Ikenberry, & Kinzie, 2014; Maki, 2004), there is less evidence that assessment results have been put to use to directly inform the *direction and scope* of improvement activities, and even less that the assessment loop has been closed—examining whether changes undertaken have produced improvements (Banta, 2009; Banta & Palomba, 2015; Kuh et al., 2015; Suskie, 2004). Students and practitioners of assessment are encouraged to do more to put assessment results to greater use to guide and inform improvement and to initiate the kinds of follow-up assessment that substantiate institutional change.

Reporting and Sharing Assessment Results

Once assessment data are collected the next step is to compile evidence in a form that facilitates data interpretation and use and to disseminate to individuals and offices that can be informed by the work. Of course the trick is to assemble and report assessment results in ways that interest stakeholders, draw findings into contexts for decision-making, and profitably inform improvement efforts. This stage of assessment work requires thoughtful attention to what and how results are reported and to whom.

The formats for reporting and sharing results vary widely in student affairs assessment. The variation is, in part, a function of the many purposes and uses of assessment. Assessment work in some instances has become an annual reporting expectation; thus, at many institutions assessment results from all units are annually compiled into comprehensive reports and submitted to the assessment office or committee. Other times, assessment projects are launched and results are pulled together in response to a particular project need, or to address a campus concern, and are only disseminated to the committee or program responsible for the project to act on the results. Assessment results may also be compiled and shared with relevant stakeholders with the goal of providing current metrics on effectiveness to inform practice. These results and other statistics about program effectiveness or performance may be posted publically on assessment webpages, and made available to anyone who is interested. Primarily in the spirit of transparency, many more student affairs units are taking advantage of websites to post results, along with a range of technology-enabled data management platforms and dashboards to increase interactivity and to continuously update and display key performance indicators for decision-making.

The variety of means of reporting also raises questions about with whom results are shared. More formal reporting may only be reviewed by administrators or assessment leadership, whereas posting results to websites could be designed to inform students, the general public and others on campus about program effectiveness and performance. Bresciani, Moore Gardner, and Hickmott (2010) assert that after collecting and interpreting assessment results, one must involve others in determining how the results will be used as well as in effectively communicating the results and decisions to institutional and community stakeholders. The effective execution of this step is critical to increasing the acceptance of the assessment process and to ensuring that results help bring about change.

Assessment Reporting 101

The most basic report on any assessment project should at least include a description of the assessment work undertaken, the purpose and goals of the work, a summary of results, discussion about conclusions or recommendations, and information about data use. Comprehensive or topical assessment reports benefit from an executive summary (one to two pages), which is a short description of findings. Assessment reports must be written in simple formats that summarize the findings for various stakeholders and are disseminated to suit their needs. Specific plans for sharing information on websites, with committees/departments, in briefings, in marketing, and soliciting feedback where appropriate are also necessary.

The conclusion or recommendation section of assessment reports should include thoughtful discussion about what the results mean in relation to why the assessment was undertaken, or to address program or institutional goals. Portland State University's Assessment Handbook (2011) provides some helpful discussion prompts for the conclusion of departmental assessment reports, including: "How do your results provide evidence for your outcomes? What do your results say about your program process and the impact of the program on students' learning and development? Based on the results, what decisions will you make or what action will you take regarding programs, policies, and services as well as improvements/refinements to the assessment process?" (p. 17). These prompts, particularly the last one about discussing planned action for improving the assessment process and for applying results, are important to address to strengthen the connection between assessment and improvement and to foster action on results.

Scheduled or Annual Assessment Reporting

Given the press for assessment in higher education, it is not surprising that most student affairs divisions across all institutions have established regular cycles and processes for conducting assessment and for reporting results. Banta and Palomba (2015) indicate that annual reports of assessment findings are required for most students affairs units, and many include follow-ups and evidence of action taken on results. For example, Ball State University's assessment reports are due by June 1 of each year, with highlights presented to the vice president of student affairs in May. All departments in Enrollment Management and Student Affairs at Portland State University are required to complete an assessment form each year to plan assessment activities and then to submit an annual report that addresses goals and outcomes and discusses how previous year's goals were met. The assessment form invites departments to outline the department vision, mission, and goals and link to student affairs and University goals, and then to specify the steps to determine the effectiveness of programs and services, approaches to gather evidence of student learning, student development, and evidence of how well the program is functioning, and how results affect the next assessment cycle.

The assessment process in the division of student affairs at California State University, Sacramento, follows a fairly structured, ongoing process coordinated and facilitated by the vice president for student affairs and colleagues from the Office of Institutional Research (OIR) (Varlotta, 2009). A reporting template ensures that relevant topics are addressed and the information is collected and disseminated consistently throughout the division. The template requires information about six steps:

Step 1: Writing the departmental mission

Step 2: Formulating planning goals

Step 3: Identifying program objectives and student learning outcomes

Step 4: Mapping out the methodology

Step 5: Collecting and analyzing data

Step 6: Using the emergent information to make data-driven decisions

These steps illustrate the most basic outline for annual assessment reporting.

The development of a common template for reporting assessment results is fairly standard in larger divisions of student affairs. For example, Oregon State University developed a shared format for Division of Student Affairs Departmental Assessment Plans and Reports (Oregon State University, 2012). This format is used to lay out plans and then to report at the end of each year. Each unit identifies and assesses one or two outcomes per year under the larger overarching goals for the department. Reports conforming to the submitted plan must specify: the type of outcome; delineating if it is a business or service outcome or a learning outcome; the assessment methods employed, and when and how assessment activities were implemented; information about results; and how results were shared and used to inform actions and make decisions. The report template provides a basic and uniform approach to planning and reporting on assessment projects.

Committed to building a collaborative culture of inquiry and accountability for acting on results, Oregon State enhanced its assessment reporting process by adding a consultation process following the submission of the report. The Assessment Council Consultants aim to assist student affairs departments and units in developing, refining and better reporting the outcomes of their work, and to help clarify and improve the assessment work. First, a consultant reviews the report employing a common rubric to evaluate the extent to which the department met the standards for assessment related to mission, goals, learning outcomes or business/service outcomes, methods, results, and decisions and action. Then, in a meeting between the consultant and department, representatives from the department present their assessment work, along with any questions or issues upon which they would like feedback, and respond to five questions: "(1) What question or questions was/were your assessment designed to answer? What did you want to learn from your assessment? (2) To what degree did your results provide you with information to answer the question you had? (3) What specific findings helped you to make a decision, alter a program or teaching method, etc.? (4) How did you use the information? What actions were taken? Who will you share this information with and how? (5) What if anything would you do differently next time?" (Oregon State University, 2012, p. 3). The meeting is an intentional conversation about the work of the department and how the assessment council members can be helpful in answering questions, and offering suggestions, related to the assessment work.

One of the core principles of Oregon State's assessment process is that "the reporting of data is necessary, but not sufficient in the assessment process." Rather, "An evaluation of the data and its usefulness in helping to answer the question or measure the degree to which an outcome was met is essential" (Oregon State University, 2012, p. 1). This emphasis is furthered by the effective use of prompts in the assessment report form that demand the thoughtful integration of results with plans to improve both the program and the assessment activities. Even more, the consultant review meeting provides support and accountability for programmatic change and to devise a plan for improving the assessment work itself.

Reporting and Sharing

Once the assessment data are assembled, communicating and sharing results is a critical step in ensuring that assessment results make a difference. The division of student affairs at Marquette University has outlined a thoughtful approach for designing and implementing assessment measures that provide evidence of program effectiveness and processes to routinely collect and use assessment data to make improvements to programs and student learning. To facilitate data sharing and use, Marquette developed an extensive, accessible repository for assessment results, including an assessment webpage featuring reports from a range of surveys including the institution's New Student Survey,

National Survey of Student Engagement (NSSE), a Graduating Senior Survey, and several alumni postcollege outcome surveys (see www.marquette.edu/dsa/assessment/). Meaningful summary statistics from various surveys are also on display. The institution's Campus Labs platform fosters the collection of data of interest to student affairs and also connects data across units to encourage administrators to make informed, data-driven decisions about strategic planning, cocurricular programming and other student success concerns. Dashboard displays of key measures increase the functionality of results, guiding decision making between academic and cocurricular units. The department also created a webpage "Your Voice" featuring information for students about what Marquette does with the survey information they collect. Student learning assessment also is tied to other forms of needs assessment and program evaluation and these data collectively inform planning and fiscal decisions.

The creation of specialized reporting to specific audiences and interesting visual displays is increasing being used in student affairs assessment. Clemson University created tailored reports about its NSSE results to reflect the interests of various constituencies including student affairs, student government, and academic affairs. Short topical reports featuring data about cocurricular involvement, students' experiences with diversity and data about participation in enriching experiences including service-learning, undergraduate research and internships were provided to audiences with vested interests in the results. Even more, Clemson created the "Student Affairs Dashboard," an informative and visually interesting display using the picture of a gear shift and the symbols "D" (drive), "N" (neutral), or "R" (reverse) to indicate progress on the goal, and a paragraph of explanation of assessment data on six student affairs goals. For example, the report for Goal 1—"Increase Undergraduate Student Retention and Engagement"—described the progress made in the quest to increase this goal. The paragraph describes how NSSE scores of interest to the campus related to positive relationships with peers, involvement in cocurricular activities, and positive relationships with administrators and staff remain strong, and to what the campus attributes these strengths, and how student affairs has invested in activities to support these results. The narrative also includes data on increases in internship postings in the career center and upturns in numbers of students completing internships. The explanation closes with next steps, including a commitment to examining data by student subpopulations to identify pockets of opportunity to decrease attrition during, and after, the first year (Clemson University, Student Affairs Dashboard https://www.clemson.edu /administration/student-affairs/documents/scorecard/10-11.pdf).

Strategies to Increase Effectiveness of Reporting and Action on Results

Assessment results can be reported and shared in many formats. Common reporting templates, dashboard displays, online data management and display platforms, and short topical reports are all useful and appropriate approaches for reporting and sharing results. However, specific considerations addressed in the reporting phase of assessment are more likely to facilitate use and action:

1. *Ensure that results are relevant.* The quickest way to ensure that assessment results will not be reported, reviewed, or used is to conduct assessment projects that are not connected to work of interest or significance in student affairs. Relevance should be central to the purposes of any assessment project. However, relevancy may need to be re-established as results are assembled and the report completed. To heighten attention to relevancy at the reporting stage, clarify the salient audiences and departments and, if possible, involve them in the interpretation of results, and then compile the results and shape the report with their concerns in mind. It is important to point out that relevancy can be affected if the motivations

for the assessment project change over the course of the project, or if findings are not what program administrators or campus leaders expected, or if campus politics intervene. Revisiting the assessment project in relation to original goals, and considerations of current campus issues may also be necessary to ensure results are shared and used.

2. *Collaborate with related departments.* To have an impact, assessment projects should involve a variety of individuals and units, including assessment experts, data analysts, program or department representatives, and so on. However, too often departments that could really be of help in terms of lending expertise or perspective, or that will be affected by or can positively influence uptake of results are left out of the assessment and reporting process. At California State University, Sacramento, the expertise of the Office of Institutional Research (OIR) staff helped accelerate the assessment process in student affairs, with OIR staff serving as one-on-one assessment consultants to the student affairs directors. At this stage, institutional research staff can help shape what gets reported to ensure accuracy and to develop processes for collecting follow-up data to assess change. The division of student affairs at Marquette benefited from a collaboration with academic affairs to create a shared dashboard display that ultimately helped facilitate communication across the division. Think broadly about individuals and departments that have a related interest, expertise, or influential role, and involve them in reporting and sharing results.

3. *Report results in digestible bites.* The most common mistake in reporting assessment results is to provide a complete, 100-page, all-inclusive report to a wide campus audience. Although a comprehensive report should be assembled, and happily provided by request, it is a mistake to distribute the report and assume that it will be read. Preparing short reports from the whole study that connect directly to the

questions or needs of a program, or that feature smaller bites of findings are most likely to generate interest and use. For example, to better communicate NSSE findings, Drake University disaggregated the data into an array of short reports and clear tables focused on college and school level results and topics that were related to the Drake mission, including: "Collaborative Learning among Students, Faculty and Staff," "Preparation for Professional Accomplishments," and "Responsible Global Citizenship" (see http://www .drake.edu/acad/studentoutcomes/). Reorganizing results from the standard issue NSSE reports into clear tables and reports organized by topics of interest to the institution or student affairs program takes some work, but is more likely to get attention. Other short reporting options include: (1) executive summaries (one to two pages) providing a quick overview of the assessment project and highlighting key findings; (2) multiple tables summarizing findings with simple explanatory paragraphs; (3) collection of a few short thematic reports (four pages each) featuring a topical collection of findings; and (4) supplemental reports written for a specific campus audience, which address only their particular question.

4. *Keep reports interesting and accessible.* Assessment reports should be reader friendly and employ a more casual tone and format than a traditional research report or dissertation. Simple, interesting graphics, including figures and tables, may do more to draw the reader in than a long narrative explanation of findings. Write clearly, with little to no jargon, and use plenty of headings to guide the reader. Including rec- ommendations or speculating on the reasons for the findings, and posing alternative explanations, may also draw read- ers into the findings. Although one school of thought about assessment reports is that the report stops short of offering recommendations, it is clear that reports that ponder what

the results mean are not only more likely to draw an audience, but are important to guiding the users of results.

5. *Develop a plan for using the report and taking action on results.* Too often, assessment reports are produced and issued without any thought put into ensuring that reports are used and action is taken on results. The best way to ensure action is to develop an implementation plan for making use of the report and how results will work their way into contexts for decision making.

Using Results to Take Action to Improve

Assessment projects revealing that a program or service is performing above established benchmarks, or at a level of efficiency that exceeds institutional expectations, can be gratifying. Assessment projects showing that, for example, students at Pennsylvania State University are highly involved in clubs and organizations, with over 95 percent participating at least once, and that findings from several years of Student Satisfaction surveys confirmed students reported high levels of satisfaction with their academic and cocurricular opportunities and with student services, with 92 percent indicating they would choose to attend Penn State if starting college again and 90 percent expressing satisfaction with their formal academic experiences (see http://studentaffairs.psu.edu/assessment), provide Penn State's student affairs professionals a reasonable level of confidence in the effectiveness of student life experiences. Even more, assessment reports that demonstrate correspondence to an established standard or outcome or higher-than-expected satisfaction levels addresses the very real demands of accountability. Yet, in keeping with the ethos of assessment for improvement, the Office of Student Affairs Research and Assessment encouraged deeper analyses of variables by student characteristics and the need to take action to address differences.

As the Penn State example suggests, gathering information and data to help student affairs units and other campus educators understand how well student affairs programs are working is an important outcome of assessment (Bresciani, Zelna, & Anderson, 2004). Such assessment reports fulfill expectations for assessment, and they can also be used to convert skeptics, gain greater support across campus, make the case for additional department support, or to request pilot funds to implement a new program. For example, Penn State's positive cocurricular involvement results can make the case for additional investments in union and student activities programs and budgets, and for prioritizing renovation projects in the student center. Even assessment projects that affirm high levels of effectiveness and demonstrate the value of a unit or services can be used to make change.

Many assessment projects are about the systematic use of information to make practical change. However, assessment projects that forefront the value for improvement are more likely to zoom in on where services or experiences are falling short or to set a high bar for achievement to motivate action on results. For example, the student affairs assessment council at Portland State asserts the intention for assessment to lead to change by describing that assessment plans should be designed with the *end in mind*, imploring departments to consider: "What do you want to see occur as a result of your program? Changes in student learning? Changes to program content or delivery? Changes in participation?" (Assessment Handbook, 2011, p. 8).

When assessment results reveal shortcomings in the quality of students' experiences, deficiencies in services, or adverse influences on student persistence and success, the need to take action on results is undeniable. Using results from assessment projects to make improvements should be the most meaningful aspect of assessment. Armed with evidence and a report indicating the need for change, student affairs professionals can proceed with confidence to implement action steps to improve programs and the quality of students' experiences.

A solid assessment project coupled with a strong interest in making improvements can lead to meaningful action. For example, the student life program at Widener University, which coordinates a range of student activities including student clubs and organizations to Family Day and orientation programs, had a history of using student satisfaction measures to assess student satisfaction and gains concerning freshman orientation (Valesey & Allen, 2009). However, concerns about program effectiveness suggested the need for a more formal assessment of the orientation program, so Widener conducted satisfaction surveys and focus groups, and convened an independent orientation advisory committee to examine results and to examine best practices at peer and benchmarked institutions and from the literature. Their assessment project revealed that while some aspects of the orientation program were effective, there were problems with unclear outcomes, poor timing of orientation in relation to athletic schedules and valued student programs, unfocused summer program goals, and a disconnect between orientation and academic requirements. Assessment results guided the implementation of changes to the orientation program, including the development of a three-day formal, mandatory program, greater emphasis on the high school to university transition, on orientation as an academic requirement, and greater faculty and student affairs staff collaboration in workshops and evening presentations. Results also helped make the case for customized orientation sessions for commuters and other student groups and where additional resources for personnel and programming might be needed. Widener was not only thoughtful about taking results seriously, but they also conducted an assessment following the changes to determine if the changes made the intended difference.

Taking action on assessment results is a challenging step in the assessment process. However, the likelihood of bringing about change from assessment results is increased when the goal to take action is embedded in the assessment project from the outset. Assessment plans must not only layout the approaches to gathering evidence but also make transparent the vision, desires, expected outcomes, and steps for taking action on results. Assessment projects designed with the end in mind and that invite departments and units to consider what they plan to do with results, is important to increasing the likelihood of bringing about change. In addition, encouraging wider sharing of results and thoughtful discussions about evidence and how it can be used, can lead to recommendations for institutional improvement and taking action when feasible. Assessment is ultimately about making evidence-based changes in programs and practices and reporting action taken and the improvements that have resulted. Let's work to ensure that meaningful change is an outcome of all assessment activities in student affairs.

Discussion Questions

1. Which is more important, assessment for improvement or assessment for accountability?

2. How does one balance assessment for accountability with assessment for improvement? Can one conduct an assessment for both purposes?

3. If preliminary results are positive, should those conducting the assessment inform interested stakeholders of the results, or should they wait until all analyses have been conducted?

4. How can one determine the type of report that various stake-holders want or need?

References

Assessment Handbook. (2011). *Assessment practice*. Student Affairs Assessment Council. Portland State University. Retrieved from http://www.pdx.edu/studentaffairs/sites/www.pdx.edu.studentaffairs/files/PSU_EMSA_AssessmentHandbook_0.pdf

Banta, T. W. (2009). Demonstrating the impact of changes based on assessment findings. *Assessment Update, 21*(2), 3–4.

Banta, T. W., & Palomba, C. A. 2015. *Assessment essentials: Planning, implementing, and improving assessment in higher education* (2nd ed.). San Francisco, CA: Jossey-Bass.

Blaich, C. F., & Wise, K. S. (2011, January). *From gathering to using assessment results: Lessons from the Wabash national study.* Urbana, IL: University of Illinois and Indiana University, National Institute for Learning Outcomes Assessment.

Bresciani, M. J., Moore Gardner, M., & Hickmott, J. (2010). *Demonstrating student success: A practical guide to outcomes-based assessment of learning and development in student affairs.* Sterling, VA: Stylus.

Bresciani, M. J., Zelna, C. L., & Anderson, J. A. (2004). *Assessing student learning and development: A handbook for practitioners.* Washington, DC: National Association of Student Personnel Administrators.

Carey, K., & Aldeman, C. (2008). *Ready to assemble: A model state higher education accountability system.* Washington, DC: Education Sector.

Commission on the Future of Higher Education. (2006). *A test of leadership: Charting the future of U.S. higher education.* Washington, DC: U.S. Department of Education.

East Carolina University, Division of Student Affairs. (2012). *Closing the loop on 2011–2012: Celebrating and using assessment results for improvement* (2012). Retrieved from www.ecu.edu/cs-studentaffairs /saassessment/upload/2011-2012-Closing-the-Loop-Assessment-Report-Executive-summary.pdf

Ewell, P. T. (2009). *Assessment, accountability, and improvement: Revisiting the tension* (NILOA Occasional Paper No. 1). Urbana, IL: University of Illinois and Indiana University, National Institute for Learning Outcomes Assessment.

Harward, D. W. (2012). *Transforming undergraduate education: Theory that compels and practices that succeed.* Lanham, MD: Rowman & Littlefield.

Kezar, A. (2009, November/December). Unexplored terrain: Is too much change happening in higher education? *Change,* 35–45.

Kezar, A., & Eckel, P. D. (2002). The effect of institutional culture on change strategies in higher education: Universal principles or culturally responsive concepts? *Journal of Higher Education, 73*(4), 435–460.

Kinzie, J., Hutchings, P., & Jankowski, N. (2015). Fostering greater use of assessment results: Principles for effective practice. In G. D. Kuh, S. O. Ikenberry, N. A. Jankowski, T. R. Cain, P. T. Ewell, P. Hutchings, & J. Kinzie (Eds.), *Using evidence of student learning to improve higher education.* San Francisco, CA: Jossey Bass.

Kuh, G. D., & Ikenberry, S. O. (2009, October). *More than you think, less than we need: Learning outcomes assessment in American higher education.*

Urbana, IL: University of Illinois and National Institute for Learning Outcomes Assessment.

Kuh, G. D., Ikenberry, S. O., Jankowski, N. A., Cain, T. R., Ewell, P. T., Hutchings, P., & Kinzie, J. (2015). *Using evidence of student learning to improve higher education*. San Francisco, CA: Jossey-Bass.

Kuh, G. D., Jankowski, N. A., Ikenberry, S., & Kinzie, J. (2014). *Knowing what students know and can do: The current state of learning outcomes assessment at U.S. colleges and universities*. Champaign, IL: National Institute for Learning Outcomes Assessment.

Leveille, D. E. (2006). *Accountability in higher education: A public agenda for trust and cultural change*. Berkeley, CA: Center for Studies in Higher Education.

Maki, P. (2004). *Assessing for learning: Building a sustainable commitment across the institution*. Sterling, VA: Stylus Publishing.

National Commission on Higher Education Attainment. (2013). *An open letter to college and university leaders: College completion must be our priority*. Washington, DC: American Council on Education.

National Institute of Education. (1984). *Involvement in learning: Realizing the potential of American higher education*. Washington, DC: U.S. Department of Education.

Oregon State University, Division of Student Affairs. (2012). *Consultation process for assessment reports in the Division of Student Affairs*. Peer Review Process & Agenda (updated 2015 - MS Word). Student Affairs Research Evaluation & Planning. Retrieved from http://oregonstate.edu/studentaffairs/assessment-formats-and-examples

Schuh, J. H., & Gansemer-Topf, A. M. (2010). *The role of student affairs in student learning assessment* (NILOA Occasional Paper No. 7). Urbana, IL: University of Illinois Indiana University National Institute for Learning Outcomes Assessment.

Suskie, L. (2004). *Assessing student learning: A common sense guide*. Bolton, MA: Anker.

Valesey, B., & Allen, J. (2009). Widener University. In M. Bresciani, M. Moore Gardner, & J. Hickmott (Eds.), *Case studies for implementing assessment in student affairs* (pp. 103–111). New Directions for Student Services no. 127. San Francisco, CA: Jossey Bass.

Varlotta, L. (2009). California State University, Sacramento. In M. Bresciani, M. Moore Gardner, & J. Hickmott (Eds.), *Case studies for implementing assessment in student affairs* (pp. 87–94). New Directions for Student Services no. 127. San Francisco, CA: Jossey Bass.

14

DEVELOPING A CULTURE OF ASSESSMENT

Making assessment part of an organization's routine is central to developing a culture of assessment, which will lead to a culture of evidence for student affairs units. Ziskin, Lucido, Gross, Hossler, Chung, and Torres (2015) emphasize the importance of establishing a culture of evidence as related to college admissions in the following way, "Further, these studies also suggest that work needs to be done to establish a culture of evidence on many campuses, a culture that would identify effective practices from those that are ineffective" (p. 370). In simple terms, a culture of assessment is an important element as institutions of higher education attempt to develop a culture of evidence. Such a culture is one where assessment projects are conducted on a routine basis as part of the organization's annual work activities and the findings of assessment studies are used to inform professional practice, to identify effective practices and areas in need of improvement. Among the questions this chapter will address are the following:

- Now that we've done a study, how do we keep assessment projects going year after year?
- How do we interest the nonbelievers in conducting assessments?
- What might we do when we run into serious resisters?

Kinzie (2010) adds that the role of senior leaders in developing assessment is central to the process by asserting, "In this sense, the influence of campus leadership on advances in assessment that drive student learning cannot be overestimated" (p. 141).

We begin this chapter with a case study that focuses on the challenges faced by a director of student activities in developing a culture of assessment in her unit. While the unit conducted a number of assessments in one year, sustaining assessments over time turned out to be a much more difficult problem for the director. After introducing the case, we move on to a discussion of what it means for an institution to have a culture a evidence that, in our view, creates a climate where assessments are expected and valued. Then we move on to identifying and discussing strategies for developing a culture of assessment in student affairs. We will point out that creating or changing a culture is a significant challenge, and will not occur in a short period of time. Creating a culture of assessment requires sustained effort, which is what we think our student activities director in the case study will find. This chapter builds on Chapter 12's discussion. To be clear about the use of the terms *culture of assessment* and *culture of evidence*, we believe that a culture of assessment is needed to form a culture of evidence. That is, the process of assessment will yield information that is used in the decision-making process undertaken in student affairs. Both are needed to meet the goals of assessment—accountability and improvement (see Chapter 1). We conclude the chapter with some questions for our student activities director to consider in developing a culture of evidence.

Developing a Culture of Assessment in Student Activities at Kersy College

Chaz is director of student activities at Kersy College (KC), a private, baccalaureate institution in the Southeast. Kersy is a selective institution and has an enrollment of 1,600. Most of its students are enrolled in liberal arts majors but the business administration program is growing and is the largest major. Much of the growth in the number of business majors is attributed to internship opportunities available to students in the state's metropolitan center, Capitol City, which is just 15 miles away from Kersy.

The office of student activities historically has been a strong unit in student affairs at Kersy and many students are engaged as members or leaders in one or more of the organizations registered with the student activities office. There has been, however, a shift in student participation in the past ten years away from student clubs and social organizations toward volunteer, internship and service-learning opportunities. Whether this shift is due to the changing values of the KC students or for other reasons is not entirely clear, though a number of students have indicated to Chaz that they participated in volunteer organizations in high school and they thought continuing to volunteer was a logical extension of what they were used to before matriculating at KC.

Chaz has four staff members in the student activities unit at KC, one of whom is a relatively new student affairs practitioner. Charlie, the newest staff member, came to KC from the state university where he had completed a master's degree in student affairs two years ago. Charlie provides oversight primarily in leadership development, offering a number of workshops and other experiences to help students sharpen their leadership skills. Charlie also helps honorary societies plan initiation ceremonies. KC has chapters of a number of honor societies and really encourages students to join when they are eligible. In these cases Charlie provides assistance to academic departments with publicity, room arrangements, and refreshments.

Sally is a long-time KC staff member who has grown up with the college. Sally originally was an administrative staff member but upon completing her bachelor's degree, she was promoted to a professional staff position. Sally primarily works with treasurers from the student organizations. She provides training for and consultation with these students, and oversees reimbursements for the expenses of student organizations.

(Continued)

Max advises the Greek-letter coordinating councils. Max was heavily involved with the Greek system as an undergraduate at KC, left KC to pursue a master's degree six years ago, and came back three years ago to fill a vacancy after the Greek advisor left KC. KC has four fraternities and three sororities. Their membership has been stable but there always is the fear, following regional trends, that membership could decline. Since the Greek-letter organizations have a significant commitment to the local community, Max also works with several student organizations that sponsor volunteer programs. These include a student group that provides tutoring for children who fall below grade in reading and another student group that provides support for senior citizens who are homebound.

Finally, Sam works with musical performances, exhibits, and speakers. KC has a robust program of concerts, often with student performers, a splendid array of visual exhibits, and a number of speakers who visit campus each year. Sam advises a large committee of students that plans many of the events. Coordinating these activities is a complex task and Sam is convinced that students learn a great deal from overseeing the various programs in the "arts" portfolio.

All of the staff are enthusiastic about their assignments at KC and are eager to work with Chaz in moving student activities forward at KC. They realize that for an institution of its size, KC has made a substantial commitment to student activities and they are convinced of the potency of the various programs and services that student activities offers to the KC student body.

A year ago KC's decennial regional accreditation was renewed and while accreditation was affirmed for 10 years, the visiting team, in its report, indicated that KC was weak in assessing student learning, both formal and informal. The accrediting body indicated that it was going to require a report from KC in three years that would focus on assessments of student learning. The accrediting body also wanted the report to indicate how assessment of student learning was going to be woven into the annual activities of the College. This directive was not a surprise and student affairs units at KC immediately began to undertake a series of assessments of the student learning that potentially resulted from the programs and activities associated with the division. Residence life took an in-depth look at the residential experience for students, campus recreation began to take steps to measure student learning from participation in intramurals and club sports, and the office that organized tutoring and learning support programs for KC students started to measure the effectiveness of the various programs it offered. Chaz and the student activities staff decided that they needed to begin to measure the effectiveness of some of the programs and services of the student activities office.

And they did: Each one of the staff organized an assessment that would align with the goals and objectives of the unit for which they had oversight responsibility. Charlie provided a longitudinal assessment of the benefits of the leadership development program from the point of view of the leaders. Sally measured the influence of the support provided for organizations treasurers from a variety of perspectives, including the treasurers, their organization's members, and the KC Controller's office staff. Max worked with the local school district to measure the value of the tutoring for the children who participated in that special program. Sam kept track of participation in the various arts programs and also asked the students who organized the programs to describe what they had learned from this experience.

The results of the various assessments were consistent with what the student activities staff members had anticipated. When compared with the literature in the various areas, no surprises were revealed. Chaz was pleased because the goals of the various programs were being met, participation levels were high, and, in short, student activities programs were accomplishing what they were designed to do. Such positive findings are not always the case. Sometimes assessments reveal that improvements need to be made, so in this respect Chaz felt lucky since the work of student activities was on track. Had deficiencies been noted, staff would need to consider developing strategies to rectify the problems, concerns, or inadequacies noted by the assessments.

(Continued)

Chaz was surprised when the VP announced at the final staff meeting of the academic year that it was time to begin to plan assessments for the next year. The assessments conducted by the student activities staff had taken a good deal of extra time, and while what was learned was gratifying and instructive, conducting assessments all over again was going to be "a tough sell" to the other student activities staff members. They had seen the assessment projects as an extra assignment for the year and they had hoped that they could turn away from assessment for a while. Besides their time, the staff felt that the extra costs associated with conducting the assessments made for very tight budgets for the year. Chaz shared these concerns with the VP, who responded that while assessment certainly could be seen by staff as something "extra to do," KC, as a consequence of the accreditation visit, had to incorporate assessment in the culture of the college across virtually all units, including the division of student affairs. The VP made it clear that all of the units in student affairs were going to have to incorporate assessment into their annual plan because failure to do so could result in a variety of problems for the college in general and for student affairs in particular. Chaz wondered how to follow through on developing an ongoing assessment plan for student activities.

What Is a Culture of Evidence?

Culture sometimes is thought of as applying to the visual or performing arts. This characterization would mean that a "cultured" person is able to identify famous musicians, composers, or artists. In the context of this chapter, we do not mean to define culture that way. Rather, we think of culture by one of the ways it is defined by Bess and Dee (2008), "the 'patterns of basic assumptions that a given group has invented, discovered, or developed in learning to cope with its problems of external adaptation and internal integration, and that have worked well enough to be considered valid, and therefore, to be taught to new members as the correct way to perceive, think, and feel in relation to those problems'" (p. 363 [citing Schein, 1992, p. 12]). Culture involves a variety of aspects including the language people use, the organization's symbols, the rituals employed at the institution, norms for faculty, staff and student behavior, the organization's values and so on. One way of thinking about a culture of evidence might be to ask the question, "To what extent does the use of evidence (data in various forms) influence how we behave at our college?" More specifically, "Are the number of drops from various courses used to initiate conversations with faculty about their instructional techniques?" "If students move in droves from one residence hall to another, what does that mean?" "Why are some Greek letter organizations flush with members while others struggle to meet their annual membership quota?" And so on.

A culture of evidence also would suggest that those responsible for various aspects of the institution typically would use available data, or collect new data, to make decisions about issues that arise. Their initial reaction to problems or concerns would be to think about the information they would need to make a judgment about the presenting issue. Their approach to dealing with problems would be to think first about the data that are needed to make the decision. For example, a simplistic approach to chronic residence hall overcrowding at a public university would be to propose that a new residence hall with 500 spaces be constructed and financed using bonds that would be repaid over 20 years. A more nuanced approach would be to study enrollment projections for the state (for example, Hussar & Bailey, 2013) and determine if the residence hall overcrowding was due to a gradual increase in the number of graduates from the high schools that are the source of the institution's enrollment, or if this increase was a consequence of temporary growth in the number of high school graduates in the state that is likely to decline in the future based on current census data. If a decline is likely, it could be difficult to pay off the bonds, so making a long-term commitment may not be in the best financial interest of the institution. The point is that data are used to make this important financial decision that will result in a multiyear financial commitment of the institution.

A culture of evidence, in our view, would result in staff thinking regularly about the availability of hard data on campus. They would routinely think about surveys that are conducted routinely by other offices on campus, the results of which are widely available. An example of this would be an institution's annual participation in the CIRP freshman survey (Cooperative Institutional Research Program, 2014), or the National Survey of Student Engagement (NSSE, 2014). The institution also might publish an annual fact book that provides a profile of the college or university, including such information as the demographic profile of students, characteristics of faculty, and sources of revenue for the institution (see, for example, the fact book of the University of Virginia, http://www.virginia.edu/factbook/).

Another foundational aspect of a culture of evidence is that decision makers rely on hard evidence in making decisions. Soft evidence, in our view, could be illustrated by the following examples:

- A telephone call from a parent of a student
- A letter published in the student newspaper
- An e-mail from a staff member
- Concerns written in chalk on the sidewalk outside the basketball arena indicating "no one cares where students sit at basketball games"

All of these examples share several characteristics. They reflect the opinions or points of view of potentially a very small sample of stakeholders. The student affairs educator has no way of knowing how widespread the concerns expressed in these examples are. A parent who calls the dean of students to let that person know that the food served in the residence hall is "unfit for human consumption" clearly has a point of view but whether the opinion is shared by many of the consumers of thousands of meals served each day is unknown. A letter may have been published in the student newspaper because it represents an outrageous point of view, that is, all of the businesses in town hate students, to stimulate more letters. A staff member writes the unit head that morale of the staff is the worst the person has experienced in the past 10 years. Maybe the morale problem is only in the eyes of the staff member and is not widely shared, or perhaps it is. A group of disgruntled students meets with the athletics director because they are unhappy with student seating at basketball games and they claim "nobody will go to the games this year." The examples may reflect a point of view or occurrence that is not the norm. The staff member may have been experiencing a difficult day and dashed off an e-mail to relieve stress. The students may be unhappy with their basketball tickets because they attempted to renew their seating assignments after the published deadline with the result being that their seats are much farther from the court than in previous years and really are looking for relief from the athletics director. These examples reflect anecdotes, to be taken seriously, but because they may not reflect conclusions drawn from a systematic effort to secure data, one can only guess at the generalizability of the information.

As opposed to soft data, hard data include information that has been collected through a systematic process that reflects the broad consensus of opinion about a given topic or may have been analyzed on the basis of institutional records, such as the Registrar's annual analysis of campus enrollment. For example, a review of the high schools from which the entering class of first year students have graduated might reveal a substantial number of students who have completed their high school education at high schools in new markets for the admissions staff. This might indicate success resulting from new recruitment strategies.

On the other hand, if the yield from new markets was small, perhaps the strategies employed were ineffective.

Yet another aspect of a culture of evidence is a willingness to accept critical feedback related to programs, initiatives, or activities within a unit in student affairs and to commit to acting on this evidence. No one likes learning that unit programs are not publicized well, that staff are not well organized, or that the result of an initiative has not achieved its desired goal. All of these examples represent critical feedback, but critical feedback is required for improvement. Careful analysis, of course, is necessary in thinking about major organizational changes, such as dropping a long-standing program or reorganizing an office. But failure to take critical, systematic feedback seriously may result in even more drastic changes, such as reassigning a unit to a different division on campus or making significant staff changes.

The last aspect of a culture of evidence builds on the previous paragraph. That is, if the data indicate serious problems, staff members need to be willing to change course. For example, maybe the approach to helping students identify prospective employers needs to be changed from on-site meetings for students with potential employers to online communications. Perhaps residence facilities need to be reconfigured to provide more apartment-style units than traditional residence hall rooms. Maybe because of work and family commitments, orientation programs for students new to campus traditionally held in June need to be rescheduled to an orientation that would be held just before classes begin in the fall. All of these illustrations represent significant changes to long-standing programs. But they may be necessary if the data suggest that changes are needed.

Assessments clearly are an important element in developing a culture of evidence. They provide important information that feeds into the decision-making process of the institution. They provide an important element in an institution's leaders' ability to demonstrate accountability to stakeholders, such as students, parents, faculty, governing board members, and benefactors. Assessments contribute to institutional transparency and provide solid evidence of institutional efforts to communicate how well they are accomplishing their goals. They also provide valuable information as units and program leaders strive to improve. Without systematic data it is very difficult for leaders to know how well they are doing, what adjustments they need to make to enhance programs, and how to determine if goals are being met. But, it takes a great more effort, in our view, than simply announcing that the organization has incorporated assessments as part of the organization's culture. We move to a discussion of what a culture of assessment means and strategies to develop a culture of assessment in the next section of this chapter.

Developing a Culture of Assessment in Student Affairs

A student affairs division with a culture of assessment would be one where undertaking assessment projects would be deeply ingrained in the routine work of the division. For example, one would not think of proposing a new initiative without including an assessment dimension as part of the proposal. Assessment projects would be undertaken routinely by staff to demonstrate effectiveness to stakeholders and also to learn how to improve programs, activities, and learning opportunities for students. In short, accountability and improvement would be central elements of administrative practice and newcomers would be socialized to conducting routine assessments of programs, activities, and experiences designed to enhance student learning. In the case study, Chaz would not have to think about convincing staff to conduct assessment projects when they had undertaken new initiatives if the student activities organization was one that could be characterized as having a culture of assessment. Rather, student activities staff would automatically build in an assessment component when proposing a new activity or program. Relatedly, they would ask questions about current programs and design assessment projects to explore their questions and act on what they learn.

Why is developing a culture of assessment an important step in student affairs? As a framing thought, Blimling (2013) asserts that " ... student affairs needs to be able to show how it contributes to the education of students, why its programs are important to students' education, why the investment in student affairs facilities and programs is worth the increased cost to students, and what system of performance measures is in place to ensure that students' money is spent efficiently" (p. 13). While the staff of the student activities department at KC embraced the assignment of conducting assessments for one year, and were pleased to learn of the effectiveness of their programs, evolving to an organizational culture where each staff person in the department will include assessment as an ongoing activity in their yearly routine will be very challenging and likely to be met with resistance. Getting staff to embrace this commitment to assessment is likely to be a major challenge for Chaz. As Hersh and Keeling (2013) assert, "culture change is hard work" (p. 9). Why? Several reasons contribute to the challenge of developing a culture of assessment for Chaz.

First, the typical routine for the student affairs staff did not include a commitment to assessment. That is, programs were developed, students were advised, activities occurred, and then planning began for the next year. In short, what was missing was an element in the program planning and delivery process that would have included an evaluation of the various aspects of the yearly routine. In addition, the staff members were specifically focused on demonstrating outcomes and did not design plans of actions to respond to the data or to take any action to change. Bresciani (2011) asserts that questions routinely need to be asked of student affairs educators along these lines: Do you contribute to student learning and development, directly or indirectly, or do you inhibit student learning and development. If so, how?

Bresciani's questions frame a different way of conceptualizing programming in student affairs at KC than in years past. Decades ago the general approach to thinking about the potency of programming or offering other experiences in which student participated had to do with determining if students had a good time by participating in an activity, or designing a program might provide a complement to the institution's curriculum, but rarely was a systematic approach to measuring student learning undertaken. In contemporary practice, thinking about advancing student learning is where the discussion about programming begins (see Kennedy-Phillips & Uhrig, 2013, for a detailed discussion of identifying learning goals for a complex student affairs program).

Second, staff members too often see assessment as an "added on" assignment (as indicated in Chapter 12), as opposed to being central to their work responsibilities. Staff members frequently regard such functions as program planning, staff selection and supervision, and facilities management as their central responsibilities. And the life of student affairs staff is full of unplanned events, such as the student who drops by an office simply to visit, the student leader who poses questions about problems encountered at a meeting held the night before, or the student in crisis who cannot wait. Unless assessment is thought of as a central activity, it is very easy to ignore this important component of the work. Blimling (2013) describes the situation this way: "Student affairs administrators are awash with cumbersome bureaucratic tasks and reporting requirements; therefore, they are understandably reluctant to undertake assessment efforts that take valuable time but appear to have little influence on the management demands of their daily work" (p. 8). Accordingly, as long as assessment is seen as something extra to do, it will be difficult to integrate assessment activities into the annual routine of those engaged in student affairs practice.

A third reason is that staff indicate that they do not have adequate resources to conduct assessment. They identify the costs associated with securing instruments, collecting data, leading focus groups, transcribing interview notes, or purchasing computing software as expenses that are not part of the unit's base budget. And the time that is needed to conduct the assessment also represents a significant resource. Consequently, they believe that they simply cannot afford to engage in assessment projects given the current assets that are available to them. These are legitimate concerns because if unit budgets are developed and resources are not identified to support assessment, the costs, while not necessarily oppressive, may result in a diversion of funds, or time, from activities that the staff believes are quite valuable. But one of the things that we do know about assessment is that start-up costs may well be greater than the costs of maintaining assessments. Swing and Coogan (2010) assert, "During the start-up phase of most higher education initiatives, there are extra costs associated with initial research and development efforts" (p. 17). Accordingly, it may be useful to remind staff that costs associated with conducting assessments are likely to decline over time. In short, the first year is likely to be the most expensive year.

A fourth reason staff may give about why they do not want to conduct assessments is that in their heart of hearts they may feel as though they do not have adequate skills to conduct high-quality assessments; or, they may feel as though after they do their best work the resulting assessment product will be criticized by faculty or others who identify methodological flaws. Terenzini (2010) reminds us, "Finally, whether one is dealing with design, measurement, or analytical issues, it will be well to remember that campus-based assessment programs are intended to gather information for instructional, programmatic, and institutional improvement, not for journal publication" (p. 44). He adds this sound piece of advice: "The most appropriate test of the suitability of a design, measure, or analytical procedure is probably that of reasonableness (citing Pascarella, 1987): Was the study conducted with reasonable fidelity to the canons of sound research?" (p. 44). Conducting an assessment and putting the resulting report on a website, distributing it at a staff meeting, or posting the resulting report on a bulletin board can represent taking an intellectual risk in that the report may draw criticism or the findings may be negative. Of course, not having an assessment also may result in criticism, though the form the criticism takes very well may be different.

All of these reasons may be valid depending on a staff member's responsibilities, personal assessment experience, or other circumstances, but the bottom line is that assessments need to be conducted for reasons that have been identified throughout this volume. Accordingly, Chaz is going to have to figure out how to get staff to buy in to an assessment culture. This matter becomes as much a supervision issue for Chaz as much as it is an issue that deals with the technical aspects of assessment. Exactly how the matter can be resolved will depend on a number of elements of the circumstance. Highlights of these elements are identified in the next section of this chapter.

Strategies to Develop a Culture of Assessment

Developing a culture of assessment is more complex than simply announcing that as of a certain date the unit will adopt an assessment culture. Nor does the accumulation of various assessment projects add up to a culture of assessment. We do know from our extensive consulting as well as leading many assessment projects that several strategies have great potential for developing an assessment culture. Among our ideas are the following.

Identify the Goals of Programs

While it may seem obvious, it is extremely difficult, if not impossible, to develop assessment projects without having goals for the initiative that is going to be assessed. For example, what are the skills one hopes participants in a leadership development program will develop? What are the desired outcomes for a living-learning community? If a student studies overseas, what are the goals for program participation? Bresciani (citing Suskie, 2004) points out when writing about outcomes-based assessment that "outcomes-based assessment is the ongoing practice of establishing succinct, identifiable, expected outcomes or end results of student learning, development, or services..." (2011, p. 323). Thus, in developing an assessment culture, student affairs educators need to start their process by identifying what they are hoping will occur in the way of student growth, learning, and development through their participation in various programs, events, and activities. In keeping with the outcomes-based framework, it is equally important to identify an improvement-oriented purpose for undertaking the assessment project; for example, what does the program hope to learn about a particular aspect of the living-learning community and how will the program use results to improve?

Appreciate Multiple Forms of Assessment

We do not believe that there is only one form of assessment in student affairs that is viable. We assert that certain forms of assessment are more likely to provide usable answers to research questions than others, depending on the nature of the experience being measured, the number of participants, and the nature of the analysis being conducted. For example, if we are interested in the perceptions of all of the first-year students participating in a summer orientation program, a quantitative study using a valid and reliable questionnaire, and employing a statistical analysis of the data, probably would be a reasonable approach, whereas a similar approach with four students who participated in a study-abroad program one summer probably would not. With the students participating in the leadership development program in the case example, asking the students to keep journals of what they had learned is likely to yield results that will help inform program planners as well as provide useful data for the participants as they reflect on this complex experience.

In short, the nature of the assessment and the goals of the project are central in determining the assessment technique that should be used. Clearly, the point of view that "I like doing one form of assessment over all others" is likely to result in assessment projects that do not yield the kind of results that are likely to be useful. Our view is that projects need to yield information that can be used for improvement as well as demonstrate accountability, but the nature and purpose of the project, as well as other dimensions of it, such as the number of participants and the nature of what is being measured, should drive the methodology.

Put Someone in Charge of Assessment

We identified this principle in Project DEEP (Kuh, Kinzie, Schuh, Whitt, & Associates, 2010). We found at institutions that have higher than predicted scores on the National Survey of Student Engagement and higher than predicted graduation rates that someone was in charge of assessment and evaluation projects. But we also learned that the responsibility for assessment was not assigned to just one person. Rather, the responsibility for conducting assessment projects was widespread among student affairs staff. Accordingly, and this blends with a culture of evidence, people *thought* in terms of developing strategies when conceptualizing new initiatives or projects.

The person in charge provided assistance in several areas of assessment. One was training. That is, if staff wanted to take on a project and they were concerned that their methodological skills were limited, the person in charge could provide training or assistance to those conducting the project, or could arrange for the assistance if the person did not have the skills herself or himself. A second would be to arrange for resources if the unit planning the assistance was short on personnel, finances or other aspects of the assessment project. A consultant might be identified as was suggested previously, or funds could be infused to purchase instruments. While the person in charge probably cannot solve all the problems that might arise, having a person available as a consultant certainly can facilitate the assessment process. Further information and details about the role of an assessment coordinator is provided by Livingston and Zerulik (2013) as well as in Chapter 12 of this volume.

Report Results

It is legitimate for those who are novices at assessment to fear that the results of their projects may reflect negatively on their programs or on them, as Chapter 13 of this book indicates. Realistically, as assessments are planned, doubts can influence the thinking of those conducting the assessment as to what might occur if the results are negative. Will a program be cancelled or radically adjusted? Are staff positions in jeopardy? Will budgets be slashed? While all of those outcomes could occur, assuming that the environment is one dedicated to growth and improvement, draconian results are unlikely.

But staff need to be assured that if they conduct an assessment and the results are not favorable, that is, goals are not achieved, improvement does not occur, students are dissatisfied, and so on, that the information will be used for improvement rather than program elimination. Ongoing negative results could lead to program dissolution, but we posit that such should occur only after repeated negative results. In our view it takes more than one set of negative results to dissolve a program.

Devote Discretionary Resources to Assessment

This element has to do with arranging for a dependable stream of support for assessment projects. We concede that when assessment projects are initiated, finding appropriate resources can be difficult. Consequently, we think that as discretionary resources within the units that are planning assessments become available, they be devoted to supporting assessment projects so that the projects do not languish because of lack of support.

Examples of discretionary resources could be salary savings when a staff member leaves, one-time funds are not spent for new equipment or travel, or revenues from fee-for-service operations generate larger amounts of income than projected.

Reward Assessments with Resources

A close relative to the previous element views the allocation of resources from a broader perspective. In this case we are referring to resources that may be available at the division level. The senior officer can support assessment projects perhaps by developing a central pool of funds that are available for those who wish to initiate projects. Those units that are diligent in undertaking assessments might be rewarded with permanent fund transfers, but with the caveat that the funds must be used for assessment projects or they will be withdrawn.

A variation on this strategy is to provide resources to meet needs or deficiencies identified by assessment projects. Resources often are thought of as monetary, but they also could mean space or staff support. Suppose, in our case study, that Sam learns as a consequence of conducting an assessment of an arts program that the publicity campaign simply is not reaching potential participants in visual-arts programs. That is, invitations to participate that take the form of generic e-mails too often are ignored by the recipients. KC has a marketing specialist who is available to help plan targeted advertising for events and the Student Affairs VP has access to this person. Meeting the advertising needs of Sam's visual-arts programs could be a way of providing resources based on the findings of an assessment project.

Celebrate Assessments

One other element that we think contributes to the development of a culture of assessment has to do with celebrating assessments. This can be done in several ways. First, senior student affairs leaders need to emphasize that assessment is a central activity in the division of student affairs. Anecdotally we have heard of situations where senior leaders discourage assessment projects of a variety of reasons articulated in this volume (see Chapter 12). Unless told not to engage in assessment activities, we think that staff, regardless of their assignment in the division, can undertake projects that assess their area or areas of responsibility. We urge senior leaders, however, to be out front in terms of leading the encouragement and celebration of assessments. That can take the form of emphasizing assessment in the division's annual report to recognizing those persons and units that have conducted assessments in the previous year at the annual divisional retreat. Second, assessment activities can be recognized in departmental newsletters or other forms of internal communications with the division of student affairs. Kind words about units undertaking assessments can go a long way in underscoring how valued assessment projects are. Third, assessment results can be placed on divisional websites or, if one prefers, announcements of the results can be placed on divisional websites with links to the assessment reports on individual unit websites. Again, this activity emphasizes how valuable assessments are in the division and provides an easy mechanism for accessing the results. Fourth, and this takes a bit more effort, assessment poster sessions can be held on campus along with a program that recognizes and celebrates the assessment projects that have been conducted in the division in the current academic year. Toward the end of the spring term is a good time for this kind of event. The institution's community can be invited to the activity and those responsible for conducting the assessments can be available to explain what was learned and what changes will result from the assessment effort.

Developing a Culture of Assessment in Student Activities at Kersy College Revisited

This chapter begins with the challenges facing the student activities director at Kersy College. Chaz was successful at encouraging her colleagues to conduct assessments during the year right after the critical accreditation report. All of the areas for which Chaz's staff were responsible conducted assessments, but what was surprising to the staff members was that the vice president indicated that assessments were going to have to be undertaken every year, not just once. While not stated by its leadership, it is clear that the division of student affairs was moving in a direction of integrating assessment into its work routine, in keeping with the recommendation of Sandeen and Barr (2006), who asserted, "Strong leadership by senior student affairs officers is the most important change that could improve student affairs' role in assessment" (p. 151). That still does not mean that a culture of assessment had been developed, because an organization's culture suggests widespread agreement on "how things are done here." *Making* people do something is very different from creating an environment where people *want* to do something, *expect* each other to do something, and *socialize* newcomers to behave that way. Chaz recognized that simply requiring staff to do assessments was very different from their agreeing that assessments were necessary to demonstrate accountability to stakeholders, as well as the key to improving campus conditions. So, what remained was establishing a culture of assessment.

Chaz considered a number of steps in beginning to establish a culture of assessment in student activities. One was to hold a retreat with the student activities staff before the beginning of the fall semester to identify the infrastructure needed for assessment projects to be conducted routinely in student activities. Another option was to schedule several half-day workshops that would be designed to help the staff to develop the skills needed to undertake assessment projects. A third could be to schedule a series of meetings

(Continued)

338 ASSESSMENT IN STUDENT AFFAIRS

with staff to identify resources to help pay the added costs of the assessment projects that were being contemplated for the next assessment year. A fourth could be to plan a trip to visit the state university to talk with a professor who had expertise in assessment to discuss various approaches to beginning the assessments in student activities and possibly invite the faculty member to serve as an ongoing consultant, though the resources to establish this relationship were not easy to come by.

In thinking through her options, Chaz was perplexed and not entirely sure how to proceed. If Chaz asked you for advice, what would you advise her to do to begin to develop a culture of assessment? How will Chaz sustain a culture of assessment after another year or two, assuming that assessments begin to be undertaken routinely by the staff members of student activities? How might Chaz affirm the strong findings that indicate the effectiveness of programs and get staff to ask new questions about their programs and students' experience for future assessment projects? What could Chaz have done to emphasize the assessment phase of taking action on results to improve? Suppose that the findings had indicated that programs were ineffective. What strategies might be used to bring about program improvement? While we have identified reasons why staff members resist conducting assessment, are there others that make conducting assessment difficult? From your point of view, of the elements of an assessment culture that have been identified, which are essential? Which are nice to have but not crucial to successfully establishing a culture of assessment?

Discussion Questions

Hersh and Keeling (2013, pp. 9–11) have identified elements of a culture of evidence on a college campus. The following elements are based on their work, modified for the purpose of this chapter and listed in question form.

1. Is there institutional consensus on student learning goals?

2. Are expectations and support for students elevated?

3. Does rigorous and comprehensive assessment of student learning exist?

4. Is the assessment loop purposely closed?

5. Do all faculty and staff have an instructional role?

6. Do continuous faculty and staff development programs exist?

7. Are academic and student affairs tightly coupled?

In examining these questions, what evidence would you need to determine if these elements have been implemented? What process would you use? Have these elements been adopted at the institution with which you are affiliated? What is your evidence?

References

Bess, J. L., & Dee, J. R. (2008). *Understanding college and university organization* (Vol. 1). Sterling, VA: Stylus.

Blimling, G. S. (2013). Challenges of assessment in student affairs. In J. H. Schuh (Ed.), *Selected contemporary assessment issues* (pp. 5–14). New Directions for Student Services no. 142. San Francisco, CA: Jossey-Bass.

Bresciani, M. J. (2011). Assessment and evaluation. In J. H. Schuh, S. R. Jones, & S. R. Harper (Eds.), *Student services: A handbook for the profession* (6th ed., pp. 321–334). San Francisco, CA: Jossey-Bass.

Cooperative Institutional Research Program. (2014). *About the CIRP freshman survey.* Los Angeles, CA: UCLA, Higher Education Research Institute. Retrieved from http://www.heri.ucla.edu/cirpoverview.php

Hersh, R. H., & Keeling, R. P. (2013). *Changing institutional culture to promote assessment of higher learning.* Champaign, IL: National Institute for Learning Outcomes Assessment.

Hussar, W. J., & Bailey, T. M. (2013). *Projections of education statistics to 2022* (NCES 2014–051). U.S. Department of Education, National Center for Education Statistics. Washington, DC: U.S. Government Printing Office.

Kennedy-Phillips, L. C., & Uhrig, K. J. (2013). Measuring the second-year transformational experience program (STEP) at The Ohio State University. In J. H. Schuh (Ed.), *Selected contemporary assessment issues* (pp. 83–88). New Directions for Student Services no. 142. San Francisco, CA: Jossey-Bass.

Livingston, C. H., & Zerulik, J. D. (2013). The role of the assessment coordinator in a division of student affairs. In J. H. Schuh (Ed.), *Selected contemporary assessment issues* (pp. 15–24). New Directions for Student Services no. 142. San Francisco, CA: Jossey-Bass.

Kinzie, J. (2010). Student engagement and a culture of assessment. In G. L. Kramer & R. L. Swing (Eds.), *Higher education assessments* (pp. 135–159). Lanham, MD: Rowman & Littlefield.

Kuh, G. D., Kinzie, J., Schuh, J. H., & Whitt, E. J. (2010). *Student success in college*. San Francisco, CA: Jossey-Bass.

National Survey of Student Engagement. (2014). *About NSSE*. Bloomington, IN: Indiana University, National Survey of Student Engagement. Retrieved from http://nsse.iub.edu/html/about.cfm

Sandeen, A., & Barr, M. J. (2006). *Critical issues for student affairs*. San Francisco, CA: Jossey-Bass.

Swing, R. L., & Coogan, C. S. (2010). *Valuing assessment: Cost-benefit considerations*. Champaign, IL: National Institute for Learning Outcomes Assessment.

Terenzini, P. T. (2010). Assessment with open eyes: Pitfalls in studying student outcomes. In F. Volkwein (Ed.), *Assessing student outcomes* (pp. 29–46). New Directions for Institutional Research no. S-1. San Francisco, CA: Jossey-Bass.

University of Virginia. (2014). *About the 2014 University of Virginia Fact Book*. Charlottesville, VA: University of Virginia. Retrieved from http://www.virginia.edu/factbook/

Ziskin, M., Lucido, J. A., Gross, J. P. K., Hossler, D., Chung, E., & Torres, V. (2015). The role of the institution in increasing college student persistence. In D. Hossler, B. Bontrager, & Associates, *Handbook of strategic enrollment management* (pp. 351–373). San Francisco, CA: Jossey-Bass.

15

TAKING A LOOK AT ASSESSMENT IN THE FUTURE: A LOOK INTO OUR CRYSTAL BALL

Attempting to predict the future can be a risky endeavor, for on one hand people can appear to be prescient if their predictions turn out to be accurate, such as foreseeing electronic navigation systems in cars (In 1958, Disney imagines the future of the highway, 2012), but on the other, they might be as far off as misguided reports of human space travel to Mars by the end of the twentieth century (Portree, 2001). So at the risk of missing the mark, such as the prediction of the common use of atomic cars (In 1958, Disney imagines the future of the highway, 2012), we'll take a crack at a few predictions for assessment in the future. We start with the conundrum of a new faculty member.

Teaching a Course of Assessment in Student Affairs

Carla completed her doctoral degree a few months ago and joined the college of education faculty at State U. this fall. She is one of three faculty members who will be teaching courses in student affairs administration and one of the courses that has been assigned to her is a course that will address issues related to assessment in student affairs. The State U. program carefully follows the recommendations of the Council for the Advancement of Standards for master's programs in student affairs; one of the courses recommended has to do

(Continued)

with assessment in student affairs. This course has been offered in previous years but adjunct faculty members have taught it. Carla took an assessment course as part of her master's program a decade ago, but her professional practice and doctoral study were outside of student affairs, so the topic is relatively new to her.

Carla realizes that one of the challenges she faces is develop a course that will stand the test of time because this may be the only course of its type that her students will ever take in graduate school. Moreover, she would like to offer a course that will be based on topical areas that are current now but also will be contemporary in the future. She realizes that predicting the future can be difficult but that realization will not deter her from trying to identify principles and practices that are likely to remain current over time. This chapter is devoted to looking at issues that she may wish to cover in her course along with providing a rationale for why they should be part of the curriculum for her course.

Definition and Purposes of Assessment

We start with the definition of assessment. If one traces assessment in student affairs literature, one will find comments about evaluation in the first (1937) and second (1949) *Student Personnel Point of View* but the term *assessment* was not mentioned. *Evaluation* and *research* were terms that appeared in each of these documents, but "assessment" was not included (National Association of Student Personnel Administrators, 1989). While the terms have been known to be used synonymously, in the world of contemporary assessment they are differentiated. Bers and Swing (2010) assert, "Assessment is not the same as evaluation, accountability, or performance standards" (p. 5). Suskie (2009), for example, characterizes the difference between assessment and evaluation as "evaluation is using assessment information to make an informed judgment..." (p. 14). One of the most powerful differences between assessment and evaluation, in our view, is that one function of an evaluation is to determine the cost-effectiveness of a program. We think that in an era of ever-tightening budgets, not only determining if a program achieves its learning outcomes (assessment) but also determining if the program is cost effective (evaluation) is necessary.

Suskie also differentiates between assessment and research. In her view, a fundamental difference is that assessment is a form of action research but is not designed to test theories. She points out that faculty and staff "aim to reap the benefits of assessment in proportion to the time and resources devoted to them" (pp. 13–14). We agree with this difference and believe that in the future terms such as assessment, evaluation, and research will be used with increasing specificity. In student affairs practice, assessment and evaluation are likely to be part of the administrative routine of most practitioners; research activity in divisions of student affairs is likely to be less frequent than the other processes though we hasten to add that the techniques used in a good assessment study should have rigor appropriate to the study.

Closely following the definition come the purposes of assessment. Upcraft and Schuh identified a number of reasons for assessment in student affairs in their first book (1996) but as the years have passed two primary reasons for assessment have emerged as being central to assessment practice in higher education: accountability and improvement, as Chapter 1 indicates. Ewell (2009) discussed the tension between accountability and improvement as being the primary reasons for conducting assessment in higher education. "Within the 'Improvement Paradigm,' the predominant ethos is a posture of engagement seeking continuous improvement and a 'culture of evidence.' Within the 'Accountability Paradigm,' the predominant ethos is a posture of institutional compliance, or at least the appearance of it" (p. 8). Though there are natural tensions between these competing purposes, virtually all purposes of assessment (assessing to determine student learning, assessing to determine student needs and so on [Schuh, 2009]) fit into one category or the other.

Differentiating assessment, evaluation, and research adds a level of sophistication to these important activities in student affairs. Developing assessment projects for accountability or improvement purposes offers a way of refining one's approach to implementing assessment projects. Determining why one is engaging in assessment is fundamental in our view, and we believe that adopting Ewell's thinking about the purpose of assessment will help sharpen initial thinking about why one should conduct an assessment study at the onset of the process. We do not believe that Ewell's elegant thinking about the purposes of assessment will change appreciably in the foreseeable future.

Assessment Methods

Historically, at least in our several decades of experience, assessment meant distributing a survey to a random sample of potential respondents drawn from a larger population and collecting the completed surveys at the end of a program, at the front desk of a residence hall, or asking students to send the completed surveys to a collection point through campus mail. Assessments tended to be quantitative in nature, resulting in statistical analyses that yielded frequency distributions, measures of central tendency or possibly t-tests, chi squares, or correlations depending on the nature of the data and the purpose of the assessment (see Chapter 8 for more detail on quantitative assessment). While this approach had the potential to yield useful data, the level of sophistication in collecting and analyzing quantitative data has increased significantly, and qualitative studies increasingly are used for assessment purposes, depending on the nature of the assessment projects.

Quantitative Projects

The days of distributing survey instruments by hand are rapidly fading into the past. Among the data collection approaches in contemporary quantitative assessment are distributing instruments by computer or PDA, asking the respondents to complete the instrument on the screen and submit their completed instrument by the World Wide Web. This approach is used by *Penn State Pulse* (see http://studentaffairs.psu.edu/assessment/pulse/). Using a web-based approach facilitates data collection and analysis and, in effect, speeds up the assessment process. Various commercially offered services are available to facilitate web-based assessments, such as Survey Monkey, an early developer of web-based surveys. Some institutions also have developed their own software so that they do not need to purchase commercially available software. Our view is that the use of web-based surveys and analysis will be the norm in student affairs assessment in the near future if it is not already.

We believe that the use of institutional and other bases, such as IPEDS, will be seen on an increasingly frequent basis in the future (see Chapter 11). The value of a data base cannot be overstated; that is, the data have been collected so issues related to developing an instrument and collecting the data have been resolved, especially by federal data bases. IPEDS, in particular, lends itself well to institutional comparisons, especially large-scale comparisons. Suppose, for example, a baccalaureate institution wanted to compare its expenditures on student services with 50 or 100 institutions in its geographic region. One approach would be to develop an instrument, send it to potential respondents, develop a database and then begin data analysis after a sufficient number of responses had been collected. Or, the institution could access the IPEDS database and begin data analysis. We think the latter approach is far more efficient, and likely to be far more accurate since institutions are required to submit data to IPEDS on an annual basis. Assuming that an institution or two might not comply with this federal requirement, it is still likely that one can have confidence in the data that are available for analysis. Other databases are available as well as commercially available benchmarking services that will compare an institution with a group of peers.

Qualitative Projects

Our view is that qualitative approaches to assessment are taking their rightful place next to quantitative assessment approaches (see Chapter 7). The key, of course, is the nature of the project itself. Qualitative projects work very well if the potential number of participants is small, if the investigators are trying to learn about how the participants make meaning of their experiences, or want to follow up on a quantitative study. Typically qualitative projects involve conducting individual interviews or focus groups, observing participants in the natural setting (such as assessing the leadership techniques used by a person conducting a meeting) or reviewing documents. Our view is that one will find more and more qualitative projects in future as students are asked to report what they have learned from such activities as service learning, volunteer projects, or study abroad.

Mixed Methods

We anticipate that assessment projects, increasingly, will involve using more than one assessment method. We can learn how students evaluate a project using quantitative approaches, such as a survey, but finding out what they have learned from an experience, how it has affected their thinking, or their planning for additional experiences, may require qualitative techniques. The richness of using mixed methods cannot be discounted and in our view, using mixed methods approaches likely will increase in the future. Without question mixed methods approaches require more time and other resources, but the value of using multiple approaches cannot be discounted. We think mixed methods studies will be conducted with increasing frequency in the future.

Reporting Results

The future, in our view, will see an increasing number of reports that will be available to interested stakeholders (see Chapter 13). Penn State Pulse has been referenced earlier in this chapter and represents a splendid longitudinal approach to reporting the results of student affairs assessments. Other examples include the student affairs assessment program at the University of Kansas (KU) (https://studentaffairs.ku.edu /departmental-reports), which makes a wide variety of reports on programs of interest available to the KU community and the student affairs assessment program at the University of Arizona (UA). A particularly attractive feature of the UA assessment program is the series of one-page reports called "Back Pocket Data" (http://studentaffairs.arizona.edu/assessment/reports.php). These reports deliver one page of information about "the impact or results of a program or service ... " (n.p.). Our view is that these examples reflect what will be expected of student affairs in terms of reporting results in the future. UA even makes a reporting matrix available to staff so that they can prepare repots specifically tailored to the needs to the intended audience (http://studentaffairs.arizona.edu/assessment/documents /ChoosingAppropriateReportingMethods.pdf). We think that in the future student affairs units will be expected to provide this kind of information on a routine basis to their stakeholders.

Ethical Issues

When we undertook assessment projects in the 1970s and 1980s we simply started the process and had no human subjects concerns, nor did we have to worry about securing permission from our campus's human subjects committee or institutional review, because neither existed. According to the U.S. Department of Education (http://www2.ed.gov/policy/fund/guid/humansub /overview.html), procedures to protect and inform human subjects were implemented, triggered by *The Belmont Report* (U.S. Dept. of Health, Education and Welfare, 1979). Seventeen Federal Departments and Agencies "adopted a common set of regulations known as the *Federal Policy for the Protection of Human Subjects or "Common Rule"* (http://www2.ed.gov/policy

/fund/guid/humansub/overview.html, n.p.). Since then colleges and universities increasingly have put institutional review boards in place to insure that the rights of potential participants in research projects are protected to the point where it is difficult to identify a college or university that does not have some form of human subjects protection procedures in place. Assessment projects are considered to fall under this umbrella; that is, assessment projects must be meet institutional human subjects requirements.

Our view is that safeguards designed to protect the rights of potential participants in assessment projects will only become more stringent in the future. Informed consent will be required for virtually all projects involving human subjects, no matter how nonthreatening they may appear to be. In the beginning of the development of these safeguards, details such as securing informed consent from participants were seen as an unnecessary burden, since assessment projects were benign and identifying participants in assessment studies was very difficult. As time has passed, making sure that participants' rights are protected has evolved into an important, necessary step in the assessment process, no different than making sure that the reliability of an instrument is appropriate. Meeting institutional standards with respect to human subjects will continue to be a part of the assessment (see Chapter 3), and if there are any deviations from current practice in the future, our hunch is that procedures will become increasingly strict over time.

Accreditation

As we have examined historical trends in this volume, one aspect of assessment has become increasingly clear. That is, the various regional accrediting bodies have included language that requires institutions to measure the learning that occurs in the out of class experiences of students (see Chapter 11). In some cases, such as the Southern Association of Colleges and Schools the language is explicit (for example, Southern Association of Colleges and Schools Commission on Colleges, 2012, section, 3.3.1.3) while in other cases the requirement is more general, such as the Higher Learning Commission of the North Central Association of Colleges and Schools, which includes student learning in its Criteria for Accreditation (Higher Learning Commission, no date, http://policy.hlcommission.org/Policies /criteria-for-accreditation.html, 4.B.2).

Our view is that the regional accreditation bodies will continue to require some form of assessment of programs, services, and student learning that result from the various dimensions of student affairs units for the institutions they accredit. The expectations of student affairs in the future, if they change at all, are likely to become more demanding. That is, evidence of student learning in particular will be required. Failure to provide this information in the future may have undesirable consequences.

Culture of Assessment

Discussions about what constitutes a culture and evidence and how to create such a culture have appeared with increasing frequency in the past 10 years (see, for example, Kinzie, 2010; Schuh, 2013; Suskie, 2009). Schuh (2013) provides this definition of a culture of assessment: "In a culture of assessment, staff members recognize that they must collect evidence systematically to demonstrate accountability to their stakeholders, and that they must use that evidence to improve" (p. 89). These authors provide a variety of ideas about how to crate a culture of assessment, what it might look like, and how to sustain it over time.

Whether institutions have developed a culture of evidence depends on a number of factors. Suskie (2009) for example, points out that what will work in establishing a culture of assessment will vary from institution to institution depending on "its culture, history and values" (p. 69). Kinzie (2010) provides nine suggestions for developing an assessment culture and further discussion of a culture of assessment is included in this volume. The question related to an assessment culture perhaps should focus on the extent to which more institutions will include assessment as an essential element of student affairs practice. Our conclusion is that we anticipate more divisions of student affairs will develop an assessment culture, but we fear that this will result more from external (meaning accountability) influences rather than coming from the division of student affairs (meaning a desire to improve). We would like to be wrong in this prediction, but the evidence points in the direction that too often a commitment to assessment has been a function of specific leaders in student affairs rather than an overwhelming commitment to assessment. Certainly, professional documents such as *Learning Reconsidered 2* (Keeling, 2006), professional literature (for example, Blimling & Whitt, 1999; Sandeen & Barr, 2006), and professional development conferences offered regularly by ACPA and NASPA emphasize the importance of assessment, but we fear that too often assessment, especially measuring student learning, is not seen as a fundamental responsibility of student affairs units. Until assessment reports are found on the websites of student affairs units that are up to date and indicate action steps planned by the unit, we think assessment will be perceived as a secondary activity for student affairs. Our view is that regional accreditation bodies will expect more in the future and will require routine assessment reports or perhaps levy sanctions on institutions that do not comply. Perhaps then cultures of assessment will become more widespread in student affairs (see Chapter 14).

Graduate Preparation Program Curricula

This chapter concludes by taking us back to Carla's dilemma, which was to develop a course that would be contemporary over time and would prepare students well for leadership positions as student affairs educators. Central to her role as a faculty member was the assignment of teaching a graduate course in assessment in student affairs. The Council for the Advancement of Standards has recommended a course related to assessment in student affairs for years (CAS) and there are no indications that this recommendation will be withdrawn in future years. So, we believe it is highly likely that a course of this type of will be part of a recommended curriculum, for as far as we can see. Such important topics as the purposes of assessment, assessment strategies and techniques, reporting results to stakeholders, and implementing change based on assessment are likely to be part of the curricula she will develop.

We think a course of this type ought to include a practical dimension. That is, in addition to learning about theoretical and hypothetical dimensions of assessment in student affairs, we also think it ought to include a field-based activity that would include developing and implementing an assessment project (see the Appendix). The campus's division of student affairs can provide sites for graduate students' assessment projects or student affairs divisions from colleges in the area, including, but not limited to, private baccalaureate colleges and community colleges, which also have the potential to host graduate student assessment projects. The practical side of this activity is for master's students enrolled in the assessment course to conduct an assessment of a program or learning opportunity that will result in a report that will be of value to the division of student affairs. The project has the potential to yield to two important results:

1. Students get to test their assessment skills in a "real world" scenario.

2. The division of student affairs receives an assessment report that it can use for accountability and improvement purposes.

Activities of this type can be extremely valuable, yielding the two results previously listed. The division of student affairs has the potential to receive a number of assessments annually

(*Continued*)

that will provide substantial evidence to the division's leadership and stakeholders. Students graduating from the master's program will have a demonstrable skill that has been field tested and should provide them with an important product that they can use, in part, as they pursue full-time employment as student affairs professionals.

We believe that we will see more activity of this type of assessment courses that are part of graduate programs in student affairs. We anticipate that Carla will adopt this strategy and will be offering a cutting-edge course as she begins her work as a faculty member.

Discussion Questions

1. How can new technologies be incorporated in student affairs assessment in the future? For example, is there a role for Twitter, Facebook, Instagram, or other technologies in conducting assessments?

2. Are the purposes of assessment in student affairs likely to change in the future? Why or why not? What evidence do you have that contributes to why you think so?

3. Are there reporting mechanisms that divisions of student affairs can use to distribute the results of assessment projects that currently are not used?

4. Do you think accreditation agencies are more or less likely to require assessments of student affairs in the future? Why or why not?

References

Bers, T., & Swing, R. L. (2010). Championing the assessment of learning: The role of top leaders. In G. L. Kramer & R. L. Swing (Eds.), *Higher education assessments* (pp. 3–26). Lanham, MD: Rowman & Littlefield.

Blimling, G. S, Whitt, E. J., & Associates. (1999). *Good practice in student affairs*. San Francisco, CA: Jossey-Bass.

Ewell, P. T. (2009). *Assessment, accountability, and improvement: Revisiting the tension.* Champaign, IL: National Institute for Learning Outcomes Assessment.

Higher Learning Commission. (n.d.). *Policy title: Criteria for accreditation.* Chicago, IL: Author. Retrieved March 1, 2015, from http://policy.hlcommission.org/Policies/criteria-for-accreditation.html

In 1958, Disney imagines the future of the highway. (2012, July 1). *Technology Almanac.* Retrieved from http://techalmanac.blogspot.com/2012/07/in-1958-disney-imagines-future-of.html

Keeling, R. P. (2006). *Learning reconsidered 2.* Washington, DC: American College Personnel Association (ACPA), Association of College and University Housing Officers–International (ACUHO-I), Association of College Unions–International (ACUI), National Academic Advising Association (NACADA), National Association for Campus Activities (NACA), National Association of Student Personnel Administrators (NASPA), and National Intramural-Recreational Sports Association (NIRSA).

Kinzie, J. (2010). Student affairs and a culture of assessment. In G. L. Kramer & R. L. Swing (Eds.), *Higher education assessments* (pp. 135–159). Lanham, MD: Rowman & Littlefield.

National Association of Student Personnel Administrators. (1989). *Points of view.* Washington, DC: Author.

Portree, D. S. F. (2001). *Humans to Mars.* Washington, DC: NASA Headquarters, NASA History Division, Office of Policy and Plans.

Sandeen, A., & Barr, M. J. (2006). *Critical issues for student affairs.* San Francisco, CA: Jossey-Bass.

Schuh, J. J. (2013). Developing a culture of assessment in student affairs. In *Selected contemporary assessment issues* (pp. 89–98). New Directions for Student Services Sourcebook no. 142. San Francisco: Jossey-Bass.

Schuh, J. H., & Associates. (2009). *Assessment methods for student affairs.* San Francisco, CA: Jossey-Bass.

Southern Association of Colleges and Schools Commission on Colleges. (2012). *The principles of accreditation: Foundations for quality enhancement.* Decatur, GA: Author.

Student Affairs Research and Assessment. (2015). *Penn State pulse.* University Park, PA: Penn State University. Retrieved March 1, 2015, from http://studentaffairs.psu.edu/assessment/pulse/

Suskie, L. (2009). *Assessing student learning: A common sense guide* (2nd ed.). San Francisco, CA: Jossey-Bass.

The University of Arizona. (2015). *Choosing appropriate reporting methods of products.* Tucson, AZ: University of Arizona Division of Student Affairs. Retrieved from http://studentaffairs.arizona.edu/assessment/documents/ChoosingAppropriateReportingMethods.pdf

The University of Arizona. (2015). *Culture of evidence: Back pocket data.* Tucson, AZ: Student Affairs & Enrollment, Management Academic Initiatives & Student Services. Retrieved from http://studentaffairs .arizona.edu/assessment/bpd.php

The University of Kansas, Student Affairs. (2015). *Student affairs departmental reports.* Lawrence, KS: Student Affairs Research. Retrieved from https://studentaffairs.ku.edu/departmental-reports

Upcraft, M. L., & Schuh, J. H. (1996). *Assessment in student affairs.* San Francisco, CA: Jossey-Bass.

U.S. Department of Education. (2011). *Information about the protection of human subjects in research supported by the Department of Education—Overview.* Washington, DC: Author. Retrieved from http://www2.ed.gov/policy/fund/guid/humansub/overview.html

U.S. Department of Health, Education, and Welfare. (1979). *The Belmont Report.* U.S. Department of Health and Human Services. Retrieved from http://www.hhs.gov/ohrp/humansubjects/guidance/belmont .html

Appendix

DESIGNING AND IMPLEMENTING AN ASSESSMENT PROJECT

The following approach to designing and implementing an assessment project is intended to be a team-oriented task. This arrangement allows the project to be structured so that each individual can be responsible for specific sections contributing to the overall completion of the project. The team member roles include a project coordinator, a data planner, and a data analyst. Our experience has been that a small-team approach is optimal, although assigning multiple people to the planner or analyst roles also works well depending on the size of the project (Biddix, 2013). Conversely, a single individual could take on all roles, although we recommend scaling the work down or extending the time frame for completion. Team members should determine roles based on individual strengths and preferences. Responsibilities for each are described in the following:

Project Coordinator The project coordinator is the team leader. He or she is primarily responsible for liaising between and among the team members and the person requesting the assessment (or a supervisor). Activities include scheduling regular team meetings and making progress reports as requested. Team meetings should include a discussion of progress to date, future plans, and current and anticipated issues. The project coordinator also drafts the final report and delegates sections to other team members, as needed.

Data Planner The data planner is responsible for obtaining data, which can involve scheduling interviews or survey locations, observation sites, or requesting existing data and/or other documents. A major responsibility is developing or selecting instruments. Despite the primary role of the planner, all team members should be involved in data collection. The data planner ensures these activities remain scheduled and on task.

Data Analyst The data analyst is responsible for leading the data analysis process for the team. This includes training other members on analytical procedures and seeking external assistance, as needed. As with data planning, all team members should be involved in data analysis. The data analyst also should create charts and graphics for the final report.

Activities related to the completion of the project should immediately follow team and role selection. We recommend following the nine steps that Chapter 2 outlines, which are relisted in the following. The purpose for following this set of directions is to provide a standardized and easy-to-follow process. The steps should be completed in sections and include a full written report with an executive summary.

1. What are the issues at hand?
2. What is the purpose of the assessment?
3. Who should be studied?
4. What is the preferred assessment method?
5. How should we collect our data?
6. What instrument should we use?
7. How should we analyze our data?
8. How should we report the results?
9. How can we use the data for improvement?

The length of the project can vary significantly based on the goals, scope, and timing of the project. For illustrative purposes, a 12-week project might look like the following:

Weeks 1–2: Complete Steps 1–3, including approvals for the project, locating and negotiating access to sites and/or data.

Week 3: Complete Steps 4–5, including recruiting participants and/or scheduling data collection sessions.

Week 4: Complete Step 6, including approval or sign-off for instruments.

Weeks 5–7: Collect data.

Weeks 8–9: Complete Step 7 and begin Step 8, including completing data analysis and outlining the final report.

Weeks 10–11: Complete Step 8 and begin Step 9, including drafting the final report and discussing the findings with the person requesting the assessment to discuss implications.

Week 12: Complete Step 9, including distributing the report, presenting the results to the wider audience (as requested), and consulting on plans to use the data for improvement.

Specific suggestions for reporting results appear in Chapter 13. For illustrative purposes we recommend following a basic framework. The final report should include an introductory page listing team members, an executive summary, a detailed description of the questions listed previously (What are the issues at hand?, What is the purpose of the assessment?, etc.) and an appendix including any approval letters, instrument(s), or other documents. Each question should include at least one paragraph, though several will require considerably more space. Results from previous assessment efforts should be noted in the introduction and, if appropriate, referenced in the implications section. In terms of format, we recommend following APA for consistency, but your department may have specific preferences. We also endorse a formal, but brief, oral presentation of results if appropriate, both to showcase your efforts and to advocate for a culture of assessment within the division, as Chapter 14 notes. Delivery and format should be discussed with the person requesting the assessment. As a final step, ensure that the report and the raw data are stored in a location that will be accessible for future use or reference, as Chapter 6 recommends.

Reference

Biddix, J. P. (2013). From classroom to practice: A partnership approach to assessment. In J. H. Schuh (Ed.), *Selected contemporary assessment issues* (pp. 35–47). New Directions for Student Services no. 142. San Francisco, CA: Jossey-Bass.

Index

and probes, 212–213; and using open-ended questions, 206
Integrated Postsecondary Education Data System (IPEDS), 261, 262, 268, 345
Intensity sampling, 130
International interventions, 87–88
International Network for Quality Assurance Agencies in Higher Education (INQAAHE), 255
Interview data analysis, 163–164
Inventory for Student Engagement and Success (Kuh, Kinzie, Schuh, and Whitt), 238
Involvement in Learning (Study Group on the Conditions of Excellence in American Education), 15, 297
IPEDS. *See* Integrated Postsecondary Education Data System

J

Jackson, S., 255
Jacoby, B., 112
Jankowski, N., 35, 78, 103, 106, 113, 256, 285, 295, 300
Jimenez, A. L., 71
Johnson, R. B., 148
Jones, E. L., 143, 171, 289
Journal of College Student Development, 16

K

Keeling, R. P., 17, 79, 111, 117, 328, 338, 350
Kelly, B. T., 200
Kennedy-Phillips, L., 10, 329
Kenney, D. R., 222
Kenney, G., 222
Kersy College: developing culture of assessment in student activities at, 318–322; and developing culture of assessment revisited, 337–338
Kezar, A., 300
King, P. M., 35
Kinzie, J., 1, 17, 30, 35, 78, 88, 103, 106, 113, 222, 227, 232, 238, 256,

289, 295, 300, 317–318, 333, 349–350
Kitchener, K. S., 57–61
Knowledge questions, 209
Kolb, D. A., 88
Komives, S. K., 257–258
Kömürcügil, H., 255
Kovacs, A., 134
Krathwohl, D. R., 85–86
Kuh, G. D., 17, 31, 35, 36, 78, 88, 103, 106, 109, 113, 222, 224–227, 237–238, 256, 297, 300, 333
Kuk, L., 9, 113, 114

L

Lamb, J., 205
Lawson, J., 226
Leadership, for assessment, 287–290
LEAP project. *See* Liberal Education and America's Promise
Learning outcomes: developing intended, 83–88; direct measures of, 89–91; frameworks for developmental and, 80–83; indirect measures of, 91–92; intended and actual, 78–80; and intentional interventions, 87–88; measuring, 88–89; shift from inputs to, 76–78
Learning Reconsidered (National Association of Student Personnel Administrators and American College Personnel Association), 16, 17, 80, 275
Learning Reconsidered 2 (National Association of Student Personnel Administrators and American College Personnel Association), 82, 350
Leveille, D. E., 297
Level, in quantitative data, 180
Levin, J., 186
Lewin, K., 225
LGBT (Lesbian, Gay, Bisexual, and Transgendered) students, 229–230, 233, 241–242